PRESS HERE!

PRESS HERE!

Managing the media for free publicity

Annie Gurton

PRENTICE HALL

LONDON ● NEW YORK ● TORONTO ● SYDNEY ● TOKYO

SINGAPORE ● MADRID ● MEXICO CITY ● MUNICH ● PARIS

First published 1998 by
Prentice Hall Europe
Campus 400, Maylands Avenue
Hemel Hempstead
Hertfordshire, HP2 7EZ
A division of
Simon & Schuster International Group

© Prentice Hall, 1998

Typeset in 11/13pt Sabon
by Dorwyn Ltd, Rowlands Castle, Hants

Printed and bound in Great Britain by
Biddles Ltd, Guildford and King's Lynn

Library of Congress Cataloging-in-Publication Data

Available from the publisher

British Library Cataloguing in Publication Data

A catalogue record for this book is available from
the British Library

ISBN 0-13-095409-8 (pbk)

1 2 3 4 5 02 01 00 99 98

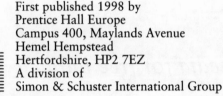

With thanks to Roger White, Delia Bartleet-Perry and Lliane Phillips, and to all the journalists who suggested their pet hates and foibles for inclusion.

CONTENTS

If you would like to make suggestions for hints and tips for dealing with the media, or you would like to change a listing entry, or add an entry to be included in the second edition of *Press Here!*, please send your comments to:

Annie Gurton, 12, Penrose Terrace, Penzance,
Cornwall, TR18 2HQ.
Tel: 01736 364787
Fax: 01736 362279
Email: annie@cix.co.uk

PREFACE

This book derives from nearly 20 years' personal experience of being a journalist and, for a short time, a PR person – I've been at both ends of the phone. In my subsequent media training courses I realised that most professionals know a lot about their product or service but very little about how to deliver that information to the press in a way that makes it most likely to be used.

The fact is that the old cliché that a picture is worth a hundred words has a crucial parallel for anyone seeking to promote their product to the press: one editorial mention is worth a hundred advertisements. The benefits of being quoted or referred to in editorial inches are almost unmeasurable. Your product or service gains an instant credibility and status that no advertisement can give it. This book is about how to achieve those column inches.

How do you promote your product, your company or yourself to the press? The short answer is relationships. Or, as the estate agents say, is 'relationships, relationships and relationships'.

You and the journalists both have a common goal and they need you as much as you need them. The journalist wants good copy and you want to promote your product. There is no reason why the two objectives can't meet. Journalists are looking for good stories, preferably with colour, flair and opinion. If you can deliver that, there is no reason why your name and product should not be up there in the headlines. While your primary objective is to promote your product, it is your personality and skill that will achieve that. Although an interview with you is a plug for your product, you and your personality are just as important.

Although many journalists spend their time seeking out news stories, many also depend enormously on stories coming to them. Indeed, many journalists depend entirely on stories arriving on their desk via press releases or through telephone calls, which they then follow up and flesh out. The idea that most of what appears in the media is the result of journalists' investigative work is false. Many journalists are waiting to hear from *you*.

The problem is that thousands of companies and individuals are also jostling competitively to make contact with journalists and be quoted or mentioned. Journalists are bombarded with calls, faxes, letters and e-mails from people wanting the same thing as you: to be mentioned or quoted in a news story or feature. And if the journalists aren't talking to you, the chances are that they will be talking to your competitors.

To be successful and rise above the crowd, you need to understand journalists, appreciate how they work and the way that they use the material they are given. Most of all, it is a mistake to think that journalists will winkle the information out of you. Much of the time, journalists are fishing around in their questions and interviews, hoping to flush out an interesting story. They are unlikely to ask you exactly the right question which will allow you to give the perfect answer that you want to see in print or hear on the radio. So, you have to develop your message in the sound-bite form journalists are looking for.

This book will give you the background information to help you understand how a journalist thinks and what they are looking for; how magazines, radio and TV stations are structured and organised so that you can deliver the right information at the right time to the right person. It also provides you with a practical methodology to extract and deliver your message.

Interview situations are also covered, where you have to seize the initiative and tell the journalist your message, while at the same time delivering the answers that the journalist is looking for. Dealing with questions from journalists so that the answers and published quotes are what *you* want to see, is a complex art. This book gives you some hints and tips for controlling the interview so that you get as much of your message across as possible, without giving the journalist an opportunity to misquote you. I've also included some fictional but realistic case studies so that you can get a real feel for what life's like for the members of the press.

Finally, we look at techniques for managing the relationship with journalists in the long term so that they continue to promote you, your product or your company. We show what you should do if you are misquoted and how to maintain your profile in the press, on radio or on TV.

Also included is a directory of PR and marketing agencies which can help you to catch a journalist's eye and get your message across.

Ultimately, you have to remember that you have no control over what a journalist says or writes, or when. Journalism is not an extension of marketing, and journalists are loose cannons. If you want to be sure of what appears in a newspaper, magazine, radio or television programme, *buy advertising*.

But you can do a lot to ensure that if you do make it into editorial column inches, it is your agenda that is being quoted. I hope that this book goes a long way in helping you achieve that.

Annie Gurton
Penzance, Cornwall
Spring 1998

CASE STUDIES

At the end of each chapter appear the ongoing stories of PR people and their products, and the diary of a journalist.

- **Case study 1: Product promotion to the lifestyle press**
  Paul Davis works for BettaProds where he is trying to promote the unique KoolWay range of kitchenware and cooking utensils. Follow Paul's attempts to promote the products and Karen Jamison, the company's managing director.

- **Case study 2: Product promotion to the computer press**
  Jessica Martin works for SoftMicro, a software house which has developed some innovative educational software called Kiddie Learn 2. Follow Jessica's attempts to raise the profile of Richard Devine, the software designer, and Professor Higgins, the company's 'independent' expert on educational software.

- **Case study 3: Diary of a freelance journalist**
  Suzie J. Ingram is a freelance journalist based in Letchworth, Herts. She writes for two main sectors of the consumer press: lifestyle and the IT industry. She also writes for trade magazines in each area, plus women's magazines, glossy monthlies and one national daily and its Sunday magazine. Suzie is grateful for good PR and likes those who give her good copy but is highly intolerant of incompetent product promotion. Like many journalists, she has a reputation for being difficult, tough and prickly to PR people. Learn from the way she deals with PR people how best to approach a journalist. Follow Suzie's diary as she details her days and meetings with people trying to promote their products to her.

CHAPTER ONE

An introduction to journalists and journalism – understanding the agenda

Introduction

No one can deny that journalists are powerful shapers of public opinion and perception. They are critical in helping consumers make decisions and choices and they can make or break the promotion of your product to your target market. Most people still remember how one small comment made by Gerald Ratner about his products was picked up and broadcast by the press, and the consequential damage to his business – that's an example of how influential they are.

This chapter helps you understand what journalists are aiming to achieve, how they work and some of the pressures they are under. This is so that you can understand how to deliver your message to them most effectively, in a way which will do as much as possible to ensure that it will be used.

You don't have to be a PR professional to deal with the press. In fact, many journalists prefer to deal with managers and executives closest to the products, customers and markets. You don't need specialist training to get media coverage – you just need to understand what journalists are looking for and then deliver it to them.

If you get your promotion to the press right, you will achieve editorial coverage far more effective and valuable than paid-for advertising. Achieving editorial coverage is not difficult – remember that the journalists are looking for stories, and you can help them!

However, it is crucial for the success of your publicity campaign that journalists know about your product and you, that they understand what your product can do, they know that you are willing to be used as a pundit, and their impression of you and your product or service is a favourable one.

To achieve this, you need to understand what sort of people they are, that there are different types of journalists and how they work, and their agenda and objectives.

What is a journalist?

When you think of a journalist, what comes to mind? The image of someone nobly and fearlessly revealing truths? A dedicated professional prepared to work long hours for little money to bring the news to their audience? Or someone determined to misquote and cause mischief?

Is a journalist a crusading, incorruptible professional supported by a fearless editor, determined to expose hypocrisy and corruption? Do they place the interests of those who require information above those who seek to conceal it? Or are they people without scruples or regard for their subjects who will print anything to gain more readers or viewers, or to further their own career? Or do they recognise their responsibility to see and hear as much as possible and pass on an accurate, unbiased picture to their readers, viewers and listeners, to allow them to have an informed impression?

Do you have a preconceived view?

There are certainly stereotypes, such as the powerful, ambitious editor, the cantankerous, conniving news editor, the seedy, shifty reporter and the chaos of a news-room. Many journalists fulfil many of these expectations, but there is no classic profile which all journalists conform to. They are all different.

The journalists' primary objective is to educate, entertain and inform.

Unfortunately for you, the way they achieve this is by using conflict, controversy and negative comment. The trick is to anticipate the journalists' need for such conflict, controversy and negative comment and deliver controversial and newsworthy information which promotes your product.

What sort of journalist are you dealing with?

It's a journalist's job to be cynical and take a critical view, and not take things at face value. So, a good journalist will automatically think, 'Why is this person lying to me?' or 'What is the true story?' or 'What is the real angle?' Good journalists are suspicious, and instinctively want to look behind the story they are being told for a more controversial picture.

Most journalists are professional and have high standards of ethics and integrity. They are under constant pressure to be fair, and most of them are.

There are also journalists who may fall into these categories:

- **The Ferret or Terrier:** They will not give up when they think they have a whiff of a story, even if it is mainly in their imagination. They will go on and on and on, pursuing individuals, hunting down leads and continuing their line of questioning until they get what they want. Sometimes, this type is accused of putting words into people's mouths or constructing the information they want in order to make the story that they are convinced is there.

- **The Bridge Burner:** Unlike career journalists who will usually respect requests to go 'off the record' or hold a story until a later date, the Bridge Burner will do anything to get a scoop or a story ahead of the competition. They have no regard for their contacts or personal relationships, putting their career and the next front page in front of everything else.

- **The Fledgling:** These are journalists fresh from media training schools or colleges, who may have practised their skills in the classroom but have no experience of real-life interviews, and possess only a very limited understanding of the industry or the specific topics they write about. This type is often a blank sheet wanting information, and is consequently often the best sort to give your views to or to tell about your product.

- **Wasters, Winos, Politicos:** There used to be at least one on every title; now they are a rarity but you still find hacks who are only good for two hours every morning and are wasted for the rest of the afternoon after a long liquid lunch. Though they are rare they are often the best journalists around and can turn in better copy in those two hours than ordinary journalists can manage in a whole day. They often have prodigious memories, so that something mentioned in passing can be pulled out and quoted later. They are often greatly underestimated and can be poisonous, difficult, untrustworthy and have enormous prejudices, as well as years of experience. Treat with care.

- **Specialists:** These are usually journalists who have been working in a particular sector, like the entertainment industry, IT or business, for many years and know just about all there is to know about the products and markets. There is not much you can tell these journalists, and they are probably the easiest to work with, provided you are not trying to hoodwink them.

They will understand the implications and benefits of your product, but are also the most likely to ask piercing questions which go right to the heart of the matter.

- **Seasoned Professionals:** These can be the most dangerous journalists of all because they have the stability and experience to demolish your efforts, claims or views with the best and most accurate arguments. They can make incisive, cunning interviewers and have so much experience on the subject-matter that it is extremely difficult to pull the wool over their eyes.

The average journalist wants to produce copy which is truthful, fair, impartial and non-partisan. However, they usually have a preconceived idea of what the story is and what their conclusion or the emphasis of the story will be. There is nothing you can do about this, except try to determine what the journalist's position and view are, and try to change them so that they reflect your message.

What does a journalist do?

Journalists observe and report, make judgements and pass comment, analyse and debate issues of public concern.

They do this by keeping themselves informed by reading all the relevant newspapers and publications. Many journalists are media junkies and often take all daily broadsheets plus specialist publications, as well as watch TV and listen to the radio.

Each journalist has a clear idea of their target reader or listener, as defined by their publication or programme and tracked by their Editor. It's one of the Editor's functions to keep their 'product' – whether print, radio or TV – on an even keel by continuing to meet the needs of their target reader or listener. This person, who is often a specific individual in a journalist's mind's eye, is their customer.

Journalists work in a non-consensual way. They are independent. They don't seek your approval or sanction for what they write or say. They are free to print or broadcast their version of a story. That means that they will publish information which they believe to be in the public interest, regardless of whether they have your approval or not. This is a basic tenet of journalism which can, at the extreme end, lead to the paparazzi type of photography and the worst sleaze features and gossip columns. But at the opposite, higher moral end it can lead to the best investigative journalism. This is a fundamental of journalism which should be respected.

What does a journalist want?

Journalists want newsworthy stories which engage the reader and make them want to read more. A good story inevitably has an element of controversy, conflict, news which someone does not want published or negative comment – or a combination of all four.

Journalists are looking for information, either as the hook for a story or to flesh out a story. Information – and gossip – are their lifeblood. They want facts and statistics to reinforce claims and statements, and these can often be used as the main hook for a story. They want opinion, passion, views and personality in the people they interview.

They want straightforward answers to their questions, and if they get those they are willing to listen to your messages about your product. They want people who are prepared and know what they want to say. And they want good contacts who they can call at any time and rely on for a good quote.

They like people who listen to experienced PR and marketing professionals with experience of the media. They usually want to present a balanced picture according to the Journalist's Code of Practice, which means getting at least two points of view for every story. But most of all, journalists are looking for a unique news story or angle.

What doesn't a journalist want?

Journalists are not looking for sales puff, vague waffle, old news, jargon or hype.

They don't want to be treated like a customer and given an exaggerated picture of your product. It is the easiest thing in the world to slip into hyperbole and start 'selling' to the journalist. You *should* be telling the journalist some of the salient points of the sales pitch, but hold back on over-the-top claims of excellence. Leave it to the journalist to come to those conclusions, if they are appropriate. Provided you have given the journalist all the best information, they will take a view, take a position, and broadcast their opinion. They don't want their opinions formed for them: that's what they are there to do.

Like you, *journalists do not want to have to deal with people who are bigoted, ignorant, egotistical, self-righteous, pushy, boring, belligerent, arrogant, smarmy, thick-skinned, sycophantic, ingratiating, over-friendly or patronising.*

Yet a surprising number of the people they have to deal with are like that. Anything less than a straightforward, business-like approach is something which journalists endure, but dislike. If you are straightforward and business-like, you have an immediate advantage over your competitors.

Does a journalist want to know about your product or about you?

The short answer is **No**, unless there is an angle which is important to their audience.

Journalists rely on people like you giving them stories, passing on rumours and offering them leads and opinions. From these seeds the journalist will think of a new story idea or flesh out an existing story. These stories aim to educate, entertain or inform their audience. Everything they do is done with their 'customer' in mind – their reader, viewer or listener.

The journalist will not want to know about your product unless it has some clear relevance or impact on the journalist's audience. You need to present the information about your product in such a way that it satisfies the journalist's need to educate, entertain and inform that audience. So you need to emphasise its relevance and impact, or positive business or social points, in such a way that the beneficial implications are obvious.

How do journalists work?

Every journalist is different and they all work in different ways. Some like to work close to deadlines and find it almost impossible to rouse themselves unless a deadline is pressing. Others prefer to be well organised.

Some journalists like to use small tape-recorders, some use reporters' notebooks, while some manage to report on a conversation without making notes at all. Remember that when you are on the telephone to a journalist, he or she is probably making notes of everything you are saying – so try and slow down and repeat the most important points when you are answering questions.

If the journalist wants to use a voice-recorder, agree and then ignore it – you'll soon forget it's there. The advantage of a recorder in a face-to-face meeting is that you can maintain eye contact with the journalist, making the interview much more like a conversation. A better, more natural flow of dialogue can be established. And it can mean that you have a better chance of *all* your words being used, and accurately. There is nothing to prevent you using a recorder too – many people do – to make sure you are not misquoted.

Who should you contact?

Ultimately, it will be the Editor who decides what goes into the publication or programme, so when you want to promote your product to the media you need to make sure that the Editor is aware of your product or service, its unique qualities, its price and what it offers. But you also need to make sure that the staff writers and freelances are also familiar with the product, because they are the ones who will actually write the copy.

So, your promotional 'push' to the media needs to be two-pronged: directed both at the Editor and at those who will produce the copy or review. It's no good just taking the Editor out for lunch or inviting only the Editor to a press conference and expecting a review, report or mention to appear. Often your budget will be better spent on the journalists who will actually produce the copy. But at the same time you cannot ignore the Editor – if he or she is unaware of your product or doesn't know what's important about it, they can remove any mention of it from the editorial.

What's the difference between staff and freelance journalists?

There are several key differences between freelance and staff journalists and it is important to bear in mind which type of journalist you are dealing with. They have different pressures and requirements, and if you are going to get publicity you must deliver to each the sort of information they want.

The most obvious difference is that a staffer works for only one title and a freelance works for several titles or programmes. In other words, a freelance offers far better economies of scale. Any promotional activity aimed at a freelance has a chance of appearing in far more places than if directed at a staffer.

Freelances are also more inclined to be professional career journalists who are committed to their jobs. They usually build up a base of regular titles that they work for, and often take on a proactive role in suggesting topics for news and features to the Editor. A staffer is more likely to be a novice straight from university or journalism school. Many staff journalists move on after nine months or a year. Hopefully, they will be promoted within the same title or transferred to another, related title, so that you don't lose touch. But many journalists will take any job as a staffer on any publication or programme when they start, regarding it as a stepping-stone to greater things.

Freelances depend on long-established contacts for commissions and stories. It's almost impossible just to decide one day to become a freelance journalist and set yourself up, and then expect to earn a reasonable living straightaway. Freelances are career journalists. They are constantly looking for new and unusual ideas for features and news stories which they pitch to commissioning editors. Time is money to a freelance because they are self-employed. This means they are often reluctant to take trips or go for long lunches. Two or three days out of the office on a trip has to result in several stories to make it worthwhile.

Is your story news or a feature?

News and feature writers have similar agendas but work to different time-scales and often work in different ways. By knowing and understanding the difference, you are more likely to deliver what they want.

A news journalist usually has a more dynamic immediate approach, while a feature writer is more analytical and takes a more considered approach.

Journalists dealing in *hard news* stories are dealing with material which is fast changing and high impact. They may need some background detail, but do not always include analysis or comment. They rarely use long quotes but like snappy sound-bites. Journalists working on *soft news* still have the news element as the dominant factor but the news is treated in a lighter style, with more padding and probably including some description and comment. Journalists on soft news stories are still often working to tight deadlines but are less aggressive in their treatment. They like to use quotes.

Journalists working on *news features* are often delivering an analysis or comment piece on an item in the news. Often a feature is longer than a straight news story. It might include description, comment, analysis, background, eye-witness reporting and a range of sources to give it depth. It aims to be informative or to open or add to a debate. It may be divided into sections, with boxes containing case studies or information. A personal view or contrary angle may be the hook of the feature, or the feature may argue a case or a point of view. The journalist probably has a week or two to research and compile the data.

Journalists working on *backgrounders* are working on a feature in which the emphasis lies not on reporting the news but explaining it or its implications. A backgrounder usually has plenty of views and opinions, giving different sides of an argument. It may set out to explain the issues behind a current news story, or be a retrospective looking back on an event.

Journalists working on a *colour feature* of the sort you see in colour supplements have a subject-matter which is not time-sensitive and is often detached from topical news. A colour feature often reflects social issues and comments on social or political changes, but lacks a strong news angle.

It is important to determine and establish exactly which type of journalist you are talking to. If it is a staff writer, you should be familiar with their title and its target audience. If you are not, *find out*. If you are dealing with a freelance, ask them which title the piece is for. They all have different deadlines, and knowing what sort of writer and which title the piece is for should tell you whether you have to comment immediately or whether you have a day or two to think about your response.

Editorial, advertising and advertorial

It is important to understand the boundaries between editorial, advertising and advertorial if you are to be successful in promoting your product to the media.

Publications vary but, as a general rule, there is a wide gulf between advertising and editorial. Unless you understand this difference, you risk upsetting the editorial staff, who are often sensitive about pressure from advertisers and the advertising department. If you fail to see the difference and move between the two groups insensitively, you are likely to fail in your efforts to achieve editorial promotion.

(In some areas of the media there is considerable overt collaboration between the advertising and editorial teams, but often the editorial content of those titles reflects such cosiness. In those titles there are usually no respected independent views and opinions. You should ask yourself: 'If I can buy editorial coverage by paying for an advertisement, is the editorial worth having?')

The primary differences between advertising and editorial are clear: one you pay for, one you do not; one you have control of, one you do not.

Advertising is the most straightforward way of getting your message across, and the easiest. If you pay for space and time, you have absolute control and you can say what you like, provided the message is, in the words of the Advertising Standards Authority, 'decent, legal, honest and truthful'. Advertising should be used in combination with efforts to persuade journalists to write or talk about your product. The message that you give to the press should be reinforced by the advertising, although the two efforts should be quite separate.

Advertising offers heavy costs, complete control but low credibility. Editorial offers low costs, no control and powerful credibility. In the grey area in between comes *advertorial*. Advertorial can be used to raise your profile as a pundit, launch you as an expert, increase awareness of the product and increase sales gradually. But advertising should be used if you want to announce specific offers or products, inform your customers about your product or increase sales immediately.

One distinct difference between advertising and editorial is personality. Media sales people require a hide like an elephant and the chutzpah to keep telephoning people who really don't want to know. People who do it have to be tough and determined and don't have to be creative, sensitive or analytical, unlike the editorial type.

Another difference is *objectives*. The editorial person is seeking to educate, entertain and inform the audience while the media sales person is seeking to achieve targets by selling advertising space. A journalist is not going to seek you out, while a media sales person will. You rarely get the two groups socialising, and they are often located in different parts of the building. This is healthy. Too much collaboration between the two teams can lead to pressure on journalists, which leads to biased copy.

Understanding these differences helps you pitch your promotion at the right level to appeal to the journalists successfully. If you ignore them and treat editorial staff like media sales staff, you're not likely to get very far.

The degree of contact and influence between advertising and editorial can vary between publishing houses and even between different titles of the same company. At one extreme there is absolutely no contact, no feature list, no feedback or flow of information from one side to the other. At the other extreme the two departments are very closely linked. You may be asked to pay 'colour separation costs' to make sure that your press release is used in the editorial pages.

Even on titles where there appears to be a clear separation between editorial and advertising teams, it is not uncommon for the editor and the sales manager to have regular meetings at which the editor tells the advertising sales team leader certain useful things, such as what features are coming up over the next twelve months and which companies are mentioned in editorial. On some titles the editor will tell the sales team manager exactly who is quoted and what is said, and even let them see copy. This is generally regarded as unethical by journalists, however.

Such collaboration works both ways. At the same meeting, the advertising sales manager may request that certain companies, people or topics are mentioned, which will give leverage for media sales activity.

Can you influence editorial if you advertise? Possibly, but you should never mention your advertising spend to the journalist and you should be extremely discreet about any pressure which you exert through the advertising team on the editorial team. Threatening to withdraw your advertising if the editorial fails to mention or quote you is often an empty, useless gesture. Even on those publications where there are strong links, these fall apart if the advertisers overtly attempt to influence the editorial. Many journalists take pleasure in *not* mentioning advertisers if they know that there is pressure in the air.

You may ask how such a situation can exist. After all, many publications rely on advertising revenue for their existence. The answer is that a good editor is a strong editor, willing and able to stand up to advertising pressure in the name of editorial independence. Those publications which have weak editors who give in to heavy pressure from the advertising team soon lose the respect of the readers, because they can see when the editorial begins to lose its independence. Gradually the publication loses its good name, and it becomes read less and less. Eventually, it loses its advertisers because none of the potential readership bothers to pick it up or believes the editorial content. It has no value and, unless the slide is checked, it will eventually close. So it is important for the long-term survival of the publication that there is separation between the advertising and editorial teams.

There are some industries and sections of the media where advertising and editorial are strongly linked and journalists have very little freedom to be critical. These are not generally respected either by the journalists or, more importantly, by the target audience, your potential customer.

What about advertorial?

Advertorials come in several flavours. The most common is an advertisement designed to look like editorial but over which you have full control, and which you have to pay for as advertising.

Usually the editorial staff dislike advertorial intensely and resist it whenever they can but they are often overruled by the publisher, who sees only the financial bottom line and is less interested in how independent the publication appears. Advertorial is sometimes sold by the media sales team, and the editorial team does not see it until it appears.

The worst advertorial uses the same typeface as real editorial and is extremely hard to tell apart, until you read it and you realise that it is pure PR puff. Some advertorial is clearly marked, with 'Advertisement' or 'Advertorial' printed at the top of the page. Sometimes it appears on the contents page. Sometimes it uses a different font and is laid out in a different style.

Some publications have a half-way stage between pure advertorial and editorial, called contributed copy. This is sometimes called an 'opinion page', 'case study' or 'viewpoint' and the copy is contributed by the 'advertiser' but they do not pay for it to appear. It will be submitted as if it were written by a journalist (freelance journalists often work with PR agencies to deliver copy which is acceptable to the editor and meets the house style and the needs of the audience). In this case the editor will have complete control over the content and will take out any excessively flattering references to the company or product. These pages are also subject to the vagaries of editorial pressure so they may be dropped at the last minute or held over.

Such pages or columns are attractive to editors because they do not have to pay for them and they are able to save on budget and spend the contributors' fees elsewhere. The difference between advertorial and contributed copy is that with the latter the editor is able to sub-edit the copy and rewrite it if necessary. The trick is to deliver contributed copy which is not full of promotional puff and is as objective as possible. Editors often look for contributed copy which is opinionated and controversial, debating topical issues.

Contributed copy can be a cheaper and more effective way of promoting your product, if you can arrange it with the editor, who will only accept it if it fits in with the editorial plans. For details of advertorial you should contact the advertising sales manager, and for details of contributed editorial you should contact the editor.

Chapter summary

Journalists

- They do not work for you. Their customer is their reader/ viewer/listener.

- They want information, stories, opinions and facts and they don't want their time wasted.
- They can be arrogant and rude and are usually creative types.
- They face different deadlines, work in different styles and have different agendas depending on whether they are news or features writers, freelances or staffers.

Also

- The frequency of a publication or programme affects the way you deal with the journalists.
- Advertising has no effect on editorial (or if it does, you should question the value of the publication).
- Advertorial can give you more control over the editorial content – up to a point.
- You need to carefully select the magazines and journalists to target for your campaign.

Remember

- Advertising and editorial are quite separate. If there is any collaboration, leverage your advertising spend by asking the media sales manager if you can talk to a journalist. Do not go direct to a journalist and tell them you are advertising and therefore want editorial coverage.
- Ask if the title is looking for contributed copy, and, if so, deliver something controversial and opinionated which makes a much better and more effective read than overt product puff.

CASE STUDIES

Case study 1: Product promotion to the lifestyle press

Paul Davis has been promoted to marketing manager of Betta-Prods, a small firm based in Plymouth which makes and sells kitchenware. It is an old organisation with 30 employees. Betta-Prods recently developed its own unique range of goods which feature an innovative insulating material called KoolWay.

KoolWay comes in a variety of forms – from hard and inflexible like metal, to soft and pliable like plastic – and was developed by space scientists. BettaProds uses it in the sides of saucepans, so the only heat comes through the bottom of the pan and the sides remain cool. It is also used in kitchen implements and cutlery, to protect the users. There is also a range of products under development specifically for babies and small children.

Paul's background is in technical development but he has taken a short course with the Institute of Marketing and feels he is capable of running a promotion and publicity campaign. He is in charge of managing the advertising campaign as well as achieving as much publicity as possible. He has no experience of working with the press, although his girlfriend used to know a journalist.

The target market is domestic and professional purchasers who buy kitchen items, and Paul's brief is to cover both the trade and consumer press.

His first task is to compile a list of prospective publications, programmes and journalists to target. He does this by subscribing to a media information service which details all the publications and programmes, and the names of all freelance and staff journalists. It is regularly updated and Paul sees it as a good investment for someone wanting to keep up to date with the press.

There are obvious publications that he needs to target, like *Good Housekeeping* and *Homes and Gardens*, plus trade publications read by professional chefs and caterers. He finds more details of these publications by consulting one of the media listings books in his local library. He does the same with the national and local press, and the broadcast media. He finds out which are his local radio stations, and where the programme-making companies are based.

He lists each of the target programmes and publications on a card filing system, and also in a database software program on his computer. Paul notes which magazines and programmes carry product reviews which would be suitable for the BettaProds range.

- **Comment**: Paul is right to start by compiling a list of target media and journalists. Next he should analyse the product's strengths and weaknesses and consider his message.

Case study 2: Product promotion to the computer press

Jessica Martin works for SoftMicro, a small computer software development company which has just launched the latest version of its educational software for children, called KiddieLearn.

The company also develops business applications, and is well established in that market as a highly respected player. The educational software was originally developed as an indulgence by the managing director, who has six young children and was unable to find the software he wanted for them. So he set about writing the software himself, and now relies on Jessica to market it.

The first version was launched two years ago, and the latest version, called KiddieLearn 2, has many improvements. It is based on the National Curriculum and has Government approval, and can be used by teachers as well as parents. There are versions for all the core GCSE subjects plus some hobby subjects.

The software is 'intelligent' and so can be used by a child all the way from the age of four up to 16. It starts with the first lessons on a subject and takes the child up to GCSE. It learns about the child as the child learns about the subject, so that if a child keeps making the same mistake the software will repeat and practise a section until the child has grasped it. It also repeats sections at the start of a new session, depending on how the child performed at the last session. It produces reports for the teacher and parent, and makes suggestions to the teacher on ancillary and supplementary work. It learns and adapts to each child's idiosyncrasies, remembering past faults and weaknesses.

Jessica was originally hired by Richard Devine, the owner of Soft-Micro, as a secretary but has shown an aptitude for PR work and he has now promoted her to marketing manager (although she still has to do all the secretarial work as well). The job was handled previously by Richard's wife Susan, but she has now left to have another baby.

Richard is very pleased with Jessica's enthusiasm for the publicity role, although she has to fit it around her other tasks. He distrusts the press, so is happy to let Jessica take over the media relations. He has an outside agency to take care of the advertising and media buying, but wants Jessica to work with them to maximise the publicity effect.

Jessica's first task is to go back through the files and establish exactly what was done with the first version of the product, which was launched before she joined SoftMicro. She finds a couple of press releases written by Richard, but which he says were not used by the press. In fact, there was very little reaction from the media except in *The Times Education Supplement* and two of the educational supplements in the national newspapers. They all tested the product and gave it glowing reviews, but Richard feels that there should have been more publicity for such an innovative product. He used the newspaper cuttings in the marketing material but has not been in touch with any of the journalists again.

Jessica compiles a database of everyone who was sent a press release before, notes who reacted to it and whether there appeared to be any follow-up by SoftMicro. She discovers that there wasn't any at all. She checks with Susan who confirms that, once the press release was sent, she just sat back and waited for the journalists to contact her.

Jessica then updates and expands the list of target publications and journalists. She telephones each publication and programme editor and asks what their deadline date is for press releases, and whether they are working on any reviews of new educational products in the near future.

- **Comment**: Asking target publications for their deadline dates is a good start.

Case study 3: Diary of a journalist – Suzie Ingram, freelance

Monday 9a.m.
The start of a new week and my first job is to run through the deadlines for copy due in the next ten days. Not too bad – I've got two 2,000-word features, a 1,800-word software product review, a 1,500-word buyer's guide and an opinion column to do, but they are all due on Thursday. As I write for two distinct industries – the home and lifestyle and the computer software industry – I have to keep up to date with a lot of issues and news.

I've already made a start on the product review and one of the 2,000-word features. I've also got a press conference invitation for Wednesday and another for Friday, plus a lunch invitation for Friday. All the events are in Central London, and as I live an hour's travel away and because of the deadlines, I make a mental note to turn down the Wednesday invitation. But if I have to go into town on Friday, I might go and see a couple of commissioning editors at the same time. One trouble with being a freelance is that unless you occasionally remind them that you are there, they tend to forget you.

That means that I will be at my desk for four days this week, and I've got a lot to do. I start to work simultaneously on the features. In my office, I create a tray for each topic and start sorting out notes, old press releases, contact names and case studies for each of the features. I also start thinking what topic the opinion piece will be on. It could be anything – it's to go in one of the Sunday supplement magazines, so I am allowed to write about anything, really, so long as it's not what I had for breakfast. I think I'm beginning to suffer from Opinion Writer's Overload – I do an average of two opinion columns a week, and it can be very hard sometimes, thinking of something fresh to write about!

10.30

First break of the day. A cup of tea while I go through the post. I get a special delivery by van because I get too much mail for the poor postman to carry. It usually takes me 30 minutes at least to go through it, although some days, like today when I've got a lot on, I only open the interesting envelopes and save the obvious press releases, junk mail and magazines for browsing later. I find that my best writing times are early in the day, so I don't want to waste the time doing too many chores. Still, better check if there are any cheques in the post.

11.00

I got side-tracked into opening all the mail after all. It's called *displacement activity* – avoiding getting on with the real task, which is writing. About 40 press releases today – it's always less on a Monday. All but three went straight in the bin, and those three I will save for some features that I know I'm going to be writing next week and the week after.

Now, I must get down to some writing.

3.00

A mid-afternoon break for another cup of tea. A phone call from an experienced PR person wanting to know what I'm working on, and asking if there is anything I need help with. I fax her my latest Features List and hope that she is able to come up with an opinionated person to comment on some of the features. Like an increasing number of freelances now, I produce a list every three or four weeks which outlines the commissions I am working on and issues I am interested in following up. Sometimes I ask for ideas for features or 'fly a kite' with certain controversial issues. If I get enough feedback then I will go to the appropriate editor and suggest that I write a feature, knowing that I have enough material and people to quote.

5.00
I put all my work to one side and catch a train down to London to go to a press party.

6.30
At the party, lots of free drinks and food, and some interesting people to talk to. The host is a PR company which has got several clients together to pay for the hospitality. I mingle, chat to other journos and meet several of the PR company's clients who might be useful in the future. Swap lots of business cards.

10.00
Catch the last train home.

- **Comment**: Suzie is obviously a busy and hardworking freelance. But she also does not suffer fools easily, and probably has a reputation for being tough and abrasive. Yet she also knows that contact with PR and marketing people is an essential part of her job.

CHAPTER TWO

What makes a story newsworthy?

Introduction

Although your primary objective is to promote your product, you need to promote yourself or a senior person within your organisation to achieve that end. News is not about products, news is always ultimately about people. Products are only important because they involve and affect people.

This chapter explains what journalists are looking for when they build a story, so that you know what you should deliver. If you understand what the press needs, then you will be able to give them the information they want in a way that will satisfy their quest for a strongly angled news story, and get you the publicity you want.

You can make the news by positioning your story so that it meets the media's requirements. They are looking for news, views and comments in the most opinionated and interesting form. Unfortunately, the journalist may not see your story the way you do. They may be looking for something which you want to hide, or they may see an angle which did not occur to you. They want to shock and surprise their readers with a juicy story, and you just want to promote your product. Yet it is possible for the two agendas to have common ground. First though, you have to understand what the journalist is looking for, which may not be what you want him or her to see. From a journalist's point of view, anything that someone doesn't want published is news – everything else is advertising. So the journalist will be looking out for – and will ignore – overt and dull product publicity.

You have to understand about the wants and needs of your target audience, and then ensure that your product can meet those demands. Learn about the 4 Ps of marketing, which differentiate your product in its market – product, price, place and promotion – and consider the marketing principles of brand management and development. These will all help you to spot key areas where your product is already naturally differentiated, and allow you to manufacture differentiating factors which can be exploited for publicity purposes.

What are journalists looking for?

You cannot just tell journalists about the product and expect them to say 'Wow'. You have to find a relevant angle and an interesting story in your product. There are a few points to bear in mind. First, it takes time to get results. It may be several months before journalists sit up and take notice. You may have to send several press releases before they pick up on one.

Second, it is out of your control. You can do the best you can, cultivate relationships, spend money on lunches and press material, and still nothing happens. Then they pick up on an angle of the story which you did not see, or you think is not important.

Third, it is an extremely competitive business. Journalists get courted from all sides, and are being wined and dined by your competitors while you are trying to build the business. You have to have persistence and a long-term plan.

Your media plan

First identify your targets, which fall into three categories:

- customers and markets
- relevant publications or programmes
- specific journalists.

Then:

- identify your story. This, for many people, is the really tricky bit. Often it's right under your nose. Stories may be all around you, in something unusual about the product, something strange about the people who make or sell it, something rare in the way it is marketed. In some way, the product might change people's lives. These things are the story you need to promote but they are often hard to see when you are close to the product and company. You have to step back from the product and look for what other people might find interesting.

Next:

- define your message

and finally:

- deliver it.

What makes a story newsworthy?

Journalists are definitely attracted by certain elements. These are relevance, information, facts and statistics, opinions and views, controversy, difference and timing.

Relevance

This is undoubtedly the most important factor. If your story or message is not relevant, nothing else matters.

Every publication and programme has a profile of its reader, viewer or listener, and its editorial contents are defined by that profile. Whatever information you give a journalist is pitched for that 'user' or audience. So consider what the reader/viewer/listener profile is, and then find the angle most likely to interest that individual. It has to be relevant to their interests and needs.

It may be a local issue, for the local weekly, or a marketing issue for the trade press. Your story may have international implications for the national broadsheets, or it may have a technical implication for engineers or programmers. You have to identify the angle relevant to each publication or programme and play it up.

Information

Information shapes opinion, and valuable and worthwhile opinions are based on clearly understood facts. An opinion without an informed background is virtually worthless. Often journalists are simply seeking information, and many of their interviews and conversations are just to provide background knowledge and facts.

Make sure you have plenty of basic information to hand when you talk to journalists. Have press releases and facts available for background information if necessary, and be ready to fax them to the journalist at any time.

Know all the angles and implications of your story and message. The journalist isn't likely to ask you exactly the right questions to elicit the responses that you want. You need to be prepared to 'brain dump' the information you have as a seamless part of a conversation or interview.

You are the expert – about your product, its market and its potential. You need to be able to talk interestingly and comprehensively – and accurately – about the whole sector that your product is targeted at.

When pitching a story to a journalist, or writing a press release, put the most important/controversial/dramatic/interesting information at the beginning. (See Appendix 3 for details on how to write an effective press release.)

Facts

Journalists frequently like to base a story on statistics, empirical evidence or research. It makes an impressive start to a news story or feature. They want to quote a source of their information. They need to anchor their story with a creditable source.

Facts and statistics give respectability and weight, and journalists will use them whenever they can. Many stories use facts or statistics as the central hook, or mention them in the first paragraph – headlines are often based around the result of a report, research or a survey.

Even if the nub of the story is not about research results, you will help the journalist by giving as much independently researched and statistical background as possible. So, whenever possible, put your story in the context of a percentage or a proportion, and give a credit for the source of your claim, where possible.

Have your facts prepared, and know

- Who? (is the story about)
- What? (is the most important angle)
- Why? (is it important)
- Where? (is it happening)
- When? (did it happen)

Opinion

Those pundits used regularly by journalists have one thing in common: they are not afraid to speak their minds. A good interviewee is someone who has views and is not afraid to express them. No one who sticks too closely to the company line or is inhibited by the risk of getting into hot water will give a quote likely to be strong and usable.

At the same time, there is no need to get yourself into trouble. Journalists love people who are indiscreet and will gossip, and you should be cautious of being led into saying something that you will regret. You have to give a balance of outspoken comment with considered verdict.

Preparation is the key to strong, quotable opinions. Anticipate the journalist's questions and think through your responses. Write them down and talk them through, so that you can give lively and interesting responses which satisfy the journalist but do not compromise you.

If you are telephoned for an impromptu comment, err on the side of danger rather than caution. It is unlikely that you will say anything really damaging, and you might be remembered for saying something outstanding.

Controversy

The media loves drama, and the essence of drama is conflict and controversy. Bad news sells newspapers, and a journalist's ears will prick up when they hear a controversial story. If you can deliver one, they'll be interested, but don't make one up. It has to be anchored in reality.

Most news stories and many features use a negative hook or are based on a premise of conflict. Journalists always 'look for an angle', which is invariably the most controversial aspect of the story. It can be a clash between individuals or groups of people, or actions or ideas which upset the norm. Good journalism will stimulate debate about a controversial issue, giving different points of view and bringing all the factors into the open.

You can anticipate this desire for conflict and suggest a controversial angle that the journalist will find interesting. In this way you can have some control over the way the journalist uses your material, and perhaps guide the journalist away from a more controversial angle that you do not want discussed. The risk, of course, is that the journalist does not stop and pursues the issue in a way which becomes detrimental to you. You need to use your judgement to know what controversy to mention and where you should hold back.

'Good' controversy includes:

- a report which goes against received opinion
- someone doing or saying something unexpected and/or upsetting
- something which somebody does not want publicised.

Difference

'Weak' news is that which is based entirely on 'soft' or 'gentle' stories and has no real news content. It's the sort of story that appears in the 'and finally' section on broadcast news, or in the trivia section of magazines, and you should try to avoid it. Your aim is to give the journalist something strikingly and notably different from that which has gone before. It is the journalist's task to deliver the information to the reader, listener or viewer in an interesting and entertaining way by emphasising the differential.

For stories to work there needs to be a 'hard' edge or difference from the existing status quo which is eye-catching and memorable. Journalists and editors are continually looking for this element of difference, and if you can deliver it to them they will come back to you in the future for further comment and listen should you call with another story.

The difference has to be new, relevant and interesting. Just having a new product is not enough, but if the new product has unique features or is dramatically cheaper or longer-lasting, then it is news. Mundane material will only be used if there is nothing more vibrant, startling and different.

Try to put an angle in your story which will interest the target audience, such as the following:

- the fastest
- the cheapest
- the first
- the last
- the biggest
- the saddest
- the most unusual.

You need to establish whether your product is aimed at a fragmented or a specialised market, and whether it will be low volume/high price or high volume/low price. Do a SWOT analysis (strengths, weaknesses, opportunities and threats) of your product and also of your key competitors. You should learn more about how your product can be differentiated.

Timing

Stories have to reach the right journalists at the right time. It is no good giving the editor of a monthly a scoop story when the title has just closed and gone to the printers. And it is no good giving a weekly newspaper a story which appeared in other weeklies the week before.

Most publications and programmes usually have a combination of features and news with different deadlines. Some have long lead times (the time between the commission and the deadline), others have deadlines right up to the time of broadcast or on the verge of going to the printers. Some, like dailies, close the evening before they appear and some, like monthlies, close two weeks before the issue appears. When you compile your listing of your target publications and journalists, make sure you include details of when they require copy, deadlines, lead times and the best days to deliver information.

Combining newsworthy elements

It makes sense to combine several newsworthy elements if you can.

So, while every story should have relevance for the audience, you can also throw in some controversy. For a local newspaper, for example, if a story about how your product helps detect pollution levels can be linked to a story about the siting of a new waste-disposal site near to a housing estate, you will be achieving two of the requirements for news: it will be relevant to the people who live locally and it will be controversial. Or for a technical journal, the hook can be that your product offers the latest way to detect pollution and is innovative technology.

It would be a bad idea, however, to 'waste' more than two newsworthy angles by combining them in one story. Better to hold the third or fourth angle for another press release two or three weeks later, to reinforce the publicity effort.

What is *not* news

Journalists will ignore:

- a very slight improvement to a well-established product
- 'news' that is old or has already been used elsewhere
- anything that is irrelevant to the reader, viewer or listener.

Targeting the reader, listener or viewer through the journalist

News stories

A news story needs to have a far sharper point to it than a feature. A news story is more likely to have a shocking or surprising headline, with some dramatic content. Headlines typically contain a lot of active verbs and dramatic, evocative short sentences ('XProduct smashes price barrier', 'Woman loses 6 stone in 3 week shock' or 'Fastest widget creates market turmoil', etc.). If you look at any newspaper front page you will see these sorts of headline, and they

indicate the kind of story that follows – full of drama and controversy, short, sharp and snappy.

Features

Features are more analytical and informative, but still need to have
an element of controversy to be interesting. As with a news story, the
journalist will take a 'position' or find an angle, or make an assumption from which point they begin their research and interviews. Feature headlines are typically more laid back, more amusing, and more
likely to include a pun.

Personality

I can't say it enough:

- people buy from people, and
- every time you promote yourself you promote your product.

If you can develop your own media personality, and create a personality
for the product which acts like a brand profile, your media campaign to
promote the product will immediately become more successful.
    A strong personality

- makes the product more easily identifiable
- makes better and strong links between the person and the
  product
- increases product prestige, as social visibility becomes more
  meaningful
- creates a positive brand image, which is the perception of the
  audience towards a particular product, and their feelings of
  expectation
- helps segment the market, and make way for product up-
  grades in the future
- comforts the audience and makes a purchase feel safe.

(See Chapter 3 for more on developing a media personality.)

Chapter summary

- The key criteria for a newsworthy story are:
  - relevance to the audience
  - interesting information

  - solid, independent facts and statistics
  - bold opinions
  - respected views
  - balanced and informed controversy
  - novelty
  - good timing.
- If there is no newsworthy angle, the press will not be interested.
- News stories need short, sharp comments.
- Features stories need balanced analysis.
- Aim to develop a media personality, for both a person and the product.

CASE STUDIES

Case study 1: Product promotion to the lifestyle press

Paul believes that the new KoolWay technology is so revolutionary that it warrants a press conference, so he sets about organising one. First he has to define the main hook of the new product's story and decides that the safety aspect is the most important and interesting to the widest number of people.

He draws up a list of journalists to invite, books the venue, arranges buffet food and decides to get an expert and a user to attend. He settles on a date four weeks away, and prepares the invitations.

To fill the role of expert Paul finds a scientist who specialises in food technology, and decides that an expert on health and safety issues would be worthwhile. He also chooses to look for a professional chef who has used the products, and perhaps a housewife. He invites each with a phone call and follow-up letter, and offers them all the complete KoolWay range for their services.

He writes four versions of a press release, with a different emphasis for the four different types of journalist he is targeting: consumer, trade, professional and health and safety. He hears from a BettaProds salesman about a possible case study of a customer who was protected from serious harm when an accident happened while she was cooking with the new products, and also from the professional chef who uses them in his kitchen and is prepared to say how much safer they are without affecting cooking capabilities. He commissions a freelance journalist to write up the stories, agreeing a rate for the job and the word length. He leaves it to the journalist to decide the style to be used, as the journalist is used to working for many of the target publications. Paul also arranges for a freelance press photographer to take a series of pictures of each of the case-study subjects and the speakers.

Paul sends out the invitations to his key journalists, publications and programme-makers three weeks ahead of the date, and telephones each one week before to see how many are planning to attend. Most say they don't know. He is concerned now, as he fears that too few journalists will show up and the conference will be a flop. So he prepares a press release to go out three or four days before the event, announcing the launch and inviting any journalists to attend. He rings around again the day before and gets 25 confirmations, out of a mailing list of 90. This is a good percentage.

Paul also plans some visits to the publishing houses and programme-makers in the next two months, and starts to telephone the publishing houses to make the arrangements. He has to make sure that a room has been allocated for a day, and then he invites each journalist within the company to attend at half-hourly intervals. He also considers whether he can arrange some kind of high-profile stunt to attract the press. He tries to think of a gimmick.

He telephones the media sales team on every publication on his list, and asks for the forthcoming features list. When these arrive he goes through them carefully, looking for product reviews that would suit the BettaProds range. He also looks for features where a person from BettaProds could comment on an issue.

Paul realises that the MD of the company, Karen Jamison, is going to have to meet the press and she has had no experience of press interviews. He checks with Karen and she is very nervous, so he arranges some media training for her and, while he's at it, a couple of other BettaProds executives. He decides to sit in on the training himself.

He also resolves that Karen's name should be appearing in the trade and consumer press as a pundit on safety issues, and rings a few magazines to see what opportunities there are for contributed items. Several say that they take opinion or points-of-view pieces, with a maximum of 800 words. Paul commissions a freelance journalist to talk to Karen and then ghost-write some pieces. He specifies that these are not supposed to be overt product marketing, but should take the form of a debate about safety issues, with Karen giving her views. Once they are written, Karen will see them and amend and approve them before they are sent off with her by-line and photograph.

Then Paul double-checks that all the arrangements are in place for the press conference, the experts and customers know where to go, and the press packs will be ready. There is a panic because he forgot to book the AV equipment, but that is resolved at the last minute.

He also arranges for all the journalists expected to attend to be sent a selection of BettaProds' KoolWay products, direct to their offices or homes. He expects that they would not want to carry them home from the press conference, so arranges a special delivery service to drop them all direct to their addresses.

- **Comment**: Paul's first mistake is to think that the KoolWay product is worthy of a press conference. He rightly tries to find the hook in the story, but the product is not new enough to ensure that the press conference will be a success. He should have realised that and opted for another way to interest the press.

He is right to get an expert on board, and he is right to do several versions of the press release tailored for each type of medium. The idea of the case study is good, but perhaps some media training with the customer in question would ensure that if a journalist contacts her as a result of the case study, she puts the KoolWay message across in the best possible way.

The journalists say that they will be attending Paul's press conference but he has no guarantee that any will turn up. He is right to get Karen media-trained, and to arrange to get samples of the products sent direct to the journalists.

Case study 2: Product promotion to the computer press

Jessica decides that a modest press reception would be appropriate for the official launch of KiddieLearn 2, and thinks about the best time and venue. She decides on a lunch-time event with a buffet. The only difference between her plans and Paul's is that Jessica's event is to be less formal.

She also decides that it would be a good idea to invite some key customers. The local education authority bought several hundred copies of KiddieLearn Version 1, and Jessica knows that they are keen to see Version 2. So she invites the head of the education department plus two or three key teachers to the press reception. She hopes that as well as showing interest in the new product, they will speak highly of the first version.

Jessica arranges to hire ten computers and have them delivered to the press reception venue, and for a KiddieLearn 2 program to be loaded onto each machine. This will enable the journalists to have a go with the new version. There will also be sample copies for the journalists to take away with them, if they want.

She also decides to arrange for a small group of journalists to visit a school where KiddieLearn 2 is being trialled, so they can talk to the students and teachers. She organises this for the week after the press reception. While the journalists are at the reception she will try to interest them in going along on the school visit. She then has the idea to arrange a nice lunch in a respected local restaurant for those who go on the trip.

Jessica tries to write a press release but realises that she is way out of her depth. The last one was not successful, but she can't see why. So she finds a freelance journalist who also writes for the educational press, and commissions her to write the press release. She talks to Jessica about the product, talks to Richard about the company and the product, and then comes back in a week with a short, succinct press release which outlines the benefits of the new product and its new features.

Jessica then asks the journalist to write up two case studies, with quotes from teachers and students.

She arranges a breakfast seminar in three weeks' time for a small number of young journalists who have recently started writing for the educational press, and decides to invite Professor Higgins, a well-known university lecturer and pundit with strong views on the advantages and disadvantages of computers in schools and the use of software for learning. The seminar will be billed as an event to discuss the issues, and Jessica also plans to invite some teachers and parents. She books a conference room in a local hotel, with breakfast being served from 8.30. She intends to have a computer there, with KiddieLearn 2 software, and also a young person who knows the software, to demonstrate it. But her objective is more to discuss the issues and hopefully give the journalists some ideas for features and quotes to be used, rather than specifically promote the product. There will also be copies of the product available if anyone wants to take one away. She makes a note to search the Internet in case there are some published White Papers on the topic, which could also be made available to the journalists.

Jessica next books a stand for SoftMicro at the Computers in Education Show, due to be held at Earls Court in three months' time. Again, she will arrange demonstration machines and make users available to talk to customers, but she decides simply to inform the journalists of the stand, in case they want to come and see a demo. She does not plan to hold a press event at the show or arrange one-on-one interviews with Richard, unless the journalists request it.

She talks to the show's organisers, however, and makes sure that the SoftMicro stand and products are mentioned in all the literature and press releases that they send out. Most show organisers have their own press activity, and anyone exhibiting should make sure that they are mentioned and involved with the organiser's publicity machine as much as possible. It's free!

Like Paul, Jessica contacts all of the relevant educational and computing publications listed in the media guide books and asks the most junior person on the team, the editorial assistant, for the current features list. If the editorial staff doesn't have one, or refuses to send it out, she contacts the advertising sales team. She also contacts some key freelances and asks them if they know what they are writing about in the next two months, and whether they need a spokesperson to talk about the benefits of educational software and computer-based training.

Finally, Jessica double-checks that everything is in order for the press reception. She rings everyone who has been invited and gets 40 per cent – over 40 journalists – confirming that they will attend. Several say that they can only spare half an hour, and Jessica makes a note to ensure that these speak to Professor Higgins as soon as they arrive. She makes sure the press packs are ready, and there are plenty of complimentary copies of the software available for the journalists to take away.

- **Comment**: Jessica continues to do all the right things, although she will have to make sure that the journalists will get something worthwhile out of the school visit.

Case study 3: Diary of a freelance journalist

I got an irritating phone call this morning from an extremely arrogant young man called Jake Smyth, demanding confirmation that I will be attending his product launch in two weeks' time. As I don't even remember receiving the invitation, I really can't say whether I will be going or not. Why should I? I asked him to fax over the invite again for me to look at, but nothing arrived. It amazes me sometimes how incompetent some of these PR people are!

Next day
An invitation to the event mentioned by that brash young man actually arrived this morning. Because of his call, I double-check it. It's from a company I have vaguely heard of for a product that I know nothing about. It gives no reason why I should attend, and as I am so busy I'm not inclined to try to find out. When he calls back I'll tell him No. If he calls back – he seemed so disorganised I'd be surprised. If he had given me a sound reason why I should attend and an indication of whether I could get a story out of the conference, I would have considered it.

Next week
I get another press release and invitation from the young man from BettaProds about his launch of their new product range, and this time I am a little intrigued. So, the products are the result of some space science research and development? And the sides of the saucepans are kept cool even while the food cooks? Sounds novel – I think I will go after all. He rings back, and I have to say I feel a little sorry for him – he sounds so desperate. And so relieved when I

say I'm going. His name is Paul. I put it in my diary, and at the same time arrange a couple of other meetings for that afternoon.

I also get a call from a young lady called Jessica doing PR for an educational software firm. She wants me to write a press release, for which I charge £300 and I try to turn it around as quickly as possible to get it out of the way. She also wants me to do some case studies for their marketing collateral. I tell her the date I can complete the job – four weeks away – and the price, which at £450 per thousand words is more than double the journalistic rates. Some people are surprised that freelances charge more for PR work than we get paid for 'proper' editorial journalism with a by-line.

I have to fit in three more features this week on computer software, and each one involves me loading and testing out two products, reading the documentation and then writing a thousand-word review of each. That's 6,000 words by Friday. It's a tough week.

- **Comment**: Suzie has another busy period, this time with a mixture of pure journalism and some PR work. She continues to give incompetent marketing people a hard time, but she also helps those she feels will learn to improve. She knows that being a marketing person is tough and journalists can be intimidating.

CHAPTER THREE

Developing your message

Introduction

'Be prepared' is not just a Scout's motto – it should become yours too! This chapter shows the importance of having your angle ready and knowing what the story will be, and explains how you can refine and develop the message that you want to get across. It also helps you prepare for an interview.

Sometimes you don't get a chance to prepare. Interviews can happen without warning and you have two options in that case: to make the best of it or to try to postpone it until another time when you can be prepared. You have to help the journalist create the news out of the product publicity that you are providing. This chapter explains how you can achieve that.

Write out your message and have the name of the journalist written down on a crib sheet in front of you when you are on the telephone. Find out something about the journalist you are going to talk to – some have specific techniques which you can prepare for; some can be trusted more than others; some are not as discreet as you might wish them to be. These are all things that a PR agency can discover. All agencies have files on all the journalists, and can prepare a profile on each for you in advance of an interview. These files have all the details and facts which might be useful, such as professional attributes, personal details and preferences, ambitions and opinions.

Should you ever refuse an interview?

Sometimes people ask 'Should I do this?' when invited to talk to a journalist. If you are trying to promote your product, the answer is 'Always!'

The only reasons to refuse an opportunity to be interviewed are if:

- you really don't think you have anything worthwhile to say
- you believe you may emerge battered
- you think your competitors may do better and your image will suffer
- you will not get a chance to respond as you'd like.

Refusing to be interviewed can appear as though you have something to hide. So, if you really believe it is best to refuse, make sure that you give a good reason and make it clear that you would be willing to appear another time. The statement 'we asked the company to comment but they declined' can be highly damning, and it is crucial to make it clear that your refusal is not company policy. Encourage the media to come back another time, and suggest topics that you would be delighted to comment on.

Media training

The quickest way to reduce fear and build confidence is with a day's media training. It can also be the quickest way to waste your budget. Many journalists offer media training because it pays relatively well. Some don't even charge a lot in the hope of attracting those not wanting to spend much on training. However, you do need a trainer with practical experience of journalism.

In media training, the old maxim applies: pay peanuts and you get monkeys. Expect to pay around £1,000 a day plus expenses, with groups no larger than five. Any less and the course is unlikely to be worthwhile. On-camera TV training, or training in a studio with lights and recording equipment, will cost significantly more.

The quality and content of media training courses are extremely variable. Expect to get a background session on the way the press works, plus hints and tips about what journalists are looking for, how they work and what to avoid doing. Expect to get at least two mock interviews each, with the rest of the time spent on developing your message and how to get your message across. Be clear about what you are getting when you book the course – some media training courses concentrate on how to dress and body language, others give a good balance of briefing and interview practice.

Choose a trainer that you can trust with sensitive information. For the training to be effective you will need to discuss the company and product strengths and weaknesses, and if you use a working journalist you need to be confident that they will not abuse your trust.

Often the best-known journalists do not make the best media trainers – different skills are required, so don't just go for the name. Look at their track record and take up references by speaking to others who have been trained by that person.

If you are dealing with the press on a regular basis, you should have a media training refresher at least once a year. See Appendix 5 for a list of PR agencies. Many of these offer media training, or can arrange it if you ask. There is also a short list of specialist media training contacts.

Research

You need to know your facts and have as many statistics available as possible before you start promoting your product to the press. You also need to know what your opponents are doing and saying.

Find out what has happened in the past with similar products, what the competition is doing and how people are likely to receive your product. You need to collect every scrap of information relating to your product and its market.

This can be done with simple 'desk research' or *secondary research*, which means looking up information at the local library, collecting newspaper cuttings and making calls to trade and professional bodies. Electronic databases are invaluable in finding out more on the competition and the market. These are available in many libraries. You should also identify the target press publications and programmes, and get the names of all key journalists, and if possible find out a little about the main ones.

You should undertake some *primary research*, which means conducting your own survey to determine likely response and market potential for your product. There are two kinds: quantitative and qualitative. *Quantitative* is a survey of a representative sample of the public to determine statistics and measurements which you can quote in your message and campaign. *Qualitative* research determines views, attitudes, opinions and insights and is conducted through lengthy interviews with a few people. All your media messages can be underpinned by this kind of information.

Consider consumer tracking surveys, which follow the progress of products once they are in the market and being used. Telephone surveys can also be used for a quick straw poll and feedback about how a product is doing and what people think about it. Again, this data can be extremely useful material for your message to the press.

Research is sometimes criticised for being worthless, but its value is appreciably improved if it is undertaken by an independent third party. If you pay for a survey or a report, its value is going to be doubted, but if a recognised agency undertakes the survey it will have some credence.

In any research:

- The questions need to be objective.
- Questions should not be closed, leading or ambiguous.

- The conclusions should be sound and relevant.
- Don't draw conclusions from unasked questions. For example, if you discover that 50 per cent of people would like to try your product, do not assume that the other 50 per cent would not: they may not have heard of it, they may be ambivalent or have no preference either way.

Develop your story

You are looking for a striking, relevant story in your product news, so that the journalist can quickly see a good hook or peg. Effectively, you have to create the story and hand it to the journalist on a plate.

Most stories come from problems. You must look for the negative aspect of a need or requirement in your audience or target market, and then consider how your product can satisfy it. Concentrate on the positive elements of your product and how it fulfils a need.

Journalists look for stories by continually scanning the news and all news sources, reading, watching and listening, and finding an angle relevant to their readers, listeners or viewers. An issue dominating in one industry can usually be translated to another industry, and a national story can be brought down to a local level.

Develop a media personality

As you saw in Chapter 2, personalities hold a lot of power to help get your product message across. People remember and associate products, services and issues with people, such as Victor Kiam with Remington, Sir John Harvey Jones with ICI or the TV programme 'Troubleshooters', and Anita Roddick with issues around conscientious beauty products and marketing. Bill Gates is synonymous with Microsoft, Larry Ellison with Oracle and Peter Davies with the Prudential.

Personalities are particularly helpful if the product is highly technical, basically dull or obscure. Remember that journalists interview the *people*, not the *product*, and people can animate issues which are otherwise worthy but dull. Even if your own personality may be shy and retiring, the journalist is more likely to want to see you as someone prepared to be outrageous, bold and outspoken.

Most industries have their media personalities, people who can be relied on to be opinionated and interesting and who are consequently called upon time and again to comment. If you can achieve this position, promotion of your product will naturally follow.

An obvious example of the successful development and use of personality is Richard Branson. Every time he appears in the media for a balloon event or to comment on his competitors' activities he promotes the Virgin brand, whether he mentions it or not. He is known to be willing to make a fool of himself for the media, and they love him for it.

If you have someone within your organisation who is naturally interesting, charismatic and something of a personality, they are the obvious choice to be the person the journalist meets.

The best personalities are authoritative figures at the top of the organisation. They have a credible track record and a breadth and depth of knowledge which creates immediate respect. It helps if they have been media trained and understand the requirements of the press. Journalists need people who are always available with a quick and opinionated comment on a range of key issues, and able to take a 'helicopter' perspective of the market and industry, rising above it and taking an overview, and not just focused on your product. A good pundit is able to deliver the quick sound-bites almost without thinking. They should be a risk-taker, unafraid of giving an outspoken view.

It also helps, but is not essential, if the personality is charismatic, photogenic and physically distinguished.

If you can build the right personality to head-up the product promotion campaign, you will find them used by the press in many diverse ways. They can appear in profile columns, on light entertainment programmes and industry chat panels. However, the personality has to be properly media trained and have a good understanding of how the press works, so that they can be relied on to work confidently with the press and deliver what they want.

Develop your message

Your message is the product's positive marketing sales slogan or your sales objectives. There is no point in having a meeting or interview without giving thought to what you want to say. An interview is your opportunity to get your product message across – but the journalist is not necessarily going to ask you the questions you might want them to ask. You have to have your messages prepared and then look for opportunities to present them.

Your message has to have:

- Credibility so that the journalist has confidence in the message and belief in you

- appropriate context for the journalist and programme or publication
- right content, which is appropriate for the viewer, listener or reader
- clarity so that the message is unequivocal
- continuity with previous and proposed press activity
- simplicity so that the message cannot be misunderstood or misinterpreted
- impact.

The best and proven way to develop and present your message is through the benefits that the product offers. To pin these down, you need to undertake a SWOT analysis of the Strengths, Weaknesses, Opportunities and Threats of the product and the market. The most positive elements can be used in the message, but you need to be aware of the worst elements in preparation for any negative questioning from the press. You cannot ignore weaknesses or threats, and you have to be prepared for the worst questions that a journalist might ask.

Prepare a matrix with the following headings:

Objectives	Facts	Sales messages	Business benefits
Company			
Products			
Services			
People			
Objectives			
Anticipated questions			

This information will be the basis for your message to the press.

- Make the message snappy.
- Use pointed phrases.
- Use imaginative comments.
- Accentuate the positive.
- Personalise your message.
- Avoid clichés and sales puff.
- Back it up with facts, specifications and statistics.

- Identify the unique features or benefits of your product and write these out in a simple list which can be in front of you if you are speaking on the telephone or be committed to memory.
- Don't qualify your messages, enlarge upon them or develop them.
- Make the main points newsworthy.
- Focus on the emotional needs of your potential customers and deliver a message based on benefits.
- Look for the unique selling points of your product and use them as part of the message.
- Draw the journalist's attention to what is novel or newsworthy. You can refer to a product as the 'fastest' or 'cheapest' if you are sure that it is, and have facts and statistics to back up your claim.
- Avoid 'latest' or 'newest', or other glib and trite words.
- Describe your product in terms of what it will do, and refer to the difference that the product will make.
- Focus on what makes the product interesting and irresistible.
- Describe the impact that this product will have on people's lives.
- Describe the way that the product will change a process.
- Describe the benefits that it will bring.
- Do not just claim that it is the best or latest.
- Build a message on your long-term objectives.

Also prepare your comments on topical issues by creating a matrix with the following headings:

	Company view	Individual view
Issues for debate		
Anticipated press questions and your answers		

Write a topic heading on the left and then the company and your individual views and opinions on that issue. Be as outspoken and controversial as you can. Then anticipate the journalist's response to your statements, and prepare a reply which continues to reinforce all your messages.

Your message and the product life-cycle

Press activity is not just associated with the initial introductory stage – it should continue throughout the product's life-cycle, changing with it. A new product needs different messages from one which has been on the market for a while.

- The first stage of a product's life, when the product is very new and only being bought by innovators or trend-setters, and still requires your considerable backing and investment, will carry a message of novelty, of being leading edge and breaking new ground. The objective is to generate customer interest and stimulate desirability, and to encourage pioneering purchasers.

- As the product begins to be accepted but is still in the growth stage, you will need an emphasis on expert opinion, with persuasive rather than informative marketing accompanying the press activity. The product will achieve wider consumer acceptance, and new features and a range of prices can be introduced.

- As it moves into the third stage of maturity, you will want to emphasise user case stories and try to maintain the differential between your product and others, such as a lower price, improved product features or extended warranty, for as long as possible. Sales will stabilise as the market becomes saturated and you may find that competition increases as other firms enter the market.

- As the product moves into its final stage of gradual decline and sales begin to fall, you can cut back the press focus and move primary press attention to newer versions or fresh products – but the original product should not be forgotten, as a demonstration of longevity. There is also the option to revive the product at this stage, perhaps by repositioning or repackaging or otherwise remarketing it.

Anticipating predictable questions

In preparing to talk to a journalist, it makes sense to think in advance of the worst, most difficult questions he or she might ask and think through your responses. There is no point in allowing yourself to be stumped for an answer when you have time to prepare. This does not mean that you should think of lies to tell, but you can consider how frank you want to be on certain topics and how you might handle questions on certain areas.

A journalist will take the position of devil's advocate, regardless of their personal opinions. Whatever you say, whatever claim you make, you can expect the journalist to criticise, make a counter-claim or ask you to defend your position in some way. The last thing a journalist will do is accept what you say at face value. The journalist may even take several perspectives on your position.

So whatever you say about your product or company, you should expect the journalist to make critical comments. Do not take this personally: the journalist is just doing their job, which is to clear away your promotional puff and sales hyperbole from the facts about the product. The journalist represents the readers, viewers or listeners, and has to put their point of view, asking all the questions that they might ask.

Anticipate contentious issues where the journalist is likely to try to ask difficult questions, then aim to be natural and relaxed rather than guarded and defensive. Rehearse your answers so that they are smooth and reassuring.

One way to start the process of anticipating questions and preparing responses is to draw a matrix like this:

Topics (suggested)	Pros	Cons
New company		
Innovative product		
Young management		
Poor share price		
Mixed routes to market – direct and indirect sales		

Fill in the boxes with the positive responses and the negative aspects of each topic. The journalist will ask about the negative angle, but you should present the positive angle in answer.

You may have to think hard and laterally to come up with all the negative angles; for example, in the matrix above, a disadvantage to having a new company is that there is no established brand, a disadvantage to having an innovative product is that the consumers are reluctant to buy something unproved, while a disadvantage to young management is that they may lack experience. There is a positive answer to each of these: a new company can provide fresh competition for a complacent market; an innovative product means that a company can jump straight in as a market leader; while young management has the freshest ideas.

You should also think through some deflective responses, such as those given in Chapter 6.

Once you have your story thought through and your messages prepared, rehearse, rehearse and rehearse. Ask a colleague to role-play the part of an investigative journalist asking the worst questions you can imagine, and see how well you can fend them off and move the conversation on so that you provide your messages as your response.

Cue cards and crib sheets

Once you have established your messages, you are in a position to be proactive about getting them across to the media. First, you need to be very familiar with your messages and opinions.

Once you have developed your messages, transfer them to cue cards, a crib sheet or some form of *aide-mémoire*. Have them handy in your desk in case a journalist calls, and read them through before an interview, if you have the chance. Devise an *interview check sheet* (see Chapter 6).

Many companies have their corporate messages pinned up on notice-boards around the building, so that all staff, at all levels, are aware of the organisation's objectives, goals, missions, targets and so forth. This is a very effective way of making sure that whoever speaks to a journalist, and at every opportunity, a cohesive, coherent company message is projected. Every individual should have a cue card or crib sheet handy in the desk, so that if a journalist calls they have their messages to hand.

Knowing the journalist

Check back to Chapter 1 where you will find the descriptions of different types of journalist. Try to categorise the journalist you are going to speak to. Despite common fears, very few journalists will spring anything particularly tricky unless they know that you have been trained to deal with difficult questions or have a public job for which you can reasonably be expected to deal with criticism from the press. Journalists often seek to comfort the interviewee, because a more relaxed interviewee actually gives more quotable copy. In most interview situations the journalist will be hoping that you deliver as much information as possible in as interesting a way as possible. They will be seeking to relax you and get you to open up, not to make you nervous and clam up.

Make sure that the journalist has your correct name and job title, if you have one, and knows the name of the product and what it does. Be sure that the journalist is briefed before you go on air, if you are in that situation. It is sometimes worth running through the main points of your message with the journalist while you are still off air, so that you can be sure that the journalist knows why you think you are there.

Press releases and case studies/user stories

You should have copies of all your recent press releases plus some user stories or case studies available when you talk to a journalist. You can refer to them in the interview, and you can offer them to the journalist to provide some background information.

A typical case study will tell how a customer's life has been changed by using your product, but it won't tell of the other products the customer tried, how many false starts there were, or detail any difficulties in getting your product to work. Those are the things that the reader will really want to know, and it is those things that a journalist will want to put into the case study.

The problem with case studies from a journalist's point of view is that they are full of the 'feel-good' factor and don't have much – if any – controversy. Too much good news quickly becomes boring, so case studies, which are often written by committee and lack journalistic flair, need to be livened up.

Therefore, while case studies are excellent sales tools, they are of limited value for journalists. Nevertheless, most journalists like to receive them, if only for the user contacts which they provide. They can be a useful way to help the journalist understand the ways the product can be used and the benefits it can bring.

If you have case studies written for sales purposes, by all means give them to journalists as well as to sales prospects, but don't expect them to be used by journalists in their entirety in their original form.

Some publications like to use case studies because they offer the editor a cheap way to fill pages and such editors are constantly looking for good ones. Even the best are almost always revised, rewritten and edited to cut out the most overt PR puff. Just remember that a 'good' case study, and one which is most likely to be used, is one that contains the minimum of product puff and lots of human interest and opinion, and the main hook of the story is laid out at the top. Remember to include the business and personal benefits of the product you are promoting. (See Appendix 3 on writing an effective press release which can equally be applied to case studies.)

Make sure that all the users quoted in a case study are aware that they may be contacted by journalists. The press might call up out of the blue and want to interview them over the phone and ask 'difficult' questions about their problem and the solution provided by your product. It is very irritating for a journalist to be given a written case study which they cannot follow up because the user is too nervous or reluctant to speak.

Have photographs available, both of the person or people mentioned and any other shots which might be relevant. Send one attached to any case studies sent to publications, but save your budget by only sending them on request to freelance journalists.

Facts and statistics

When you are preparing for an interview you should invest considerable effort to make sure you have as many facts at your fingertips as possible. Anticipate what the journalist might ask, be prepared with the right responses and be ready to back up every statement with facts and figures.

Have ready all possible facts and statistics relating to your target market, the competition, their products and market share, new products coming down the line from your competition and from yourself. It is important to know as much about your competition as about your own product and company.

Know what your targets for revenue and growth are, and whether they were achieved last year. Be ready to talk about the size of your company, and whether you will be recruiting, by how many and what the new employees will be doing.

You also need to be able to put these facts into context, interpreting them for the journalist in the broad picture.

Simplify all figures, such as rounding up or down to the nearest whole number, reducing fractions and decimals to nearest whole numbers and only using one or two numbers as examples. Use percentages, which is often the most graphic way of putting a figure across.

Use graphs where you can, and any other visual representation of your figures and statistics.

Chapter summary

- Prepare and take control.
- Do not allow the journalist to control the agenda.
- Answer the questions but also get your messages across.

- Have your messages reduced to short, snappy quotes and memorise them.
- Use cue cards or crib sheets.
- If nervous, get media trained.
- Journalists want clarity and opinions.
- Journalists want points of view delivered with feeling.
- Journalists want information.
- Journalists do not want PR puff, hyperbole or sales talk.
- Research your competitor's publicity campaigns.
- Spot and develop the story.
- Develop your media personality.
- Develop a message which indicates the relevance for the journalist.
- Change the messages as the product ages.
- Do your homework on the journalist and the publication or programme.
- Be prepared to supplement the interview with background information.
- Have as much research material and statistics to hand as possible.

CASE STUDIES

Case study 1: Product promotion to the lifestyle press

The day of Paul's first press conference arrives. The event is timed to start at 11 a.m. and he arrives at 9.30. He checks the speaker's podium and the platform and makes sure everything is in place for the speakers. He makes sure that the AV system is properly in-stalled, all the press packs are in place, and the hotel is going to serve a buffet lunch as soon as the formal event finishes. He makes sure that fewer chairs than the number of journalists expected are placed in the room, with more in a side room ready to be brought in if necessary.

At 10.15 Karen Jamison arrives and the three speakers turn up between 10.30 and 10.45. At least there are no problems with speakers not showing up! There is Mrs Jones, who uses the BettaProds products at home, Mrs White who works for the local council on health and safety matters, and Mr Junker, who works for the local college lecturing on food sciences. All have been briefed and had a run-through of their presentation the day before.

The invitations asked the journalists to arrive at 10.30, and the week before the event Paul had received 25 definite acceptances out of 90 journalists invited. He was disappointed by the low num-ber, but it could have been worse, he thinks. By 10.45 only three journalists have turned up and Paul is getting very nervous.

He gives the three journalists coffee and introduces them to Karen and the three speakers. Karen has now been media trained, so knows a little more about what the journalists are looking for. She is still nervous, but once she starts talking to the three she begins to relax.

At 10.50 another couple of journalists trickle in. Paul asks them if they know why the rest haven't turned up. 'There's another event on over the other side of town,' says one, and Paul's heart sinks. By 11.10 there is a total of ten journalists, and Paul announces that the conference will begin. Karen and the speakers take their places on the platform, and at 11.15 Paul kicks off by formally introducing Karen.

Each of the speakers makes a fifteen-minute presentation, about how revolutionary, innovative and remarkable the KoolWay tech-nology is. Paul deliberately planned to keep the presentations short, but still, by 12.15, everyone in the audience is looking very restless. One journalist slips away just before noon, and Paul makes a mental note to call him later and ask if he needs anything more.

Paul asks whether there are any questions, but no one responds so he signals for lunch to be served. Only eight journalists stay for lunch and then leave as soon as they have finished eating. They all take a press pack and all seem pleased that by attending the press conference they qualify for the free selection of BettaProds pans and kitchen utensils.

Afterwards, Karen is furious. 'All that money we spent!' she says. 'How much did this cost?' Paul admits that the price per head of journalist is extravagant. 'I managed to speak briefly to three journalists, and I'm sure most of them only came so they could get the free products.'

Paul knows he was wrong and admits his mistake. Basically, the story was just not strong enough. He did some things right – the gift of products to those who attended at least ensured that some turned up, and the experts and the user were well received. And, after all, it wasn't his fault that there was another event elsewhere in town.

But it is a bad day for Paul and the BettaProds publicity campaign.

- **Comment**: Paul is reaping what he sowed. His first mistake – that of thinking that lots of journalists would find it worth coming to a press conference to be told about a product which, although innovative, is not earth-shattering – is coming back to haunt him. Otherwise he's done everything right. The press conference was well organised, but he didn't think through at the beginning what the journalists would want to get out of it.

  The fact that lots of journalists said they would attend but then failed to show up is a common experience. There can be many reasons why this happens, and is another reason for being very cautious about opting for a full-blown press conference. The fact that journalists leave immediately after lunch means nothing – they are busy people and won't want to stick around and chat for long.

Case study 2: Product promotion to the computer press

Jessica is also nervous about her first press event. In fact, she was so nervous the week before and so unsure what she was doing that she contacted a PR firm and asked them to help her with the event. She contacted three, one based near SoftMicro's offices and two which specialise in the computer industry. All pointed out that it was very late to ask for their help, but all agreed to do it. The local firm wanted to charge £1,200 and the two specialist firms both asked for £1,000 each to step in and make sure the event went smoothly.

Jessica chose the agency which had two former journalists on the staff. Their first job was to make sure that there was a strong news story for the journalists to take away from the press reception, and worked on the messages that SoftMicro wanted to put across to the press.

The PR person in charge of the SoftMicro account, Joe Probe, quickly ran though Jessica's list of invited journalists, and made phone calls to those he knew. He went straight to the point and told them briefly that the event would be interesting and there would be a story for their viewers, listeners and readers. He added a few more freelances to Jessica's list, and also rang them to tell them that the product was interesting and there was a good hook to the story. At the end of the day he had 30 definite yes's, another 25 probables and only 10 definite no's, because of deadlines or a clash with other events.

Joe asks Professor Higgins and Richard Devine to get to the venue at 9.30, although the first journalist is not due to arrive until 12.30 at the earliest. Joe has asked a specialist media trainer to attend, and for more than an hour they run through SoftMicro's strategy, its objectives and the messages that Richard and Jessica want to get across. They also brainstorm the worst questions that a journalist might ask, and work out some credible and honest answers. Joe does some role-playing with Richard and Jessica, pretending to be a hostile journalist with whom they have to deal.

At 12.15 the first journalists trickle in, and by 12.30 there are 25 standing around, chatting, talking to old friends. At 12.45 Joe asks for quiet and tells everyone that he is representing SoftMicro and says a little about KiddieLearn 2. In five minutes he runs through the main features of the new version and the implications for the education market. He then introduces Richard and Jessica, and Professor Higgins. The food is then brought out and journalists eat, drink, circulate and talk to the SoftMicro people and to each other. Sometimes they are talking about the product and sometimes they seem to be talking about completely different topics.

At about 1.45 the first journalists start to leave, with a press pack and a sample disk of the software. Jessica and Richard personally say good-bye to each one. Joe tries to make a note of what each journalist wants in terms of follow-up. At 2.30 there are still ten journalists standing around drinking, and the Professor has to leave.

Eventually the event finishes at 2.45, and everyone is extremely pleased. 'We'll have to wait and see whether we get any coverage,' says Richard, 'but I thought it went rather well.'

- **Comment**: Again, Jessica does everything right. It is sensible to call in the experts to help with a specific project, and journalists are often more receptive to calls from ex-journalists, who know better what to say and how to say it.

Case study 3: Diary of a freelance journalist

A day in Central London today. I've got three press events and a lunch, plus a teatime meeting with a commissioning editor.

The first event is a breakfast seminar with some American analysts, being hosted by an American accounting software house. These are sophisticated people that I've met before, and I know that the quality of the hospitality and debate will be high. I take my tape-recorder. I don't usually use a recorder, but I expect the pace of the conversation to be rapid and I want to take part, not just take notes.

I have to drag myself away at 10.45 to get across London to a West End hotel where young Paul is launching his saucepans. Ah, the life of a journalist is such fun!

I get there just as everyone is taking their seats for a formal presentation, and I very soon regret not passing on this one and staying with the analysts for longer. I was really getting some good future-view stuff there, and this is soooo boring! Speaker after speaker, droning on and not saying much at all. The customer speaking about the product is fairly interesting, and so is the food scientist expert, but there's a lot of padding. I think about leaving, but spend fifteen minutes quietly writing up some notes on the breakfast seminar, and hope that the BettaProds launch gets betta.

It doesn't, so I slip out before the end. I give my card to Paul and ask him to send me a set of the products anyway. I dash over to another part of the West End to the SoftMicro lunch. Ah, this is good. Not much formal chat, a nice lunch, and a couple of old journalist friends I haven't seen for a while. It is a good event, although I can't remember much about the product. Still, I take a review copy and I'll have a look at it when I get back to my office.

Now on to meet the commissioning editor – a lady on one of the Sunday supplements. I run a couple of ideas past her, and she says she'll think about them. I also ask if she has anything planned that I can do for her, and she gives me a piece on kitchen safety for their Kids Supplement. By 5p.m., I'm on the train and heading home.

- **Comment**: Note how Suzie has to juggle several events and invitations, and prioritise them. She will choose the ones which seem most likely to produce the best story and the best quotes. Like most journalists, she likes events with analysts available to talk to, and she definitely needs to know that it is worth going. If the analysts are any good, she will be sure of an independent comment. If they are no good, or the events are disappointing because they don't deliver what they promised, she will remember those companies and marketing people next time – and avoid them.

CHAPTER FOUR

Making contact and surviving

Introduction

By now you have learned how you need to find out about the journalist, how to identify the newsworthiness in your story and how to prepare your message. Now you are ready for the most daunting part of the process of promoting your product to the media – making contact with the journalist. This chapter will prepare you by giving you as much background information as possible about deadlines, the best ways to make contact and how to pitch your idea.

There is no easy way to do it, and it is not helped by the fact that journalists can be arrogant and intimidating, and – because they are often busy and under pressure – can be brusque in their manner. This is unfortunate but true, and it is easier to deal with if you expect it. Just bear in mind that it is not personal – the journalist is probably under a lot of pressure and gets a lot of calls pitching ideas all the time.

Remember too that journalists need people like you to give them ideas and stories and, provided you make your story interesting for the target audience, it stands a good chance of being used.

Who does what in the media?

The tasks and responsibilities accompanying basic job titles vary according to each publishing house, broadcast company or channel, and each publication and TV or radio programme. There are no hard-and-fast rules about who does what in the media, and the job specifications will sometimes be radically different on different publications, in different publishing houses, on different programmes and within different production companies. But here are some commonly accepted explanations for each job title.

- **The Publisher** of a newspaper or magazine is usually promoted from the sales side, and has overall responsibility for promoting and commercially managing the title. The publisher decides the overall size of each issue (the pagination) and the ratio of advertising and editorial. Too much editorial and the publication will not make money; too much advertising and the readers lose interest. The publisher also promotes and manages the marketing of the title.

- **The Producer** is the equivalent to the publisher in the broadcast media.

- **The Editor** (print) is the person with overall and legal responsibility for the content of the publication. The editor decides the contents but often has too many management jobs to do much writing. Some editors only have time to write the Editor's Foreword, and spend the rest of their time in meetings, dealing with staff, planning issues and so forth. **The Director** is the person responsible for individual broadcast programmes, comparable to a magazine or newspaper editor.

- **The Editor** (broadcast) is the person responsible for cutting and editing the film or tape and generally putting a programme together.

- **The Sub-Editor** is the print equivalent of a broadcast editor, cutting and shaping the copy to fit the space and the house style. The 'subs' have the power to completely rewrite copy if it does not conform to the house style, and may accidentally cut out something which you might consider crucial in the process. There's nothing you can do about that. Subs are also responsible for headlines and captions, and one of their most critical jobs is ensuring that all the contents are legal.

- Other print staff include the **Production Editor** who is responsible for liaising with the media sales team and ensuring that all pages are filled to meet the section deadlines, **reporters or journalists** who put together the news stories, **Staff Writers** who are the journalists responsible for producing the day-to-day words, small filler pieces of copy and some captions, and **Freelances** or the self-employed journalists working for several broadcast and print publishing houses.

- In TV **Researchers** play an important role, and to a lesser degree in radio. They hardly exist in print journalism. Their functions vary, but usually their job is to find the right people for the journalists to interview. They back up the journalist by uncovering information, finding suitable case studies, etc. They can be overruled and are prone to making promises they can't keep.

The important point is that an approach to a newspaper, magazine or programme needs to be double-pronged. There is no point just talking to an editor, whose main task is to plan and manage the title. The editor may be responsible for commissioning features and sanctioning news stories and features, but probably writes very little. The editor needs to be aware of your product, but you also need to target those who will actually write the copy: the staff writers and freelances.

Similarly, in broadcast programmes, you need to make sure that you are talking to both journalists and directors, and possibly programme editors too. In the broadcast media, researchers are also important, and often decide exactly who will be called upon for quotes and opinion.

Variations in frequency of publications and programmes

All types of media – print, radio and TV – have different types of publication and programmes, the main division being between dailies, weeklies and monthlies. There are also specials, documentaries and supplements to mark special occasions. All need copy to balance the advertising.

Some publications and programmes are strongly news oriented, while others, such as the supplements to the Sunday newspapers, have a lead time of a month or more. Generally though, modern technology means that deadlines are closer than ever to the date and time of broadcast or publication.

- Dailies often work on tomorrow's news today, working on the fastest-moving stories right up to the deadline but finishing less time-sensitive features earlier. At most they work on stories with a two-day lead time. Any longer than that and the news is old.

- In a daily radio news programme or daily newspaper, deadlines are hourly and news comes in right up to the moment the issue closes. Stories are sometimes carried over, but often by the next day the story is too dated. Local radio is often looking for stories each morning, if you can get to them early. A fax and then a phone call are often enough, provided you have a story to back it up.

- On a weekly magazine, the features are often 'tied down' or 'go to bed' two or three weeks before the issue closes, while the news pages may not be 'put to bed' until the last minute. The publication will appear one or two days after closing, and work will start on the next week's issue before this week's is out.

- Monthly publications often have features written two months before they close – which is often three months before the 'book' appears. (Magazine publishers often refer to the magazine as a book or as 'the product'.) The 'lead time' between closing and appearing is often two or three weeks, because they are printed cheaply, in sections, between other more important jobs. Consequently monthlies rarely have topical news, often preferring instead to run news analysis.

Knowing what sort of publication the journalist is working for makes a difference to the way you respond to them. If you get a call from someone working on a news story for a daily or a weekly, you know you will have almost no chance to get back to them with further comment or information. You have to respond fairly fast. A journalist working on a monthly, on the other hand, may have more time for research. However, whatever type of publication the journalist works for, you should aim to react as speedily as possible – if you do not give them the comment they want, they will move on to someone else who will.

Journalists may need you to give them comment, but there are plenty of other people out there like you, keen to talk and promote their products. A journalist is not going to wait for long for you to call them back, before moving on to finding another spokesperson. So, even if you know the journalist has a fairly generous lead time and deadline, respond as quickly as you can to their request for comment.

If you are trying to sell a product story to the press, hope for a day when there is no dramatic late-breaking news. Your story is likely to get spiked and forgotten. Or you can try to pick a time when there is less likely to be dramatic news, such as a Monday, the morning after a bank holiday, or days in July and August. The Press Gazette and the Press Association give advance notice on events which are known to be taking place, and which might generate news coverage.

Choosing publications to target

With many hundreds of publications and programmes, it is important to specify the names of each title or programme and identify the principal journalists on each that you want to target.

Many publications have declared or vested interests, or take certain political positions even in an apparently non-political area.

Trade publications in particular are often overtly left-wing, cam-
paigning on behalf of their readers against the vested interest of the
suppliers. You need to be aware of the publication's or programme's
attitude, if there is one. This can usually be detected by reading the
editorials.

Many programmes and publications have spread their areas of
interest, so you need to check with each who their target audience is.
Publications which were once technically focused now often look at a
broader range of issues, and there has been a rise in programmes
which run a broad range of debates and issue-led features. This
means that you have to cast your net as wide as possible when you
are selecting which publications and programmes to target.

There is no point targeting publications which are clearly outside
of your market, but you should select all obvious titles, and all broad-
based publications which include references to areas covered by your
product.

To decide, ask yourself:

- who will find your product interesting
- who will be affected by your product.

You have to take a coolly analytical approach – do not allow your
personal tastes to affect your choice. Just because you do not like a
particular publication or programme does not mean it is not influential.

Once you have decided on the key titles, familiarise yourself with
each individually and closely. One complaint of journalists is that
people contact them obviously without having read the title or
watched the programme.

Making your contact list of journalists

There are various press guidebooks and media listings which specify
newspapers and publications broken down by geographical area and/or
area of specific interest. These are available in local libraries. You should
create a list of target publications, with key journalists, and radio and
TV programmes, with programme editors and key researchers. Specify
the key publications for key criteria, such as locality or market specifica-
tion, and target key journalists for the same reasons.

A scatter-gun approach is a waste of everyone's time. You should
make sure that you are approaching a journalist who is likely to have
an interest in your product or you, and that you have a story prepared to discuss with them. Some journalists will be specialist, some
general, some will have a community interest or may be industrial or

IT correspondents. Each needs the story to be pitched in a way which appeals specifically to them.

Have a database or contact file of all target journalists and keep it regularly updated. Record all professional and personal details that you can extricate. Even small pieces of information about their preferences, hobbies and ambitions may be useful in the future. Check with your database before and after each meeting, first to be familiar with the journalist you are about to talk to, and then to debrief yourself and record all supplementary information you may have discovered during the interview. Keep a record of every conversation and meeting. Also record every press release sent, and any follow-up activity.

Do not contact a journalist without being familiar with the publication or programme that they represent. Journalists are not impressed when you do not know their target audience or details of the contents of their publication or programme. They will expect you to be familiar with what they do and who their target is. They don't like people who don't do their homework. You can find out direct from them by calling up and asking the straightforward question: 'Who is your magazine or newspaper aimed at?' Better still, you can get a copy or watch the programme. But don't ask them who their target audience is in the same conversation while trying to pitch your product to them. Find out first, then go back later with your story. Remember that you are targeting your audience – your potential customers – through the journalist.

Preparing to make contact

Do not contact the journalist on the spur of the moment. Think through your approach as part of an overall strategy and work out what you are going to say beforehand. Find out the deadlines that the journalist is likely to be working towards. You must do your homework so that you know the publication or programme intimately and – just as critically – the audience profile. If the journalist detects that you have not actually read the publication or ever watched the programme, they aren't going to be encouraged to listen to what you have to say. Also:

- anticipate what the journalist might say and prepare your responses
- have your messages written down in front of you.

Lastly, do not just arrive at a journalist's office without telephoning first.

Making contact

See Chapter 5 for some of the most common ways of catching the journalists' attention, including press releases. Those are mainly broad, general, scatter-gun methods, however. If you have a good story and a strong message which you genuinely think will be of interest to the journalist's audience, you need to make *personal* contact.

There are several ways to make personal contact:

- telephone (for more details see 'Pitching the idea' below)
- post
- e-mail (for more details see Appendix 3 on distributing the press release)
- voice mail (for more details see Appendix 3)
- fax (for more details see Appendix 3)
- web sites (for more details see Appendix 3)
- in person.

Each journalist will have a preference about how they like to be contacted, and you need to know what it is – otherwise you risk their wrath. They may act like prima donnas, but unless you get it right they are liable to disregard your product and news story. As you want them to use your story more than they want to use it, they are in the stronger position. You have to play the game by their rules.

Some prefer e-mail; others prefer fax. Some hate e-mail and never read it; some read their e-mail but don't bother to download it. Others like to receive case studies, some like to get photographs; some dislike both and sling them straight in the bin.

When you are compiling your contact list of journalists, it should include the details of how each journalist prefers to receive stories and pitches. This information you can get from the journalist – but only ask them once, and then do it the way they request. Don't think 'Most journalists want their press releases by e-mail, so I'll send e-mail press releases to everyone' because a lot will still prefer post and will ignore e-mail. Journalists find it irritating when they repeatedly tell people how they prefer to receive information, only to be ignored.

Telephone

The most feared and terrifying challenge to anyone trying to promote a product is their first 'cold-contact' telephone call with each journalist. Journalists are extremely busy and telephones are extremely immediate. You must have exactly the right approach or the journalist is liable to be rude.

If you remember that the journalist is getting hundreds of press releases and a similar number of phone calls each day, you realise that you have to get your call just right. (See the section below on 'Pitching the idea' for more about telephone techniques that work.)

Post

Letters can also be a personalised alternative to the press release. Use the same principles of concise writing – given in Appendix 3 – and have the letter checked by a professional writer for faults.

Make sure that you are getting across all the important points in the first paragraph. Enclose a photograph if you have one. Make sure your mailing list is up to date and regularly cleaned. A wrongly addressed press release probably goes straight into the bin, and is not opened by anyone.

E-mail

Protocols and courtesies in e-mail communications are the following:

- Put a summary of the e-mail in the first sentence.
- Keep the message as short as possible.

Avoid sending e-mails which have long lists of recipients at the beginning. Send e-mailed press releases so that each individual recipient gets one addressed to them alone.

Voicemail

Voicemail is another technology which has changed the face of business but should be used with care with journalists. Never leave a long and complicated message – just your name and a return phone number, and perhaps a quick indication of the purpose of your call.

Remember to check your messages regularly, in case the journalist has called you back.

Fax

Like e-mails, faxes should be as short as possible. Don't send a fax unless the journalist requests it, or you know it is their preference. Many journalists dislike faxes because they have to provide the paper to receive the information. They particularly hate faxes of more than two pages.

In person

Never just visit a journalist unannounced, but, providing the journalist is expecting you, a quick visit to explain the story or pitch in person can sometimes be effective. Many journalists appreciate being taken out for a drink after work or a quick lunch. Make the purpose of the meeting as much to develop the relationship as to tell your story. Keep it informal.

Pitching the idea

Pitching is something that freelance journalists, marketing and PR people often have to do on a regular basis. Pitches are made to features and news editors, editors and staff journalists, who are all continually looking for story ideas. PR people usually do it with more obvious 'selling', which irritates commissioning editors and may even influence them *not* to take the story. If the story is good, it will be considered. When you pitch, the journalist will make a snap value judgement about whether this is a good story which will stand up; whether this is a story which might be used in connection with another story; or whether it has no value or interest.

Confidence is the key when pitching an idea for a story. Unless you believe it, the journalist certainly won't – it's the sizzle that's as interesting as the steak, as they say. They are unlikely to take the story exactly as you pitch it to them, however. Instead, they are likely to try and find their own angle and other people to comment on the topic.

Here are some other factors to bear in mind:

- Journalists are expecting to receive suggestions from people like you with a vested interest. They get them all the time. Make sure that you declare your interest from the outset, and do not attempt to mislead the journalist into thinking that you are independent. If you are involved with promoting and marketing a product, make your involvement crystal-clear from the start. They will not think any less of you, and it will not necessarily detract from the validity of the story or its potential to be used. They will be critical of the story's validity from the start and will immediately subject the idea to scepticism. This is their job. Better to reject a dud story immediately rather than later.

- The journalists are bound to want to talk to your competitors as well as to you, and possibly independent analysts and specialist pundits too. If you can suggest an independent analyst they may take your suggestion, or they may want to use their own expert.

- When you call, be aware of their deadlines as well as the specific profile of their audience. Have your crib sheet to hand, outlining your key messages and the main features of the product, and its implications for the audience.

- Avoid wasting a journalist's time. Always have something specific to say when you call and get straight to the point without overly courteous preambles. Unless it is a press day when they are bound to be exceptionally busy, journalists are usually willing to listen to most stories in the hope that they will find something that will interest their listeners, viewers or readers. They need you because they are continually looking for good new stories. So they will give you a chance, but you must come straight to the point – don't waste their time or expect flowery pleasantries about the weather. They can be extremely brusque but don't take it personally. Be business-like and don't over-sell.

- A successful pitch is explicit about the interest of the audience in the story. A pitch which is just a basic 'We've launched a new product' invites the response 'So what?' – and you have to deliver the answer to that question, whether it is asked for or not. Remember that the journalist is bound to take a view opposing whatever you are saying, but that is what they are *supposed* to do. Don't take it personally.

- Make sure that you do your homework and are fully prepared before initiating the call. The first thing to ask is: 'Is this a good time to call?' Don't just launch into your pitch. Say 'I'll just take two or three minutes of your time to suggest a story to you', and then very quickly run through the idea. Have a press release ready to send the moment you put the phone down after pitching. Follow up sensitively.

- The journalists are likely to be busy when you call – it is a matter of *how* busy. They will say if it is a bad time: in that case, say you will ring back later or next day, and do call back. Again, don't take it personally. Then quickly summarise your proposal for a story. You suggest an idea, and the journalist develops it. You don't have to flesh out the story completely or write the headlines. That's the journalist's job. They are just looking for leads and stories.

- As the pitch proceeds, listen to what the journalist is saying. You can stop halfway through and say, 'Is this interesting for you?' If the journalist asks questions, try to second-guess the journalist's specific interest, and respond to that.

- Successful pitches are well organised and prepared:
  - there is a basic structure
  - the interest and relevance to the audience are clearly apparent
  - the language is simple and direct.

You have to present the right information in the way which is most likely to appeal to each individual journalist (see Chapter 2 on newsworthiness):

- Avoid familiarity, which is the curse of many professional PR people. Unless you genuinely know the journalist well, treat them with reserve and respect. Remember that sometimes journalists get dozens of pitches each day.

- Avoid jargon. Words that you may commonly use all the time at work are utterly impenetrable to someone outside your area of expertise, and it is very important to cut out the jargon words. People who use jargon are often insecure and need the comfort of showing off that they belong to an esoteric world. They often use too many words to say too little.

- Translate technical or trade-speak to consumer-speak by re-placing abbreviations, acronyms and unnecessarily complex words or phrases with simple ones. Many firms and organisations also have an internal jargon which is impossible for an outsider to understand. It is very easy to get into the habit of using complex words to describe simple ideas or features. Techno-speak, marketing-speak and company-speak should all be avoided.

- If you keep your communications simple and unfussy, the journalist is more likely to listen to what you have to say. If a journalist is unable to understand, they are not always likely to bother to enquire. They will sometimes pretend they understand. If they do have to ask, they are unlikely to feel better towards you. Always speak and write in clear, jargon-free terms.

- Avoid clichés, those vivid verbal phrases which are amusing or appropriate the first time you hear them but quickly pall like a bad joke.

Making your story: the pegs, hooks and angles

Every story must have a 'hook' – this is the most interesting angle relevant to the journalist and which the journalist will use to interest the reader, viewer or listener. These will obviously vary according to the different media.

Sometimes people send out fairly bland press releases and different journalists will find different hooks or pegs, according to their different readerships. But you can help the journalist by pointing out the obvious pegs, and these can be stated in the standfirst under the headline.

But don't be surprised if some journalists, especially those with a strong news sense, identify a peg which you didn't see, or would prefer them not to see. For a journalist, some of the best stories are those which some people don't want printed, so they will be looking for an angle which may not be your preferred choice.

Present the pegs that you have identified clearly when you present a story – it will help to interest the journalist, and will also make sure that you focus on the angles and make you sure that there is a newsworthy element. Otherwise you may find yourself trying to interest the journalist in a story which is a non-story, because there is no hook or peg. If the journalist turns around and says 'So?', you know you haven't got a strong enough peg. For example, if you are launching a widget, it needs to be the fastest, cheapest, most colourful, most extraordinary in some way, to set it apart from the other widgets – otherwise there is no story.

Offering exclusives

There is a running debate among publicity professionals about whether or not to offer a story to key journalists on an exclusive or 'scoop' basis in the expectation that they will give it high-profile coverage.

There are several risks with this strategy: first, you may give the journalist an exclusive story and they may not use it. Just because they have been given it as an exclusive does not mean that they are obliged to use it. Some accept 'exclusives' and then do not use the story, and there is nothing you can do. You have no control over what they write about, and, even if they write the story, it may later be spiked by the editor. If that happens, then you are in a quandary and releasing it to the other members of the press becomes a difficult decision. They may not want it because it has already been passed over by the key publication, and by the time they get it the story may not be so new.

On the other hand, if the story is a good, strong one, you will not need to offer it to any journalist as an exclusive – they will all want it anyway.

So, generally, do not attempt to select key journalists, programmes or publications and try to promote your product by 'selling' the story as an exclusive. If it's a good story, they will want to use it.

Dealing with attitude

It is only human nature that journalists quickly become aware that they are 'flavour of the week' because they are continually being contacted by PR and marketing people trying to suggest stories or give information about their new products. Journalists get several hundred press releases each week, and often have many invitations to lunches and receptions. This can quickly lead – especially in novice or junior journalists – to an arrogance and brusqueness which can be downright rude. You, however, have to deal with this in a polite and charming way.

Journalists often have many preconceived views, opinions and attitudes which may clash with the message you are trying to get across. They often start with a premise, which may be wrong.

Try to back up your message and views with as much information, facts and interesting opinion as you can find. Sometimes no amount of information will change a deeply entrenched attitude. Dealing with a negative attitude without arguing is a complex skill which you should try to master by having your message well rehearsed, simple and clear. You should also practise and polish your responses to obvious criticisms. The more you say, the more selective the journalist can be about the information they choose to use, so stick to your primary message and amplify it rather than add to it.

A journalist will not change their attitude simply because you tell them that your product is the best, the most innovative or the cheapest. The journalist will deliberately be taking the critical viewpoint, looking for problems and difficulties. They will be aiming to try and ask all the questions which their viewers and readers might like to ask, and make obvious comments so that hypocrisy and cant are uncovered.

In a broadcast interview, the audience will quickly detect if the journalist has an unfair attitude or preconceived views, and sympathy will be with you.

Deadlines

All publications and programmes have deadlines, and it is important to know what they are. They can mean different things, and they can even be a false date set to make sure that copy is received in time. A deadline is not the final time that you should deliver information, however: it is the final time for the journalist to finish the piece.

The rule of thumb is: any deadline should be ignored; set your own deadline several hours or days earlier. Deal with journalists' requests as soon as possible.

Sometimes a deadline given is the absolute final date for which copy has to be written, pages subbed, recordings edited and the product ready to be broadcast or printed. Sometimes it is the deadline for a particular piece or story, or for the entire publication or programme.

Many journalists work against tight deadlines all the time. Deadlines generate a sense of urgency which in turn produces an intense and creative atmosphere. Deadlines can also encourage interviewees to comment without thinking too hard – which means that, by claiming they are working against a tight deadline, journalists may get a quick, unrehearsed and off-the-cuff statement, which is often good copy. So sometimes journalists will say that their deadline is tight when in fact it is not – it's one of the journalists' oldest tricks.

Whatever the real deadline, you have to take the journalist's word at face value. If the journalist says their deadline is two hours, two days or two weeks away you have to accept that, and aim to deliver your information or comments as soon as possible, not as close to the deadline as possible. You may have a great story but deliver it at the wrong time and so it will not be used.

To ignore a deadline or deliberately call on the day on which a publication or programme closes is suicide. The journalist is likely to be rude, and will remember you if you ever call again. No one minds one genuine mistake, but twice is not forgiven easily.

When you draw up your list of publications, programmes and journalists, also have a list of deadline days, and days which are good or bad for contacts or meetings. A weekly publication, for example, will probably close on a Wednesday, so its journalists will be frantically busy on that day. On the Thursday they will be quieter, and looking around for new stories for the next week's issue.

If a journalist calls for a comment but says that the deadline for the story is, say, three days away or next week, you should still aim to deliver the comment as swiftly as possible. Just because the journalist has several days to write the piece does not mean that they will not want to write it and finish it as quickly as possible. There are plenty of other people they can also speak to, so if you are asked for a comment, make it a rule to get back or respond as immediately as you can.

What happens to the information you provide?

Most written or e-mailed material sent to journalists ends up in the bin. This may not be because the material has been badly presented. There are other reasons which are completely out of your control:

- It may not be relevant for that journalist or that publication or programme.
- It may be only that it is not relevant *that week*.
- There may be other stories which were deemed more interesting.
- It was not eye-catching.
- The hook was not sufficiently evident.

Giving information to journalists is a lottery which relies on factors outside your control. You have no control over the mood of the editor, the events taking place or your competitors' activities.

The process on many magazines and newspapers is that the editor is often the first to see the press release or to receive the pitch phone call, and instructs the staff or freelance journalist to follow up the story. Sometimes journalists are free to follow those stories which they think most important, and then they tell the editor what stories they have gathered. The final decision whether to include the story almost always rests with the editor.

The same goes for radio and TV: the editors and reporters work together to decide which story to follow up.

Once the journalist has written the piece, and the reporter has prepared their report, the sub-editor or editor then proof-reads it and checks it. They want to make sure that it is:

- appealing to the target reader, viewer or listener
- timely
- newsworthy
- not libellous or inaccurate
- fair, with the right balance of views
- in good taste.

Why was your story not used?

If you have contacted a journalist and pitched an idea, only to find that the journalist has not shown interest or has shown interest initially but not followed up, ask yourself these questions:

- Does the story interest the target audience?
- Is it relevant to the audience?

- Is it old news?
- Have I rung on the day the publication goes to press?
- Is there not really any good hook, angle or peg?
- Is the message confused or unclear?
- Is the choice of words inappropriate?
- Have I made unsubstantiated claims without the back-up of facts and statistics?

It is important to get it right, because an attempt to communicate with a journalist which fails means:

- loss of time
- loss of respect
- loss of your confidence
- loss of the journalist's confidence in you
- credibility slip
- increased difficulty for you the next time you try to call
- ultimately, a failed attempt to pitch a story or invite an interview will lead to loss of business.

Maintaining the long-term relationship

It is far easier for you to make contact with a journalist with whom you already have a relationship, so try to cement and build relationships whenever you can.

Human nature also makes it harder for a journalist to write critically about someone they know, despite the fact that whether they know someone should be irrelevant in their pursuit of the truth and information.

Get to know your local journalists and those who are critical to your specific industry in the trade press. Find out what each journalist is interested in, and what they are looking for in a story. Call them up and ask them out for a drink, or for lunch. It need only be a quick one to break the ice and for you to discover how they think and what they want.

Once you have made contact with a journalist, keep the relationship going (see Chapter 8 on following up). Ask them out to dinner, to lunch, keep a flow of stories going.

Remember that when you make a telephone call to a journalist, have a note of what you want to say in front of you and do not lapse into chit-chat. Keep the conversation short and to the point, and do not open with lots of pseudo-friendly questions like 'How are you?' or 'How was your weekend?' These will only irritate. Get straight to the point. Even if you have already met the journalist several times, do not be over-familiar or waste time on meaningless pleasantries.

So, it's not working . . . ?

If, despite repeated efforts, the journalist is plainly not interested in you or your product or story, you should ask yourself what you are doing wrong. Given that the journalists are continually looking for stories, and are running stories from your competitors and other product providers, you are obviously doing something seriously wrong.

It may be that your pitches are not relevant, but it is more likely to be that you irritate the journalist. They get contacted by hundreds of people each week, and it is easy for them to slip into an arrogant, dismissive way of dealing with people.

They probably dislike spending time with people asking about their health or discussing the weather. They will certainly dislike a sycophantic, ingratiating tone. It may be that the journalist thinks you have called without taking the time to do any research about them, their title or what they might be interested in. If you feel that they will not be interested in your product or your views, it is better not to call.

Sometimes a fresh face is a good start – consider passing the media relations work over to a colleague or an outside agency, or get someone else to deal with that particular journalist.

If you don't like the journalist, the feeling is probably mutual. Although few journalists will ignore a story because they don't like the marketing person or the PR officer, it certainly doesn't help. Don't take it personally – you can't win 'em all.

Chapter summary

- Be selective about the titles and journalists you target.
- Don't be emotional about your choice – just because you don't like a publication or programme, doesn't mean it isn't read or watched by hundreds of your potential customers.
- Have a database of publications and programmes detailing copy deadlines, special columns, feature sections, whether they use case studies and opinion pieces, etc.
- Build a contact database of journalists, detailing all their preferences (whether to send press releases by post or e-mail,

whether they like to be called with comments, etc.) and issues that they specialise in.

- Be familiar with all the publications and programmes that your key journalists work for.
- Have everything worked out before you pick up the phone.
- Don't call on press day.
- The journalist will want to hear from you – but not if you have nothing to say.
- Don't ramble and use pleasantries. Don't even ask 'How are you?' unless you mean it. Get straight to the point.
- Listen to what the journalist says.
- Make sure there is a clear hook to the story which is relevant to the journalist's audience.

CASE STUDIES

Case study 1: Product promotion to the lifestyle press

The day after the event, Paul rings up all the journalists who said they'd come but didn't show up and offers them the complimentary samples of the KoolWay products. They all accept. He sends a press pack with each of the samples.

He then sends a press pack to all the journalists who turned down the invitation to the event. He reckons that, for the cost of the postage, it is worth the chance that one or two of them might follow up on the story.

He also calls all the journalists who came to the event to see if they want anything else. One wants a photograph of Karen and another wants some technical details about the development of KoolWay.

A few days later, out of the blue, one of the journalists who did not attend the event but was sent a press pack telephones. It is Jane Marples, a freelance writer who contributes to several leading glossy consumer magazines and writes a regular column on domestic matters in one of the Sunday supplements.

Paul takes the call, and is completely floored. He has no idea how to handle the call. Paul says, 'Can you fax over your questions and I'll get our MD, Karen Jamison, to fax back her answers?' 'Er, no thanks,' says Jane, and hangs up.

A few days later another journalist calls, this time one who was at the press conference. 'I was wondering if you had another sample of your KoolWay products,' he says, 'for my colleague.'

'No, sorry,' says Paul. 'We don't have enough to give more samples out. Anyway, if I give one to your colleague, how do I know that they will write about the products?' 'Thanks anyway,' says the journalist, and hangs up.

A week or so later Karen asks Paul what coverage there has been as a result of the press conference and Paul is ashamed to admit that the mentions were limited to a couple of fillers on the new-product pages of the trade press and one piece in a new-products page of a consumer magazine. He doesn't dare tell Karen that all three magazines are demanding colour separation costs, for printing a photograph to go with the story.

- **Comment**: Paul's follow-up is fine, especially sending press packs to all those journalists who didn't turn up for the press conference. But he should have known how to deal with the call from Jane Marples. He should have established what she was writing, who she was writing it for and what her deadline was. Then he could try and find something newsworthy for her. His reaction to the journalist who called asking for a sample of the product was truly awful. Unless the products are extremely valuable, you should always make sure that the journalist can have one if possible, if only for a short-term loan.

It's not really surprising that Paul got almost no column inches from his press conference – there was no story to report. Even those inches he did get he had to pay for, and paid-for editorial has about the same value as advertising.

Case study 2: Product promotion to the computer press

The day after the press reception, Joe calls all the journalists who attended, thanks them for taking the trouble to be there and asks if there is anything more they need. Several say they'd like to interview Richard and Professor Higgins, so Joe sets up the calls.

He is able to brief Richard and the Professor before each conversation, informing them about what type of story the journalist is doing, what sort of publication they are writing for and therefore who the audience is. The local radio and TV stations also want to do some interviews, and again Joe is able to brief the pair. He also leads them again through any difficult questions which could reasonably be expected, and coaches their replies.

All the interviews go very smoothly. For the telephone and radio interviews Richard keeps a note handy of the key messages that he wants to get across, and by the time it comes to the TV interview he feels confident and relaxed and doesn't need the notes. The Professor thoroughly enjoys his role of independent expert and takes the opportunity to poke fun at some other competing technologies and other companies in the field of educational software. Several journalists encourage him in this, and Joe has to signal to him not to go too far.

Two weeks later, Joe submits a report to SoftMicro with his bill. He also presents a selection of the cuttings achieved, with four small fillers in the national newspaper educational supplements and a long interview with the Professor in the *Guardian*'s educational pages. There are also product reviews in the IT trade press and several features about computer-based training (CBT) which feature both Richard and Professor Higgins.

Over the next few months Jessica finds several mentions of Soft-Micro as a provider of innovative educational software, and several journalists ring up Richard and the Professor to ask their views on various topics. Richard finds these difficult at first, but Professor Higgins particularly relishes them and speaks loudly and strongly about the need for CBT to be supported by teachers who under-stand the power and effect of computers. He believes that com-puters have a role but will never replace teachers.

Jessica is so pleased with the press reception that she starts planning to take a group of journalists to a school where Kiddie-Learn 2 is being used with some particularly difficult children, and begins to organise the breakfast seminar for a group of young journalists to discuss the issues raised by CBT.

- **Comment**: You can tell that Joe is a professional. He briefs everyone, knows all the journalists and deals with them in a professional manner, and the resulting column inches certainly justify his charges.

Case study 3: Diary of a freelance journalist

First thing in the morning I get a call from Paul of BettaProds en-thusiastically asking when the piece about the KoolWay range is going to appear. I'm tempted to tell him 'never because it was so dull', but bite my tongue. It is better to try and train novice marketing and PR people rather than just give them a hard time without ex-plaining what they are doing wrong. I'm about to point out why the press conference was a waste of my time and his money, when I remember the commission for the piece on kitchen safety. Perhaps someone at BettaProds can comment on innovations in kitchen safety matters, I suggest, and Paul says that he can get someone to talk to me about that.

Ten minutes later his MD, Karen Jamison, calls to talk to me but obviously has no idea what about. I have to spend time telling her the angle of the piece – I'd just told Paul and he should have briefed her. Then she has no immediate opinions or views – in other words, she's wasted her time and mine with that call. I then get on the phone to some other experts on health and safety issues, and they quickly give me the words and views I need. I also talk to a research agency for some statistics, and the piece is beginning to take shape in my mind. Half an hour later Paul rings back to see how the interview with Karen went. I am rather curt with him, I'm afraid. As far as I'm concerned it is too late for that feature, unless she's got something really outstanding to say. People just don't realise that, while I'm looking for views and opinions, there is always someone else ready with a quick viewpoint for me to quote. I don't have time to wait around for incompetent people to get their act together.

I also take a look at the KiddieLearn 2 software, which I picked up at the lunch yesterday. I didn't speak to any of the SoftMicro people, but give the MD a call and chat through the product features with him. A very helpful man, and he seemed to give a balanced view, not just a sales pitch. I start writing the product review and finish work at 7. I didn't get a chance to open the post at all today. There is a large pile getting bigger every day – tomorrow I'm going to have a session and clear the decks.

Last thing, I go online and check my e-mail. About ten personal messages since I logged on yesterday, plus a few press releases. I e-mail all the press release senders, saying I prefer snail mail (ordinary post) for press releases. I don't have the time to download them all, although I know some other journalists prefer to get press releases electronically. Different strokes for different folks. A couple of the senders are people that I've mentioned this to in the past and I make a mental note that their PR isn't much good.

- **Comment**: Can you see why journalists find marketing people like Paul so irritating? He has no understanding of the pressures Suzie is under or what she is looking for. She wants to write about KoolWay but he is, unwittingly, making it hard for her. If Karen had been briefed to say something outspoken and opinionated, Suzie would almost certainly have quoted her.

CHAPTER FIVE

Catching the journalists' attention

Introduction

To promote your product to the media you first have to catch the journalist's eye and then you can deliver your message. This chapter looks critically at the different ways to gain attention and deliver the message. The main thing to remember is to tell the journalist all about your product but do not sell it to them: they are not customers.

Attracting the journalist's eye is not easy. You are not alone in wanting the journalist to notice you and your product. A typical magazine gets several hundred press releases every day, each one from someone wanting to talk to a journalist about their product or service. You have to be positive, proactive and have an attractive spin on your story. On the positive side, once one journalist starts picking up on your story you are likely to find others following suit. So one piece of editorial might lead spontaneously to others. And, in your favour, journalists are continually looking for the next news story. They live in a news vacuum in which they can get disconnected from the people that they are writing about, and rely on people like you to keep them up to date.

By taking a strategic approach and selecting the most appropriate method of catching the journalists' attention, you will achieve the publicity that translates into sales leads. If you can succeed in making the media aware that you are available to comment on certain issues, and they know that you make a good commentator, there is a high probability that you will be asked repeatedly for your comments and to appear on panels and so forth. Press coverage is like a rolling stone – the more you get, the more you gather.

A mixed strategy

No efforts to interest a journalist in your product or story should be made in isolation. You need to have the following:

- objectives – with your targets laid out within desired time-scales

- a strategy – of how you are going to achieve your objectives
- a plan – of how you are going to set about the strategy, with time-scales, and
- tactics – to anticipate obstacles and work out your responses.

You must know what your objectives are and what you want to achieve. You must take a strategic approach, with a plan for how you are going to contact the journalist, what you are going to say, and how you are going to follow up. And you need to work out your tactics in terms of the timetable, activities and message contents. Then you need to go on the offensive to communicate your message to the media. To accomplish this you need to do more than just churn out press releases – you need to initiate and cultivate personal relationships.

First decide what your product offers that matches the needs of the market. Then refine your press messages so they are strong and effective, and promote your product to your customers by using these messages via the media. Your press efforts can also be synchronised with an advertising and promotional campaign, even though you will have no control over what the journalist will say or when.

Try not to draw a journalist's attention to your promotional spend – not only might this be regarded as crass, but most journalists and editors deliberately avoid a close association with advertising. Others recognise that a link is a commercial reality and expect it. Generally, those publications with close links between advertising and editorial are not well regarded or respected (see Chapter 1 on advertorials).

Setting objectives and costing it out

Regardless of how big or small your company is, every media strategy needs to have targets which can be quantified and judged. Media exposure is harder to evaluate than an advertising campaign where there is a tangible spend and tangible returns (sales), but the same principles apply.

Work out how much your press activity costs, in terms of the time you spend working on it, taking and making telephone calls and conducting interviews. This can then be compared with the sales directly arising as a result of the editorial.

However, bear in mind that editorial coverage does not always result in immediate sales, and more often has a slower, more subtle effect of raising your potential customer's consciousness of the product.

You can also measure the column inches or broadcast seconds, and give these a value. For example, one minute on local TV news, five minutes on local or national radio, a total of 10 column inches of press spread across trade and consumer titles, and a total of thirty product mentions in various press, can be worth £10,000 per year. These exposures can be compared with the cost of buying similar advertising space, to arrive at a realistic figure.

Many journalists, even those from the same industry or type of publication or programme, can work alongside each other. But in many other situations, journalists working for different publications or programmes are in direct conflict and are therefore highly competitive.

They don't like going to small press meetings together, they don't always like sitting near to each other, and they are very defensive and protective about the angle they intend to take on a story. Sometimes they socialise and get on well – up to a point. Ultimately, they don't want other journalists to know what they know. They are secretive about their contacts and are reluctant to reveal their sources of information.

If you are sending out invitations to small press events, you should try to be aware of any potential conflict between members of the press, either personal or professional. At a large conference any rivalry or antagonism can be absorbed, but you might find that you have problems if you invite journalists from titles which are in direct competition to a small press lunch or a seminar. Journalists from directly competing titles will be unwilling to discuss the product or to question you in front of the others, mainly so that the other journalists don't learn anything specific from the debate. If one journalist has a particular angle they will be very reluctant to give the competition any clue about the approach they want to take, and will remain silent and in ignorance rather than give the competitor an idea about the way they are thinking.

Journalists who are in direct competition, either in the titles for which they work or the areas which they cover, appreciate discreet one-to-one briefings rather than larger groups where several of their competitors are also present. It is usually all right to invite several journalists who do not compete directly for a small lunch briefing.

If it is impossible to avoid inviting competing journalists to a small event, do not despair – it is not the end of the world. It happens to them all the time. What will probably happen is, as mentioned above, that they will be reluctant to ask any questions in front of their competitors which will give an indication of the way their minds are working, or what they see as the main angle for the story, but it will not stop them covering the story. In fact, if they know their competitors are writing a particular story they will feel the need to cover it too, provided there is a newsworthy relevance for their audience.

There are exceptions to this: some journalists like to show off their knowledge and interrogation skills in front of their peers. Also, if there is an approaching deadline, they will be less concerned about 'giving the game away' by asking probing questions in front of journalists from competing titles.

The recommended way to deal with competition between journalists is simply to ignore it. If there is any conflict or rivalry, just aim to treat every journalist and publication equally. Don't give any preference or advance information to any one title or individual, and try to ensure complete even-handedness in giving out information, pictures and products for review.

Some companies select preferred journalists and titles and give them special advance knowledge, pictures or products, hoping that the selected journalists will choose to regard the 'special' briefing as a scoop and give the story high-profile coverage. Unfortunately this strategy can fail on two counts: first, the selected journalists may not rise to the bait and may choose to ignore the product or give it scant coverage. Second, the 'other' press may feel affronted and not report it at all, even when they are given all the information. For these reasons 'advance briefings' are a risky and complex strategy and are not usually advocated. Trying to 'play off' the journalists against each other, or trying to secure a high-profile editorial coverage by promising exclusives in this way, frequently backfires.

Reaching the media

Personal contact

The most common ways of initiating personal contact are the following:

- telephone
- post
- e-mail
- fax
- web sites.

You could use one or more of these approaches if you want to pitch a story to journalists. Remember that they will not just expect you simply to tell them about your product, but will also be expecting you to suggest a story in which your product could be mentioned and give them the main hook or angle.

Like the press release, the personal pitch depends almost entirely for its success on your opening words. If you haven't got their attention in the first few seconds, you've lost them altogether.

Telephone pitches can be a good way to personalise your product. People buy from people and it is important that your product has a human appeal to the journalist – you.

The trick is first to catch their attention. Then create interest by explaining how your product is relevant. Turn the interest into a desire to hear more and promise action in the form of a demonstration of the product or an interview to discuss it.

If you really believe you have a good, newsworthy story, pitch it three times before you give up. Telephone or e-mail, send the press release and then follow up with an offer of more help or an interview. If the journalist doesn't bite after all that, forget it.

Press releases

(See Appendix 3 for detailed guidance on writing an effective press release.)

Think of a press release as a begging letter saying, 'Please ring me!' It's strange, then, that they can be some of the most boring documents you can imagine.

Many freelances get 40 to 80 press releases a day. Many trade publications get around 300 a day, and the national newspapers get more like 500 a day. Most go straight in the bin. They are opened quickly, glanced at and an immediate decision is taken. Some are so badly written, or the message is so obscure, that it takes considerably longer than the regulation fifteen seconds to judge whether it is interesting or not – by which time the journalist is highly irritated.

Press releases fulfil a function for you as well as for the journalist. They:

- make you think your story through carefully before you talk to the press
- give you a permanent record of what you say and do
- help you argue a case or put a point of view.

And for the media, a press release will:

- give a distilled overview of the story
- provide a permanent record of the story for later reference
- summarise the information and views that you want to communicate.

To help your press release hit its target, it's useful to call the day before it is due to arrive to warn that something genuinely newsworthy is on its way. Press releases *have* to be newsworthy or relevant – only telephone in advance if there is a *real* story. Then, after you have sent the press release, you can call the day after it arrives to see if the journalist needs anything more (but see Chapter 8 on why you should not call up just to see if the release has arrived, or to ask whether the journalist will be using it or when it may appear).

Journalists know that press releases are the most common source of news stories and feature ideas, so some people get them right. And journalists *do* look at them for leads and information. But most are *so* boring that they are not read beyond the first half-page.

Perhaps many press releases are so bad because they appear to be written by committee – all individuality and colour subbed out by writing and rewriting, and passing for approval around the office. Some of the best press releases are those written by PR agencies – because if there are any mistakes the agency gets it in the neck!

As the journalist glances at the headline on a press release he or she is asking, 'Is this interesting to my readers/viewers/listeners?' – and the answer has to be right there in the headline and standfirst. If you haven't hooked the journalist with the headline and standfirst they won't even bother to read the first paragraph, and if they read that first paragraph and don't know immediately the story's angle and importance, they won't bother to read any more.

Target your press releases as best you can. It's a good idea to write four or six versions of every press release, to make sure the technical press gets the technical releases, and the consumer press gets the consumer angle, etc. Make sure that the headlines and standfirsts of each are specifically targeted with the most relevant angle for each journalist's audience. It is crucial to keep your mailing list up to date so that all the right journalists get the release.

The procedure in many editorial offices is that the lowly editorial assistant opens all the mail. Even those addressed to specific individuals are opened centrally. Then the pile of press releases is passed around the office, starting with the editor. People take out press releases that they find interesting. It is worth sending two – or at the most three – copies of a press release to an editorial office, but often more than three duplicates are immediately binned by the editorial assistant. In some offices individuals open the mail addressed to them personally, but this is the exception. There is rarely any value in addressing a press release to every member of the editorial team.

If your press release isn't used, don't be tempted to redate it and send it out again. If any journalist picks it up the second time around, and uses it, they are not going to be pleased when they discover that it is actually old news. If you want to re-release a press release, have a good reason for doing so and mark it clearly on the front page, with the original date of the release clearly tagged.

If you have personal contacts among journalists you can certainly call them with the story – don't just rely on the press release, which may get lost in a pile of others.

Press conferences

Many people launching a product think that a press conference is the essential first step in attracting the attention of journalists. In fact, conferences should only be used when there is a major news announcement.

Press conferences are full-scale set-pieces which take a lot of time and money to organise. They are risky because you can never be sure who will turn up or how they will react.

The first step is to consider carefully what you are planning to tell the journalists and whether there is a better, more effective and cost-efficient way of imparting the story. If you have any doubts about whether to have a press conference – don't. Find another way.

If you do decide to run a press conference, consider carefully the date, making sure that it does not clash with press days (the date that publications close – always busy for journalists) or any other event. Think about the timing: mornings are best, early in the week and early in the month. Think about the venue: make sure it's easy for the journalists to get to and offers comfort and style without being too flash. You don't have to spend lots of money.

If possible, invite customers and independent analysts or commentators who are willing to talk to the press. Many journalists will not go to a press conference where they think they are going to get a sales pitch, but will consider going when they know that an independent analyst or customer is going to be there.

Make sure the guest list includes everyone you might ever want to attend. You are only going to hold a press conference every blue moon or more rarely than that – so you may as well invite everyone you can think of (except family and friends – keep it professional). The drop-out rate is usually high – a 20 per cent attendance rate is very good, and 5 per cent is not unusual.

Send invitations about ten days to two weeks in advance, with clear details of when and where. Give some details on the invitation of what the journalists are going to see, what they might get out of it, and whether independent parties will be there. Include a reply-paid card or fax-back form. Whether they reply or not, you should call the day before to establish whether they are still intending to come. Even those who affirm may not show up on the day. It may be for a good reason, but they are unlikely to let you know that they're not going to show. Expect attendance to be far less than the number that confirm their invitations. Unfortunately, it is common for journalists to accept several invitations for one day, perhaps in the optimistic hope that they can cover them all. Also, you don't know what other stories may break on the day of your event which will prevent journalists attending.

Call up the day before 'to make sure the journalist knows where the event is being held' and offer to fax over a map of the location. This should give you a last-minute feel for who intends to attend. You can also offer to book one-to-one interviews after the main press conference.

Hold a rehearsal, particularly if you have speakers who are unused to presenting. Don't assume anything – double-check everything. Make sure that all the presenters, users, experts and analysts know where they are going and what time they are supposed to be there. Confirm the catering, AV and seating arrangements, and have a technical run-through on the morning. Put out fewer chairs than number of people expected – better to have to pull out extra chairs than have chairs unfilled, but allow for journalists not wanting to sit too closely together. They might want to make notes that they'd rather the other journalists didn't see.

Keep the event short, especially the formal presentation. Anticipate a crisis, such as the AV system breaking down, the software crashing, or a speaker suddenly and unexpectedly unable to be there. Have a contingency plan.

The event can be a breakfast, lunch or tea. A buffet is preferable to a sit-down meal, because it gives individuals more flexibility to move around to meet people, and they can leave if they need to without fuss. A formal lunch would be appropriate for a small group of similar-minded journalists, but for several dozen a buffet is more practical. Hospitality should be good but it need not be too lavish.

Make sure that there are telephones available for journalists to use, and some journalists might like to be able to plug in their portable computer. They might also want a direct line with a modem socket.

The plan for a press conference should be something like this:

- **Arrive** (give an arrival time ten or fifteen minutes before you want to start – no longer or you will have a group of irritated journalists ranging around).

- **Sign in** and coffee. Give each a name badge.

- **Formal presentation** with product demonstration and questions. Keep the formal presentation to a minimum and make it as slick as possible, without using gimmicks. Journalists are not keen on speeches. It is better to have people doing things than saying things. Have a user or analyst available for questions – journalists like to speak to an independent third party. These individuals should be trained and rehearsed and be prepared to answer questions from the press. Prepare them for any awkward questions which you think may arise, and rehearse their answers.

- **Drinks and lunch**, with opportunities for one-to-one discussions.

- **As they leave**, give each journalist a press pack containing press releases, drafts of speeches (in case they want to quote the speaker), names and contact details of all speakers, customers and analysts who attended, photographs, plus a complimentary copy of the product if appropriate. You can also include copies of the presentations and speeches and biographies of the speakers. Do not include press cuttings or reprints of previous press coverage or you will kill the story dead. These indicate both that the story is not new, and that the papers the cuttings are taken from are regarded by you as more important than those represented at the conference. (Some PR professionals believe that the press pack should be given to journalists as they arrive at the event. The advantage of this is that they can use the pack contents for notes, and it can be useful to be able to make notes about a presentation on the hand-out material.) You should offer the journalists the option of having the contents of the press pack on CD-ROM, or having it e-mailed to them. You should also put the contents of the press pack on the Internet.

- **Do not overload** the journalist with irrelevant material. You could just tell them that biographies and transcripts are available on request. Avoid including sales leaflets.

If you are inviting US speakers or journalists, be aware that in the USA it is common practice for journalists to applaud at the end of a press conference. In the UK journalists do not do this, which can be very disconcerting for American executives who are not warned of the way the UK press behaves. In the USA it is also routine for journalists to stand and state the publication they work for, but in the UK they often just ask their question without introducing themselves.

Many journalists record press conferences, and extracts may be used for radio and TV broadcasts. Everything which is said at a press conference is 'on the record' and can be published.

Follow up afterwards, making sure that each journalist has everything that they requested.

Avoid non-disclosure agreements (NDAs) and embargoes. An NDA is a variation of the embargo and both are equally disliked by journalists. The NDA is a quasi-legal document in which the journalist agrees not to write about what they see or hear. Many journalists refuse to sign them: what is the point in telling a journalist something and then asking them not to use it? But although journalists don't like them, they do have their place. For a company trying to promote a story and a product, it can be useful to inform the media before the launch, yet they may not want the launch publicised before they are ready. It is also sometimes useful to give a journalist a briefing in a more relaxed atmosphere some time before an official launch, because it gives them time to research and write the story in advance.

The question you have to ask is: What are you going to do if a journalist breaks an NDA? There are no legal sanctions you can resort to, while threatening not to give the journalist the story next time is likely to be self-defeating. A better strategy might be to give trusted journalists an 'off-the-record' briefing, after you have struck an agreement that they will not use the information. However, the same principles apply to off-the-record statements as to NDAs: you cannot be absolutely certain that the journalist will not use them, and there is nothing you can do if they break the agreement.

Press receptions

A press reception is less formal than a press conference and is an opportunity for you and your colleagues to meet a group of journalists who may be interested in your story or product, usually in an informal location such as a wine bar. Like all business contact, face to face is always best and press relations after a personal meeting are always easier. If you are located some way from where the journalists are based, a one-off press reception can be a good opportunity to meet individuals whom you would otherwise always just talk to on the phone.

Sometimes it is necessary to offer journalists some kind of inducement to attend, which may take the form of a bottle of champagne, for example, or the opportunity to meet an interesting celebrity or reputable analyst. They should certainly be offered a complimentary copy of the product, if that is appropriate.

Press receptions are often arranged in a side room at exhibitions, where journalists may be reluctant to visit stands or the stands are manned by salespeople unskilled in talking to the press. You should be prepared for any question about facts and statistics and expect some questions on any topic, just like an interview. Answer them if you can, but otherwise offer to get back to them next day or whenever is convenient. Remember, everything is on the record.

An example of a press reception is when a PR agency invites all its clients and all the journalists it can think of, and gets the clients to pay for a venue and food in the early evening. The journalists go along after work, have a drink and relax, and chat to the clients. The clients should be warned not to overtly promote their products at such a meeting: the primary objective is to get to know each other and create relationships. Conversations should be casual, but everything is potentially on the record. Business cards are exchanged, and the journalists are refreshed and hopefully have some ideas and have made useful contacts. The clients will be feeling more confident and relaxed about talking to those journalists in future.

One-to-ones

Another way to get your message across to a select group of journalists is to arrange a series of individual private meetings with them, perhaps an hour apart. You meet them singly, and present them with your product and story. This can be a good opportunity to target the right journalists precisely and make sure that they know about your product.

One-to-ones are often held in hotel meeting-rooms, and are a more formal alternative to a lunch. Some journalists like one-to-ones because they feel they are getting an exclusive story specifically geared for their readership. Others dislike them because they have to work hard to uncover the hidden story.

When you hold a one-to-one, make sure that you have something prepared to say. Do not simply invite the journalist in, sit them down and say, 'Now, what do you want to ask?' You invite the press there to tell them your story and to promote your product, so point out the newsworthy elements of the product and hand the journalists their angle or hook on a plate.

The worst type of one-to-ones have one journalist and three, four or six people on the 'other side'. This can be extremely unnerving and the journalist can feel that they are being swamped with a false 'feel-good' story. Such one-to-ones are 'sold' to the journalist as an 'interview opportunity' but often they are forced to spend the whole time viewing a presentation. There is often little opportunity for dissent or cross-questioning. A better alternative is to invite two or three journalists together, from publications or programmes which do not clash.

When building your database on each journalist's preferences, it is helpful to find out their feelings on one-to-ones.

Workshops or seminars

Workshops and seminars are increasing in popularity because they are more informal than a press conference and journalists get real value out of them – usually knowledge or information.

Workshops are typically presented as an opportunity to learn more about a specific topic from an expert on the subject. They are particularly attractive to novice journalists trying to master a complex technical topic.

Workshops and seminars are most successfully arranged for breakfast time (9 a.m.) so that the journalist can have breakfast and learn about an issue, and perhaps get a story idea, on the way in to work.

Make sure the journalists have a chance to speak to users and others connected with the product, and leave with a press pack of information, photographs and, if possible, a sample of the product.

Exhibitions or shows

Shows and exhibitions are good places to launch new products to the public, and it is worth making sure that journalists get invited just in case they have not heard of or seen the product. But, contrary to popular opinion, they are not such good places to meet the press. Regard exhibitions and shows primarily as opportunities to promote your product to potential customers, and any contact with journalists as icing on the cake. Many people wanting to promote their product to the press like to take the opportunity of exhibiting at a show to invite journalists to the stand to see, feel, touch and try the product.

There are some points to look out for, however. Journalists know from experience that most people working on show stands are there to sell and do not have the time to talk to the press. Many shows are so huge that it is difficult to predict where you will be at any time, and so journalists are often reluctant to make exact meeting times. Some journalists don't even bother to go to shows because they have already seen most of the products being launched to the public. They don't expect to see anything new.

Many marketing professionals like to organise press conferences on the first day of trade or consumer shows, and some do get a good press turn-out, but, like all press conferences, it is a risky gambit. The value of such conferences is generally regarded as dubious. For example, there may be other conferences or some spectacular event happening on the show floor, or the key journalists may not be attending the show at all.

Sometimes journalists like to attend show press conferences and one-on-ones to make contacts, but do not expect to get good stories.

The press offices at many shows are traditionally regarded as good places to find many journalists together. Strictly speaking, press offices should be a rest room and a haven where journalists can relax and receive refreshment without being plagued by marketing and PR people. Sometimes PR people and non-journalists are barred from the press office, but these days most show and exhibition organisers allow anyone into them. In fact, many journalists retire to bars rather than go into the press office where they know they will be tormented by PR and marketing types.

Sometimes journalists are offered lures to get them to visit stands, such as a bottle of champagne for simply turning up and leaving a business card. Presumably the marketing people are hoping to get a few minutes' time with them, but they have no guarantee of getting value for their champagne.

Facilities visits

Depending on what type of product you are promoting, it might be appropriate to invite a small group of journalists to tour the factory or see your retail outlet. However, you should only do this if there is genuinely something unusual and worth seeing.

Journalists, being cynical and busy creatures, need to have a good reason to make the effort to leave their office and you should make sure that you offer them something special, some unique value that they can get out of it. You need to be sure that they are going to get a story, with a strong hook. A simple visit to a factory is not going to be newsworthy.

A good facilities visit, for example, combines the launch of a new product or some other newsworthy announcement with an invitation to an all-expenses-paid outing which includes a tour of a factory or shop.

Media tours

If you have a product and story to promote, you can go to the publishing houses and journalists by undertaking a media tour. This means going around the publishing houses at pre-arranged times and having meetings with and making presentations to the journalists in pre-booked meeting-rooms.

You have no guarantee that they will put the time in their diary, but they are more likely to attend a meeting in their own office building than if you invite them to a press conference or reception, for which they have to travel away from their office and sacrifice several hours of valuable time.

An example of a media tour is when a computer software vendor books a meeting-room within a large publishing house, and sets up a demonstration of the product in the room. Journalists and editors are invited at half-hourly intervals, to enjoy refreshments in the meeting-room and to try the product. They only have to leave their desk for a short time, and the vendor is on hand to explain the benefits of the product. The journalist should also be offered a free, non-returnable copy of the product for them to try out at their convenience.

A variation of the media tour is the roadshow, in which you take your product to venues where it will be exposed to your target audience. You can also invite journalists to roadshows, but do not expose them to the undiluted sales pitch which you give to prospects.

Press hospitality

A traditional and popular way to get to know journalists better is to take them out for lunch or for a drink in a pub. This can be a very useful way of understanding the journalist better and improving the lines of communication. You can learn more about what the journalist wants and how you can best deliver it to them, and the angles they are looking for, by a couple of hours' hospitality.

Do not spend the whole time talking about your product. Hopefully you will get a few minutes to mention it, but the time is just as effectively spent talking about wider issues and what the journalist is looking for. Regard it as an opportunity to get to know the journalist better, not as a chance to ram your product down his or her throat.

Unless otherwise agreed, everything is on the record, however relaxed the surroundings. Be careful not to become too careless in your gossip unless you want to be quoted. Remember: you should assume that nothing is ever off the record.

You should pay for all hospitality. If you are working with American companies or US journalists, you should be aware that in the USA journalists are not allowed by many editors to accept such hospitality, or gifts or trips, because they believe it is unethical and opens them to corruption. This is not the case in the UK and the company promoting the product would be expected to pay all the journalists' expenses. Do not be embarrassed by this – the journalist would be more embarrassed if you expected them to pay or go Dutch. The UK journalists will expect you to pick up all the bills but will not feel obliged to give a more flattering review or mention. A very few UK publications, programmes or editors take the same view as the US journalists and frown on any hospitality or gifts. If you are unsure of the protocol, ask. As a rule, remember that it's only a bribe if you try to keep it secret.

Features lists

Features lists are your opportunity to react to something proactively, rather than trying to approach a journalist cold. Many publications and most radio and TV stations – and also some individual freelance journalists – produce lists of forthcoming features they are planning to cover.

The features list may be for the next week or for the next year and is an invaluable tool for those wanting to promote a product. The lists tell you the topics, titles, issues and subject-matter which the journalist will be expecting to cover, and it is up to you to respond to these lists. By responding at the right time and delivering interesting and opinionated views, not just boring sales information, you stand a good chance of being mentioned. Features lists tell you that a feature on a certain topic is extremely likely to be run, although at the end of the day anything can happen: the editor may have a change of mind and change the date of the feature or not run it at all.

The main purpose of a features list is that the sales team can sell advertising space around a feature on a specific topic, although on many titles the connection goes further and high-spending advertisers are given priority in the editorial coverage. You can use features lists to your advantage. If you know that an editorial feature is coming up which relates to your product or market sector, you can seek out the journalist writing it and try to give them some interesting comment which they can use.

You can get a features list from the sales team and then follow up through the editorial team to find out who is writing the feature and what the deadline is. If the editorial team is reluctant to tell you, the media sales team may have the information you need. Once you have the journalist's name and number, contact them, first with a press release and then with a phone call, and interest them in your product and your views. Have a clear idea what their audience is and the likely angle of the feature. They are probably looking for input and views and are likely to welcome your call, although you cannot be sure. They may tell you that the piece is written already, or they may have all the information they need.

Some editors refuse to produce features lists, claiming that they compromise editorial integrity and independence, and it is certainly true that those titles which have no influence from the sales team have better editorial with more controversial, independent and less sycophantic copy.

You may get a call from the advertising team if you have spoken to a journalist, and sometimes they insinuate that unless you advertise in the publication, your editorial mention will be dropped. This is rarely the case and there is almost never any true reason for you to advertise just because you are mentioned in the editorial. This is pure blackmail and you should resist it.

On the other hand, if you are placing an advertisement, it is worth asking whether you can speak to a journalist. On some titles the journalists are under pressure to talk to advertisers and will try to run editorial that positively mentions you if they know you are advertising. But the safest way to leverage your advertising is through the advertising team, not by going direct to the journalist.

Product round-ups and reviews

Many publications run editorial surveys and reports of product types, groups or categories, and if you are trying to promote a product, inclusion in such round-ups is critical. You should establish which of your target publications or programmes do such reviews, contact the editor and ask whether they are planning a review in which your product would be suitable for inclusion.

Some publications automatically review new products, and you should make sure that the editor or reviews editor has samples of your product for consideration. Depending on the product, they could either just be sent a review copy, a sample, or be offered a demonstration at an appropriate location.

If the journalist asks for a demonstration, try not to 'sell' the product's virtues. Remember that the journalist is probably extremely familiar with the type of product and your competitors, so will be aware of any overt sales hype. Just point out the key features and let the journalist try it out. Make sure that you provide all appropriate and relevant sales literature, brochures and manuals.

If a review or product round-up appears and your product is not included, contact the editor or reviews editor immediately and politely point out the omission. Obviously, by that time nothing can be done about the original editorial, but the reviews editor may consider a second editorial which includes your product.

Gifts and freebies

In the UK, few journalists turn down the offer of a gift or a freebie provided they come without strings. UK journalists rarely refuse gifts and freebies on the grounds that they might compromise their independence and integrity. At Christmas in particular, many journalists receive corporate gifts such as port and Stilton, wine and other give-aways. These are usually gratefully received, but without any feeling of obligation to favour the provider in the new year. Most journalists are grateful for gifts, tickets for corporate hospitality events, etc. at any time of the year, but there needs to be the strict understanding that they are given and received without any expectation of editorial publicity.

In America the situation is quite different. It is a dismissable offence on most US titles for their journalists to accept freebies. Most US publishing houses give their journalists an allowance so that they can pay for their own meals and travel to events and meetings without relying on the hospitality of a PR company or someone seeking to promote their product. Some UK titles take a similar view, although they are in the minority.

As with hospitality, if you are unsure of the protocol with particular titles or journalists, ask. They will not be offended. It is only a bribe if you attempt to disguise it.

Stunts and teasers

Stunts are great – when they work. Sometimes a stunt can be painstakingly arranged and appear to be successful, only to be completely ignored by the press. Or worse, the stunt can misfire, and that becomes the story – negative rather than positive.

Those who advocate stunts believe that conventional ways of getting a journalist's attention are just that – too conventional. They say that paper-based press releases get lost in the crowd of the hundreds which arrive every day, and a stunt makes a bigger impact. They also provoke interaction between the journalist and those seeking publicity, and create an individual and memorable impression. These possible positive outcomes have to be balanced against the risk of disaster, which can easily take over.

If you decide to arrange a publicity stunt, you still need to make sure that you have an underlying message which the press will want to hear. It helps if there is a topical theme which needs to be appropriate for the product and segment of the press.

The problem with stunts is that they are as vulnerable to the curse of the unexpected as press conferences. You can do your best to ensure that they do not clash with other events, but there is always something which no one could have predicted to make it all go wrong, like a travel strike or a thunderstorm or some other disaster. It helps if the stunt is arranged around the middle of the day or early evening – in other words, mealtimes, when journalists are most likely to be available and willing to leave their offices. Choose a location which is handy for the journalists and make the invitation alluring without giving too much away. You need to make it clear that the journalist is going to get a story, and it is not going to be a waste of time. However much fun the stunt is, the journalist still wants to get a good story with a distinct hook.

On the plus side stunts can create excellent photo opportunities, and will possibly interest radio and TV journalists as well as print press, because of the novelty and visual aspect.

A *teaser campaign* is a version of a stunt, and is equally liable to be effective or a disaster. Like stunts, teasers are hard to evaluate and can have a distinctly negative effect. Many journalists are irritated by them, ignore them, or worse, react with hostility. For other journalists, they work.

There are various types of teaser campaign. Some are a series of press release mailings in advance of the true release, which are supposed to whet the journalists' appetite for a story. Others are a series of small anonymous gifts which lead up to and culminate in the full story. Generally speaking, they are not recommended: if you have a story, tell it to the journalist – don't waste everyone's time by telling half the story. If the story is interesting, the journalist will follow up, regardless of any teaser campaign.

The principle applies to both stunts and teasers: if the product is interesting it won't need tricks to catch the journalists' eye. But if your product is extremely dull and you are having trouble finding a strong hook for the story or unique message, then a stunt may be the only way of catching their eye. However, once the press realises that the product has little to offer they are likely to reject the story anyway, regardless of the stunt or teaser.

The secret is to know your journalists, and know which might be receptive to a stunt or teaser and which will be annoyed.

Opinion pieces

Some editors use opinion pieces because they are a free way to fill copy space. It means the editorial budget can be saved and spent elsewhere. A good opinion piece will discuss a topical issue but will not over-mention your product or company. Many freelance journalists will write opinion pieces, usually based on an interview with the subject. The usual rate for this is £350–£450 per thousand words the normal rate for PR writing. This usually compares favourably with the advertising rate for a similar space.

The benefit of an opinion piece is that you get a fairly large chunk of editorial space in which to get your view across, and it significantly helps promote you and your product. It also helps to promote you as a pundit and your company as one which has radical or strong views on topical issues.

You usually get your name as the by-line, or at the bottom of the piece, and sometimes the name of your company and a contact telephone number. Sometimes you have a chance to have your photograph printed too, but you do not have any editorial control. Opinion pieces go through the usual editorial subbing process just like any other copy, and will be changed and edited to make them match the house style.

If, once the opinion piece appears, you are unhappy with any changes that have been made to it, you have no comeback unless they create an inaccurate impression. If you want complete control over the piece which appears, you need to be considering advertorial or advertising (see Chapter 1 on advertorials).

Do not offer opinion pieces or any contributed editorial to more than one publication at the same time. Offer it to one, then wait and see whether it will be used before offering to anyone else. An editor is likely to be extremely angry if the same piece appears in another title at the same time.

Sponsorship

If you want to promote your product to the press, and through the press to a wider audience, participating in sponsorship opportunities can be a good way to catch the journalists' eye and publicise your product's name to your market. There are often sponsorship opportunities at a very local level, either of local sporting events or of local arts. There may also be sponsorship opportunities which are specific to your target market, or associated with a relevant trade or industry.

If you are investing in sponsorship, make sure that you personally attend every event and seek out every opportunity to meet the press. Do not necessarily try to talk about your product – see it as a chance to get to know the journalist better, and suggest another meeting or interview to discuss your product.

Contributed articles

Some editors will only publish or broadcast original features or news stories which they have specifically commissioned, but others will fill some of their space with contributed pieces. It helps them save their budget, or frees up funds which can be used elsewhere. Ideally, the contributed piece will not mention your company or product too overtly but the emphasis will be on an issue or a view which is, coincidentally, connected with your product.

Before spending time and effort on producing an article, contact the editor first and establish that they do accept such pieces. Sending unsolicited work is almost certainly a waste of time. Once you have established that they use contributed work, you need to know the word count and whether there is a preferred topic to be covered and anything to be avoided. Have the target reader clearly fixed in your mind, and write for them.

Again, as with opinion pieces, do not offer a contributed article to more than one journalist at a time. They are likely to be extremely upset if the same piece appears in other publications or programmes at the same time. Only offer it around when you are certain it is not going to be used, and then to only one other journalist at a time.

Letters to the editor

Letters for publication are one of the most overlooked areas of opportunity for those seeking to promote their product. You get several column inches of your own point of view, without criticism or comment from anyone else, and your name and company name at the end. Again, avoid being too overt in promoting your product – it makes a better read and subtlety can be just as effective if you talk in an opinionated way around surrounding issues.

However, the general rule is: 'Don't nag, don't argue and never expect an apology.'

Chapter summary

- Failure to plan is planning to fail. Draw up a strategy, a plan and some tactics. Don't just write a press release and send it off.

- Decide which method is best for you to contact the press – or which combination of methods – and stick to your plan. Your options are wide: press conferences, receptions, tours, one-to-ones or sponsorship. Choose for a reason.

- Define those objectives for the next three and six months which are measurable:
  - How many press mentions?
  - In which publications?
  - How many interviews?
  - How many sales as a direct result of the publicity?

- Have a plan for contacting the press, who you intend to contact, how and the order in which you want to contact them.

- Develop some tactics for keeping your product in the media for the next six months.

- Work out tactics for dealing with difficult questions from the press. Most awkward situations can be anticipated.

CASE STUDIES

Case study 1: Product promotion to the lifestyle press

A month after the press conference, Paul is thinking of other ways to make the press aware of the KoolWay range and get BettaProds in the news.

He has a meeting with Karen during which they decide on some key issues being discussed in the press on which she can comment. They use some lateral thinking to find these topics, settling for some which have nothing to do with kitchen goods or the catering industry, or health and safety.

Karen feels that she has strong views on European monetary union (EMU), on women's role in the workplace and on the difficulty in getting staff with the right skills. Taking these three areas, she and Paul work out and write some strong comments and views.

Then Paul goes back to the media directory and selects 80 journalists he knows write about these issues. Some are freelance and some write for specific titles and programmes. He prepares a series of press releases on each of the topics, leading with Karen's views.

He starts with Jane Marples, the journalist who rang after the press conference, and quickly explains to her that Karen has some strong opinions on some topical issues. She is immediately interested, and narrows down the three areas to one which she is writing about in the near future – women's role in the workplace. They arrange a telephone interview, and late that afternoon Karen calls Jane, with her cue card in front of her carrying her three key messages about KoolWay and BettaProds that she really wants to get across.

They have a friendly conversation – Karen says afterwards she would be reluctant to call it an interview because it was more like a chat with a friend. They cover a broad range of areas including Karen's background, her family arrangements and how she manages her two children, and her feelings about running a company of 30 employees. Jane also asks about KoolWay and the range of products, and Karen manages to mention all three of her key messages. It wasn't difficult, although she realises she cannot be sure that Jane will use any of them.

Afterwards, Jane wants to talk to one of BettaProds' other employees, and Paul sets up an interview with a warehouse manager. She asks him how he feels about being employed by a woman, and he is able to say what a good company BettaProds is to work for, and that the MD being a woman makes no difference at all!

Two weeks later a feature appears in the local newspaper and two weeks after that a major survey is run in one of the Sunday supplements, both written by Jane Marples. She quotes Karen in both, and has a picture of her in the local paper. The angle of the two pieces is slightly different, and the one in the Sunday supplement is shorter and other people are quoted, but there is a box-out describing BettaProds and the KoolWay range. The local piece is almost exclusively about Karen and BettaProds, as a local company run by a woman.

- **Comment**: Paul is right to try and establish areas where Karen has her own strong views and to try to match those with the journalists and publications/programmes. With this approach he is more successful with Jane Marples, and the resulting interview between Jane and Karen is productive for everyone.

Case study 2: Product promotion to the computer press

Jessica continues with her plans for a breakfast seminar and to take a group of journalists to a school which uses KiddieLearn 2. At first she thinks that, having seen how Joe managed the press reception, she would be able to do it herself, but after a couple of phone calls she realises that it is far harder to call a journalist and interest them in attending an event than she thought.

She calls Joe again, and they arrange for Joe's agency, Probe PR, to handle her press relations on a permanent, full-time basis. Probe PR has five people working for it and has around 20 clients, all connected with the computer industry. Joe is the managing director.

They have a meeting at which Jessica and Richard outline what they want – which is basically as much editorial press exposure as possible. Joe tells them what they can realistically expect and how much he will charge. The retainer fee is £2,500 a month plus expenses, which Richard feels is a lot for SoftMicro to afford at this stage. But Jessica persuades him that if they are to achieve sales they need the publicity, and it is worth using a professional for the next six months.

Joe also introduces Jessica and Richard to Sasha, who will be handling their account. Sasha has only recently joined Probe PR, but Joe reassures Richard and Jessica that he will be overseeing Sasha and directing everything that she does.

Over the next week Sasha spends a few days with Richard and Jessica, familiarising herself with KiddieLearn 2 and the innovative features it offers. She is very enthusiastic, although Richard is concerned that she knows less about the product than Jessica, and doesn't appear to know the journalists personally.

The next event scheduled is the visit to the school, which Sasha is instructed to organise. The plan is to take eight journalists to a special school in Central London which has been using KiddieLearn 2 since it was in Beta version. Richard knows that they are extremely pleased with the software and the results shown in the children's performance, so is confident that there will be a strong, positive story.

The eight journalists are from the IT and educational press – five staffers and three freelances. Sasha writes the invitations, follows up with phone calls and reports that all eight are expected to attend. She also arranges for a table to be booked at an Italian restaurant near to the school for lunch.

On the day, the journalists are due to arrive at 11.00, but by 11.15 no one has turned up. Sasha, Richard and Jessica are standing around waiting, with the headmaster of the school. Sasha is twittering, 'I'm sure they said they'd come, I can't think what's happened to them.' She gets out her mobile and starts ringing round their offices.

By 12.30 it has transpired that, of the eight, six were never definite about turning up, and then at the last minute they chose to do other events. Sasha maintains that other events are outside her control, but Richard believes that she did not make the SoftMicro event attractive enough. The remaining two journalists said that they attempted to find the school but got lost and returned to their offices.

When Richard gets back to his office he is furious with Jessica, who calls Joe and is furious with him. Joe is extremely apologetic and promises to give the SoftMicro account his personal attention in future. Jessica says that she will not pay for any expenses incurred by the fiasco at the school.

Joe and Jessica agree that they will proceed with the breakfast seminar, and Joe starts planning it.

- **Comment**: Jessica has made the same mistake that Paul made: thinking that journalists would come along without the likelihood of a story to take away. At least Joe makes sure that there is a story. But Joe has made a mistake too, of putting the inexperienced Sasha on the account. You have to watch the PR agencies and see they don't do this.

Case study 3: Diary of a freelance journalist

A newspaper editor rings and needs a quick news analysis story. He wants 800 words in three hours' time. He gives me a lead, which is based on a report from the Institute of Directors that claims that few accounting software products are going to be EMU-compliant in time. The result is going to be widespread accounting chaos.

He faxes me a copy of the report, and I need some pundits and respected business people to comment on it. I make a list of the type of people I would like to see comment from – a software developer, an exporter, a business person and so forth.

While I'm thinking about it I go through the stack of press releases and come across a couple from people and firms who might be able to comment on EMU compliance, even though their press releases are about something entirely different. One is my old friend BettaProds, who I believe imports and exports. I give their PR person, Paul, a call, but he seems unable to cope with an enquiry which doesn't fit in with his train of thought. Luckily he puts me straight through to Karen, and this time she is a far better spokesperson.

She talks openly about the existing problems of being an international business, and the difficulties of running multi-currency systems, and says that it is possible that her business will collapse unless the EMU issue is sorted out one way or another. This is a good, strong view and I put her opinion at the beginning of the piece. I ask her to send a photo of herself to the newspaper. Then I call Jessica at SoftMicro and talk to her about EMU, but she admits immediately that she is out of her depth. Fair enough. She puts me through to Richard, who also gives a strong view on the problem of making software EMU-compliant, this time from the developer's point of view. Apparently it's not their fault, but is down to the EU, which hasn't yet defined all the parameters for compliance. That puts another spin on the story. Again, I ask him to send in a photograph of himself, and he says he'll get Jessica to do it.

Paul from BettaProds rings back asking to see the copy before I send it to the editor, so that he can make sure that I have 'quoted Karen accurately'. I tell him no, and he is rather surprised. Where do they find these people!?

The piece is fairly easy to write, especially after a quick interview with a government minister and a spokesperson from the Business and Accounting Software Alliance, which gives the official position on EMU compliance.

Once that's out of the way, I go back to the feature on kitchen safety. I'm struggling here, because I need to talk to some people who have had accidents. I go online and put up a message asking people who have experienced kitchen accidents to give me a call.

Next day
When I log on to my e-mail there are five messages from people talking about their kitchen accidents, and then the phone rings with four more who want to talk about faulty products and danger areas. Great! I'll be able to write a comprehensive and balanced piece fairly quickly, at this rate.

- **Comment**: You can see how Suzie uses press releases, and how she remembers who has been a good commentator in the past. But Paul shows his inexperience by asking to see the copy before it is published.

Chapter Six

The interview

Introduction

In an interview situation you need a cool head and must keep your messages clear in your mind, and concentrate on getting them across.

If the interview goes well, you will get free publicity, enhance your company image, spread information about your product and improve your own career. Your aim is to provide information quickly, accurately and succinctly. Few people manage to achieve all three, at least at first, but this chapter will show you how it can be done.

Things to bear in mind

Interviews are an opportunity to promote and profit. There is more at stake than simply 'raising the profile of the company and product': there is hard cash to be made from successful dealings with the press. The value of a positive two-minute interview broadcast on local radio is virtually immeasurable, and so is a print interview in the right specialist media.

The problem is that you are playing the journalists' game, in their territory, using their rules. You have little control, but if you understand something about the rules they use and the agenda they are working from, you can turn the opportunity to your advantage. If you don't take advantage of an opportunity to talk to the media, your competitors surely will.

Most journalists are looking for information and opinion, and they are all looking for good copy. Often interviews just feel like a chat, but don't be lulled into a false sense of security: remember that the journalist is subsequently free to print or broadcast anything you say. So don't get *too* frank, but be opinionated and assertive.

The journalist will be far more experienced and confident than you, but if you are nervous try not to let it show. The journalist will think that you are trying to hide something and may try to dig even deeper. On the other hand, journalists are unlikely to bully those who are obviously nervous. They are more likely to be tough on those who appear arrogant, pompous and cocky.

Interviews are the medium by which you get your message across to your potential customers, even if you don't talk much about the product. In some interviews, you may be talking about apparently unrelated topics. You may not be able to mention the product name once, but even so it is not time wasted. The point is that any opportunity to publicise the name and raise the profile and exposure of the brand is worthwhile.

Every interview is different. They can be friendly, adversarial, emotional or entertaining. They can be for hard news, research, investigation, information or back-up. Most are straightforward exchanges of information, and few are like the grilling that you see on Newsnight or hear on Radio 4. Those are extremely high level, and it is very unlikely that you will receive that kind of treatment.

Some interviews are extremely short – particularly telephone interviews – while some are long and others are positively leisurely. Interviews over a lunch are typically long, rambling affairs with plenty of time to build the relationship as well as make comments and quotes.

The journalist's approach

Journalists will prompt, challenge or say nothing as techniques for encouraging the interviewee to say more than they might want. Interviewers are allowed to be tough-minded, sharp and sceptical, but they should also be informed and not partisan. For example, the BBC requires its journalists to be: 'not aggressive, hectoring or rude, but tough-minded, sharp, sceptical, well informed, and not partial, committed or emotionally attached to one side of the argument'.

Remember that the journalist will ask questions on behalf of the viewer, listener or reader, and the questions they ask may not reflect their own opinions or views. The journalist will have an image of their viewer, reader or listener in mind and will present the sort of questions that that person might be likely to ask. It is the journalist's job to ask questions on behalf of the viewer, listener or reader. They are like the little boy in the story of *The Emperor's New Clothes* – boldly asking things which others are too afraid to mention. Journalists often have in mind 'the man in the saloon bar' or 'the man on the Clapham omnibus' on whose behalf they are directing their questions. So do not be surprised if the journalist's questions appear naive or innocent and keep your answers equally simple.

The journalist will act as devil's advocate, asking questions which seem to imply the worst possible criticisms and which no one else wants to voice. Remember that the journalist does not necessarily want to make you appear in a bad light, but is just attempting to get the best story. They usually want you to perform well.

If you are attempting to promote a product you are unlikely to face the full force of an interrogative political interview. Politicians put themselves in the firing line, but those trying to promote a product are not viewed as potential targets in the same way. The journalist is likely to question any assumptions or claims you make, saying, 'Yes, but . . .', and you will be called upon to explain your proposals, but you will not receive an aggressive grilling unless you make false claims or the product is flawed or dangerous.

Even a novice hack journalist will not let wild claims go unchallenged or accept unsubstantiated assumptions. Journalists are independent, with a duty to challenge what you are saying. Their objective is to expose your weaknesses and discredit your claims. You should expect this and should not take it personally.

If you persist in avoiding a question the journalist is likely to rephrase and re-ask it until you provide an answer. They will try to annoy and fluster you by:

- making provocative statements
- overstating the opposing view
- swinging between opposing viewpoints
- teasing and baiting with outrageous comments
- asking and saying irrational things which are bound to irritate.

You should expect all this. The journalist should not be deterred by position, money or power from making probing remarks or asking revealing questions. They are not doing a good job unless they are sceptical, cynical and bold. Expect controversy and argument – expect to be cross-examined and criticised. Do not be surprised by familiarity, insolence and cheek. The journalist is unlikely to be downright rude but if he or she is insulting, don't take it personally.

Some journalists deliberately cultivate their reputation for being aggressive, but they are just looking for interviewees who are interesting, passionate about their subject and opinionated. Usually they know that the best way to get a good comment is by being polite but firm. The key is to try to relax and enjoy the experience. Respond calmly, ignore the most absurd comments and correct the most ignorant. An interview is like a game and, provided you are prepared and keep cool, you can win.

Classic techniques

Two examples of classic interview styles can be seen in the techniques of Radio 4's John Humphrys and Sir David Frost.

John Humphrys' method is interrogative, aggressive and overtly combative. He is usually polite but very forthright. He will continually interrupt, is impatient and can appear to bully. He comes to every encounter with a contrary view, and is highly cynical, world-weary and sceptical. Like the other master of this style, Jeremy Paxman, he can be sneering and verge on the insolent. He can be extremely scathing and caustic, and appears to go for the jugular at every opportunity. He is also very well briefed and has ample background information.

Sir David Frost's method is apparently nicer, appears to be more friendly, and aims to make the interviewee relax. However, this affable, softly-softly approach is deceptive. He is just lulling his subject into a false sense of security. He knows that he can elicit just as many revelations by using kid gloves as with a baseball bat. He is also extremely well briefed, with excellent levels of background information. This type of journalist is just as dangerous as the John Humphrys type.

Some journalists take a deliberately relaxed approach and prefer to have completely informal, unstructured, apparently cosy chats rather than formal interviews, but remember that everything you say can still be used and reported. Appearing relaxed and friendly can be a subterfuge to make you lower your guard. Inviting interviewees to share a confidence can also encourage people to speak out.

The objective of both styles is to get you to say something which is accurate but is not what you wanted to say. Your objective is to deliver your messages clearly and strongly.

Interview Check Sheet

Prepare a one-page form to ensure that you maintain control of the interview, and have the information you need at the end. This will act as an *aide-mémoire* when you review your interviews, and act as a prompt for delivering follow-up information to the media.

Have your three main messages at the top and tick them off as you successfully get them into the conversation. Have several Interview Check Sheets run off, with your current messages printed at the top, but update them regularly. Your messages should be overhauled and updated at least every six months, if not more frequently. Have them handy in case a journalist calls, and make sure you use one if you call a journalist.

Your Three Main Messages: . . . .
. . . .
. . . .
Name of Journalist: . . . .
Date of Interview: . . . .
Publication *(or, if freelance, probable publications)*: . . . .
Deadline: . . . .
Topics Covered: . . . .
Specific Questions: . . . .
Answers: . . . .
Follow-up: . . . .

Telephone interviews

Many telephone interviews are extremely short, which can be disconcerting. It means that you have to focus your thoughts on the message you want to get across, as well as listening carefully to what the journalist asks.

Telephone interviews can be impersonal as well as extremely fast, which is exactly why journalists like them. By contrast, going to a press conference takes several hours and a face-to-face meeting is more difficult to leave.

If the journalist calls for comment, you may only have a minute or two before the journalist says, 'Thanks for your time', and hangs up. Try to extend the interview in order to get your message across, but better still have your messages carefully prepared in succinct statements to achieve the best possible effect and stand the most chance of being used.

Some people find telephone interviews difficult because of the lack of eye contact. Others like the fact that they can have their cue cards in front of them, to make it easier to get their messages across.

If it is any consolation, telephone interviews can be just as awkward for the journalist, because they are unable to see your face and read what you are *really* trying to say. They are probably making notes and trying to write while balancing the phone on their shoulder, and trying to think of the next penetrating question.

Remember to smile and use arm movements as though they were in the same room. Standing up while talking on the phone can help give confidence. Suggest a face-to-face meeting in the near future.

Face to face

A face-to-face situation can be formal, casual, over a meal or a drink, arranged or impromptu. They usually last longer than telephone interviews, which are more abrupt without seeming rude. In face-to-face meetings there are more protocols and social niceties to observe.

Many people prefer them because you can see the journalist's body language and understand better their objectives and agenda. On the other hand, it is harder to make notes, receive prompts or use your cue cards.

The journalist will be noting all aspects of your body language, such as whether you have your arms folded, when you nod, shrug or hold your hand over your mouth (a sign that you are lying). Even if the interview is not being recorded for broadcast, and the journalist may not even be in the same room, be careful to give the right body-language indicators and avoid bad habits.

Taking control

The journalist will try to take full control of the situation, but it is important that you are not pushed into a defensive position. There should be an equal balance of pushing and reaction. Interviewees are often defensive and react to everything the journalists say without asserting themselves. The aim is to be in control of your responses, not to allow yourself to be flustered or bullied, to answer the questions and still get your message across.

To be assertive you have to ask questions and feel confident enough not always to answer all the journalist's questions exactly and fully if it is not in your best interests. You have the right to refuse to answer, although to do so is to turn down an opportunity to get your message across, and you risk irritating the journalist. You should attempt to answer the questions and then flesh out your answer by introducing your messages. Use the journalist's questions as a lever to lead into the message that you want to get across.

When you first start talking to the journalist, it is all right to ask certain things, such as the following:

- What is the interview about? (You may not be the right person to comment on its subject.)

- Why does the journalist want to talk to you?

- What sort of publication (and therefore reader) is the interview for? (This helps you deliver the right level of technical or business content, and helps the journalist too because they don't then have to steer you to the right level.)

- Is it news or a feature? (Then you know whether the journalist is more likely to want a snappy comment or a more leisurely backgrounder or analysis.)

- What is the deadline? (Then you know whether you have to respond immediately or if you can get back later in the day, or later in the week, with more information.)

- What is the angle? (It is all right to ask the journalist what sort of angle they have in mind, or what they think the hook or peg will be. This too will help you deliver the right sort of information – either strongly agreeing or disagreeing with the journalist's premise.)

- Who else has the journalist questioned? (It is acceptable to enquire who else the journalist has spoken to, or intends to speak to. That will also give you a better feel for the angle and what you might say that will be controversial and quotable.)

- Where did the journalist get the story from? (This helps you determine whether the journalist is friendly.)

If your interview is arranged in advance, make sure that you have been through the process of checking who the journalist is and what the angle is, and run your messages through your mind. Remember too that it's all right to ask the journalist other questions, such as whether they know what your competitors are doing. The journalist probably has a finger on the pulse of your industry, and they usually like to gossip. Sometimes it is possible to trade or swap information – but don't push your luck!

If a journalist calls unexpectedly

You are sitting at your desk, working on something. The phone rings and it is a journalist you don't know. *Don't panic.* You need to take control of the situation by finding out a few basics, and then you can 'buy' yourself time to think. You don't have to answer the journalist's questions immediately.

First, using an Interview Check Sheet, make a note of the journalist's name, title and phone number.

You can also ask:

- which publication they are working for (from this you will know

– whether it is daily, weekly or monthly and
– what sort of audience it is targeted at
and you will realise the level at which to pitch your answer, and what kind of information they are likely to be looking for)

- what their deadline is (so you know whether you have to give them the information immediately or can get back to them in a few hours or next day).

Do not ask the journalist to fax the questions over. Why? Because the journalist probably does not know exactly what the questions will be. They will have some idea in mind, but interviews are not usually highly structured. Like conversations, they change track and double back, go down cul-de-sacs and take unexpected turns according to the interviewee's responses and the journalist's thoughts.

Ask these questions and add these notes to your Interview Check Sheet:

- What is the angle? – if you know this you can deliver the right response
- Who is the audience? – if you know this you can pitch your responses to the right level
- What's the worst question? – if you know this you can have your response prepared
- What's the first question? – if you know this you can think through your first answer.

Once you have this information, you will be better able to answer the journalist's questions.

If you still feel lacking in confidence or nervous, it is all right to 'buy' yourself a few minutes time by saying 'I just need to check a few facts with my colleague', or 'I'm just about to go into a meeting, can I call you back in 10 minutes?' Take the time to think through what you want to say, and then return the journalist's call. You risk the phone being busy when you try to call back, but you will feel more in control.

If a journalist calls and is unsure about your involvement with the product, declare your interest at the outset. Do not attempt to mislead the journalist into thinking that you are an independent analyst, a pundit or a customer if in fact you are attempting to market and promote the product for your own advantage. Your position is perfectly respectable and – provided you give the journalist clear and honest information – extremely valuable.

Listen to the journalist and deliver your message

You need to determine the journalist's 'view' or 'position', as, practically every time, the journalist will have one from which they are working. It is usually a negative assumption. You have to discover what this is – don't work in the dark. You can ask what the angle is, although they may not tell you, and you can often tell from the line of questioning or the name of the publication where the journalist is 'coming from'.

You cannot avoid the journalist's questions. You must not try to talk 'over' the journalist, or blindly push your message irrespective of the journalist's actual questions. You have to give the journalist an acceptable answer to their questions, and then move the conversation on so that you can state your message. If you persistently avoid the questions and push your own response, the journalist will probably think that you are trying to mislead her or him.

If you are too pushy in your message the journalist may also think you are:

- biased
- trying to spread propaganda
- trying to exaggerate the features or abilities of your product
- spreading misinformation which benefits you
- confused
- not as knowledgeable as you are pretending to be
- afraid to speak the truth for some reason
- deliberately hiding important facts or information
- trying to be more outgoing than you would normally be, to curry favour.

Dealing with questions

Answering the questions

- The journalist wants you to listen carefully to what is asked and give an answer to that question. Don't just launch into a prepared answer which totally ignores what the journalist has said. A crucial part of being a good interviewee is to be a good listener. Once you have absorbed what the journalist is asking, and as you are answering it, think how you can skew the answer towards the message that you want to convey.

- Try to establish a rapport with the journalist and don't bother with trivial greetings. Get straight to the point. You should have your messages prepared, written out and rehearsed, but avoid copious notes because they are confusing.

- It helps if you can memorise your messages and just have brief prompts if necessary, but don't allow yourself to become stilted or sound as if you are reading the messages from a script. Rehearse your material but don't learn it absolutely by heart – allow some room for spontaneity. Try not to let your material come between you and the reader, listener or viewer.

- Keep sentences short and simple, and learn the facts, not the padding. You should know your key points and practise saying them. You want to be as concise, succinct and as clear as you can. Try not to use three words when one or two will do. There is no need to be afraid of using emotional language, and if you can, illustrate your words with good visual descriptions. Avoid flowery, waffly styles of speech and avoid jargon – use plain English.

- Be opinionated and be a tub-thumper with strong views. It helps if you can make it personal by putting in anecdotes, but keep them simple and short. You might also try to use metaphors and analogies to illustrate your points.

- It's best to assume the reader, viewer or listener has no knowledge and keep it simple – but do not patronise. Avoid being predictable and don't worry about making the journalist worried about what you might do or say. Try not to actually do anything which will embarrass or backfire on you, but it is good to be memorable. If you feel passionately about a subject, let it show.

- Explain the thought processes which lead to your views – don't just give conclusions. You are more likely to persuade the journalist if you explain everything clearly.

- It is important not to lie or deliberately mislead. You needn't tell the whole truth, but do not say anything which gives the journalist a wrong impression – he or she will never forgive you or trust you again if you deliberately give false information. If the journalist asks you something that you don't want to answer, try to lead the conversation on to another topic.

- Round figures up or down to whole numbers – these are more dramatic and more easily remembered. Avoid fractions and decimals.

- Mention the name of the company and product as often as you can – don't just refer to the product as 'it' or to the company as 'us' or 'we'. You'd be surprised at the number of people, particularly those who work for large companies, who can go through an entire interview without mentioning the name of the company or the name of the product once!

- The journalist is probably making notes so try not to speak too fast and repeat key words or phrases. It helps if you can reinforce your points and repeat the key messages. If you have a good sound-bite, say it several times.

- Ultimately, you can always stop the interview. You don't have to go on if you are feeling uncomfortable or you don't trust the journalist.

- Conclude with a summary of your main points.

- Think positive thoughts – you are less likely to freeze or say negative things. You are more likely to perform better if you are enjoying yourself. Practise, plan and enjoy.

- Most are fairly polite but some journalists can be insulting or rude, sometimes deliberately and sometimes inadvertently – if you are offended you should tell the journalist so, politely and calmly, and try to steer the conversation to safer ground. *Whatever you do, don't lose your temper*.

- There are also inevitable human personality clashes: you may simply not like the journalist or they may not like you. There isn't much you can do if there is mutual dislike, except to try to be as polite as possible.

- If you feel you are not getting anywhere or you think the journalist has switched off – don't persevere. You can't win them all.

Open and closed questions

A good journalist will ask open questions which trigger a good response in you. They don't want monosyllabic 'Yes' or 'No' answers, so they will not ask closed questions to which those are the only responses possible. They are likely to ask a lot of open questions which begin 'How?' or 'Why?' because these give you the chance to give an opinion or to be controversial, and to give a full and fleshed-out reply.

The journalist will not want you to ramble, so try to answer the question in a fairly short way, then expand on your answer, integrating your message if you can, and finally sum up with another direct answer to the question.

The journalist will avoid asking questions which can be misinterpreted and will try to be as clear as possible. There are unlikely to be questions which you find difficult to answer, perhaps because you do not have the information available or because it puts you out of your depth.

Another common comment from the interviewer – said with the aim of getting you to expound – is, 'Why do you say that?' This can also be a good opener for you to put across your message or views. They may also ask you to 'Give an example' or say, 'Tell me what happened after that', or 'Tell me how you feel about that.' These are all good open-ended questions for you because they open up the opportunity for you to convey your message.

Interview tricks

Journalists can be sneaky and manipulative. They know various techniques they have either been trained to use or developed themselves over the years.

These are the common ones:

- simple questions
- complex questions
- over-friendliness
- switching from friendly to hostile
- bullying and hassling
- misleading
- making assumptions
- appearing to end the interview
- using third parties
- putting words into your mouth
- silence
- claiming pressure from deadlines
- slipping in a surprise last question

Simple questions

The journalist might ask you a question which you feel is incredibly simple, or even rather stupid. Don't be surprised or hint that the journalist really should know the answer.

What's going on? First, the journalist is representing the listeners, viewers or readers and may feel that some do not understand your product, and by asking a simple question she or he gives you a chance to explain it. It may be that you are talking to an educated audience while the journalist knows that the audience may not understand or may be 'the man in the saloon bar'. Anyone involved with a project, product or company risks being too detached from public understanding because they are so immersed in their subject. It is easy for such a person to forget that not everyone knows so much, or is so interested, in that subject. So the reason for asking a simple question may be to bring your answers down to a basic level so that 'the man in the saloon bar' understands.

Or, second, the journalist may be asking a simple question in the hope of tricking an unprepared response out of you.

Either way, you should answer as politely, simply and fully as you can. Do not patronise. Deal with simple questions by imagining that you are explaining things to your granny, or someone else completely new to the subject. Remember that you are talking through the interviewer to a wider audience. If you are prepared and being honest, you will find it easier to deal with the questions, and you will come across in a positive way.

Sometimes, of course, the journalist asks a simple question because they want a simple answer, and that's what you should aim to deliver.

Complex questions

The journalist may ask you several questions in rapid succession, or combine several questions into one. This is another technique to throw you off balance. It sometimes confuses people and prevents them thinking too much about their answers.

Stop the journalist and go back over the question, calmly taking each point one at a time. Tear the question apart and take each element individually. Do not allow yourself to be hustled. You can control the pace.

Over-friendliness

A good way to get people to relax is to make them think that you are their friend and on their side. So journalists will appear to be very sympathetic, making comments like 'How awful' or 'That must have been awful for you.'

The interviewer may express outrageous sympathetic surprise, and is perhaps indignant on your behalf. They may say, 'That's terrible, you poor thing', and again you can be led to believe that the interviewer is a friend.

By appearing very sympathetic and friendly, the journalist makes you feel that you have the ear of someone prepared to listen to your woes and complaints, and you may find yourself talking about things which you had not meant to discuss. If the interviewer starts sounding less like an interviewer and more like a sympathetic friend, beware! They are just trying to lull you into a false sense of security. Ultimately, the journalist is there to get a good story, and will use the super-friendly approach to get you to talk unguardedly.

Some interviewers will barter information, appearing to share knowledge or an intimacy. This makes people feel that they have to give back some information in return, and encourages people to volunteer news, fact or gossip.

Switching between friendly and hostile

A more sophisticated technique is to vary the emotional temperature by moving from sympathy to aggression, hostility to receptiveness. This can be disconcerting, but emphasises the fact that the journalist is not a friend but has an agenda and is doing a job which is not necessarily in accord with yours. A sympathetic approach at the beginning can make an interviewee relax, but an aggressive approach later on can produce the best responses for the journalist's purposes. Then a switch back to friendly can end the interview on a good note, and make the interviewee willing to be questioned another time.

Bullying/hassling

There are several ways in which a journalist can bully the interviewee. One is to put several questions together to make a complex and aggressive question. Another is to say that there is a tight deadline and a response is required *now*.

Be calm and stick to your message. Deconstruct a complex question and resist the temptation to make any comment to be included before the deadline. You can counter this approach by taking your own notes or recording.

Misleading

The interviewer may make a deliberate mistake which you feel you have to correct, thereby inadvertently giving the information you were perhaps trying to hide. They may set you up to make a response. For example, the journalist may say, 'I hear that you earn £50,000 per year', and you might be tempted to respond quickly with 'No, it's only £35,000', when in fact you had no intention of discussing income. A better response would have been, 'No, that is far more than I earn, but I am not prepared to discuss the exact figure.' That should also stop the journalist from making more guesses. Correct the mistake, but do not volunteer information. Use positive words, and do not repeat the misleading words.

Making assumptions

Another technique for winkling out more information than you may be prepared to give is by making assumptions. The interviewer makes a statement which assumes that something has happened, or is going to happen. Sometimes they are just guessing, sometimes there is a grain of truth in what they say. Sometimes an interviewer will state something which is assumed or guessed as a way of testing out their theories.

You don't have to accept the interviewer's inaccurate appraisal of a situation. You should correct the interviewer and put them right in your answer.

An assumption should not be allowed to stand unchallenged. It must be dealt with immediately and firmly and you must not allow it to continue. There is no need to be rude or to argue with the interviewer, but you must put the record straight. If you can fall back on facts and statistics, or refer to an independent third party or a report or survey, so much the better.

Unless you correct the assumption, if you just allow it to stand, the journalist can validly take it to be the truth. You may even be quoted as agreeing with the statement – this is known as 'passive endorsement'. Sometimes the assumption may be something you are also expecting to happen, but you still need to make it clear that it is just an assumption and is not fact.

Appearing to end the interview

Pretending the interview is over is another trick journalists use. They may close the notepad or start to chat about something inconsequential. The interviewee invariably relaxes, and often that is when the best material comes out.

Interviews are not over until the telephone is put down, or you or the journalist is down the street. All the time you are speaking to a journalist you are potentially on the record. So be careful – the interview isn't over till it's over.

Using third parties

Some interviewers will try to distance themselves from a question by saying something like 'Some critics may say . . .' or 'Your competitors may claim that . . .' or 'Opponents might argue that . . .'.

This is a technique to de-personalise the question, and to distance the interviewer from a hostile or difficult question. Attributing a statement to a non-specific expert or competitor is a way of testing contradictory opinions and a device to get you to state your position clearly.

Sometimes the third party may be real, but the technique can also be used as a straightforward trick. The journalist may say, 'Professor John Smith of the University of London says that your product . . .' or 'I was talking to one of your customers the other day, and he was saying that your product doesn't work as well as you say it should.' The journalist may not have spoken to a customer at all. You can then say, 'Well, perhaps you would tell me who that customer is, because I'd like to make sure they are happy.' The chances are that the journalist will duck and dive, being unable to give you the name. They may say they want to 'protect their sources'. Respond then by dealing with the complaint, saying, 'Well, I haven't spoken to this customer or to any others who have said that, and all I can do is repeat that in our tests, our product . . .'

Deal with these questions as though the journalist had asked them on their own behalf or, if you actually know the third party who is being quoted, address your response to them. It can be a way to display your wide understanding and knowledge of a topic. You can say, 'Yes, Professor Smith's work is highly regarded and I have read his thesis with interest, but in my view . . .'

Putting words into your mouth

You may find the interviewer tries to put words into your mouth, perhaps by saying, 'Are you saying that . . . ?', 'Would you agree that . . . ?' or 'Would you say that . . . ?', and then making a statement which is an assumption of your view.

Unless you disagree, the journalist will assume that you concur and are passively approving of the statement, and may go on to say so in print or broadcast. As with a misleading statement, unless you are happy with the words, deal with the issue immediately and say, 'No, I would not say that.' Do not allow an inaccurate statement to stand uncorrected.

Silence

Unless the journalist is doing a live interview for broadcast, it is quite common for them to use the silence technique. This is the old sales-person's trick in which he or she will just keep quiet and, knowing that people cannot bear a silence, will wait until the other person makes a response.

So, for example, the journalist may say, 'I hear that 100 people are going to be made redundant at the factory which makes your product', and you should immediately respond with 'No, that's not true at all, I don't know where you heard that.' A clever journalist may then keep quiet until you jump into the silence gap and say, 'Well, maybe ten or twenty people are going to be laid off, but that is nothing to do with the sales figures of my product' – and the journalist has got the information they wanted. The journalist was simply using a combination of 'kite-flying', or saying something outrageous, with the silence technique.

Pressure from deadlines

The journalist may try to encourage you to make a hasty response by saying they have a deadline. She or he is more likely to get a juicier reaction and a 'better' quote if you reply off the cuff, but you do not have to be hurried. There may or may not be a deadline – you can't afford to take the risk. Say you will call back in five minutes and use the time to call your PR agency and/or gather your thoughts. Then call back. Few journalists work to a five-minute deadline, and if that is what they have, and you miss the opportunity, it is probably better to do so. A remark made in haste is most likely to be regretted.

Sneaking in a surprise last question

Just when you thought the interview was over, the journalist might ask you something completely unexpected and apparently unconnected with the main thrust of the interview. It may also appear innocuous, so be careful. Many people have been caught out replying in an off-hand way to a question which appeared to be an afterthought.

If you feel unsure, say so. Say, 'I'd need to check on that and get back to you.' Don't think that it is not part of the main interview and will not be used simply because the subject-matter is quite different.

Putting yourself across

Journalists meet a lot of people, and you need to focus your mind and work on your charm and personality so that you and your product or service are remembered.

Your product or service is important – that's why you are being interviewed – but it is more likely to be you and your personality that the journalist, and the journalist's viewers, listeners and readers, recall. Remember: people buy from people.

- Look the part – whatever the dress code, make sure you conform.

- Maintain eye contact. Be lively in your conversation.

- Try not to get flustered. Stay calm. Think of your messages.

- Be brief. Be positive.

- Work at radiating a pleasant, interesting and interested personality.

- Think 'communication', and project yourself.

- Concentrate on the interviewer. Be convinced and you will be convincing.

- But don't overdo it – you will appear false and pompous. Trying too hard can make you look very insincere.

- Be pleasant and responsive – remember you are really talking to the viewer, listener or reader, not the interviewer.

- Get your main points across by saying, 'The most important issue here is . . .' or 'The main point to remember is . . .'.

Dealing with questions you don't want to answer

If you are promoting a product you can be fairly sure that the main purpose of the interview will be to elicit information. The interviewer will probably focus entirely on areas you want to talk about, but it may be that he or she is also interested in a topic or angle you would rather not discuss.

If you can possibly discuss the matter, try to do so, because to avoid answering looks suspicious. Give an answer which is as full as possible. Journalists are more sympathetic to people who come clean with them. But if you definitely cannot discuss the matter, perhaps because it is outside your area of responsibility or it is *sub judice*, be equally frank about the reasons for your reticence.

It may be that:

- you do not know the answer
- you know the answer but don't want to give it
- you know the answer, would like to give it, but are prevented from doing so.

The journalist will understand if you cannot answer because it is beyond your remit, or if there are difficult negotiations under way, or it is in some other way sensitive. They will accept a straightforward explanation, especially if it comes with a promise to talk about the matter at a later stage when it is less sensitive. But the journalist is still required to ask the questions, and to push you as far as they can, on behalf of their readers, listeners or viewers. Respond with charm and courtesy, and the journalist will not persist.

This may be the time to go off the record but this is a risky strategy unless you know the journalist well. You should start from the belief that anything you say may be used regardless of your request to go off the record. Think what you want to see in print and say it, even if it consists of 'X was unable to comment.' The worst thing you can say if you want to avoid a question is an unqualified 'No comment'. It is invariably taken to be a concealment, and the journalist is likely to come back immediately with 'Why don't you want to comment?' and will not just leave it alone.

One way to handle the situation is with a frank 'I'd like to answer that question but unfortunately I can't because . . .'. This can work if there is a valid (if not entirely truthful!) reason why you can't answer, such as it is beyond your remit, or you need to check with the company secretary or your boss. Obviously this can't work if you *are* the boss, or if it is your job to know the answer.

If you are asked a question to which you do not know the answer or one you are not allowed to answer, be frank and say, 'I'm sorry, it's not policy for someone in my position to answer that question, but I can get someone who can to contact you after the programme' or 'I'm sorry, I don't know the answer to that, but I will find out and let you know later.' It is better to be honest about any limits to your knowledge than try to bluff or make it up.

Another response is to deflect rather than hide. Anyone who has heard politicians on Radio 4 in the mornings will be familiar with the technique of simply not answering the question being posed, but giving an unrelated answer. You can say, 'That is a very good question, but that is not the real issue. The real issue is . . .'. You should not overdo this technique because it becomes irritating for the listener or viewer, and can alienate them.

A skilled journalist will simply repeat the question, and keep repeating it, until you are forced to give a direct answer. If the full answer is embarrassing for some reason, just give as little information as you can get away with, but make sure it is honest. Then try to move the conversation on to something else. Do not be tempted to lie.

A stalling technique is to repeat the question, giving yourself time to think. Or you could say, 'Let's put this into perspective . . .' and then proceed to explain the situation from your point of view.

If you do not want to answer a question it is better to stall or avoid than to refuse to answer. Such refusal is as bad as a 'No comment' response. It tells the journalist that they are near to something very sensitive and they are therefore likely to keep at it like a dog at a bone until they get something juicy. The only way that you could say 'No comment' is by qualifying it with something like: 'I can't comment on that until I've had a chance to . . .' or 'I'm not the best person to speak to about that, you should talk to . . .' or 'I'd like to answer that once I've had a chance to check with my colleagues . . .'.

If you find yourself saying something that you don't want to say, or being led down a path where you don't want to go, stop and say, 'Hold on, let me put that another way . . .' or 'Hold on, let's start that again . . .' and take it from the top. Whatever you do, don't lie or embellish your answers. It is more embarrassing to be found out after you have exaggerated than to admit straight out that there is something you don't know.

Another technique is to throw a question back at the interviewer. It takes an aggressive and controlled interviewee to manage to throw the journalist off balance in this way, but it can be done. You do not want to antagonise or irritate the journalist, however. You have more to lose than they do.

Remember that you know more about your subject than the interviewer does, and even if the journalist appears to be well informed, you are the expert. That is why they are talking to you. But if you appear to be dodging the question by deliberately concealing or avoiding, the audience's sympathy will switch to the interviewer. If you are being as honest and frank as you can be, within the restrictions imposed on you, the audience will be on your side.

Commenting on the competition

You may find that a journalist is more interested in your views on your competitors than in you or your product. They may ring you up because they are writing a story about one of your competitors, and they are looking for comment. They may ask what you think about your competitors' activities, their new products or the way they are running their business, because one of the ways that a journalist finds a story is through negative comment.

This is one time when it is not good to be too strongly opinionated or have an outspoken point of view. You can be fairly sure that they are most interested in negative comment. Be cautious.

It is generally regarded as bad form to comment too critically about your competitors. It is a cheap way to get press coverage, and in the long term does you no favours. It does not make you look good. Unless your criticism is balanced and fair, it is better to move the reply on to talk about *your* product or company. It is a better tactic to positively promote your own position than to attack an opponent's.

So, to the questions 'What do you think about Company A's new product which they say is going to dominate the market in six months?' or 'What do you think about Company A's strategy to use cheap labour in the Far East?', you can respond with 'Well, I think it is a very interesting development, but more interesting is what we at Company B are doing with our new product' and then continue to talk about your product/company. In other words, side-step the question. Try to avoid being drawn, unless you have a balanced comment to make, such as 'Well, Far Eastern manufacturing does have some interesting benefits, but I think we at Company B would find that such a strategy would conflict with our policy on human rights.' In that way you have made a comment on the question, but you have also introduced your message. On the other hand the journalist may ignore your statement, recognising it to be a corporate marketing message.

If a journalist comes to you claiming that a competitor is saying this or that about you, you can ask for more details about what they are saying and you should deal with it point by point. You have no right to see the journalist's notes or to ask for transcripts, but courtesy and the journalist's Code of Practice might make the journalist oblige. Don't respond by making wild allegations about the competition. Think positively about your position and assert your views over those of your competitors. Prepare by anticipating your competitors' views and opinions, and have responses ready. Have a short, positive statement which reinforces your message.

Dealing with hostile questioning

If you are talking to a journalist because you have a product you are trying to promote, you are extremely unlikely to encounter any aggressive or hostile interviewing. They are reserved for political interviews or for crisis situations. You are far more likely to be talking to a journalist who is mainly hoping that you will keep giving them lots of interesting and opinionated material, and will not be too nervous or quiet.

But you should expect the journalist to criticise what you say. You cannot expect them to allow your statements or claims to stand un-challenged. That is their job. Journalists are also encouraged to prompt, challenge or say nothing as techniques for encouraging the interviewee to say more than they want. Interviewers are also allowed to be tough-minded, sharp, sceptical and should also be informed, not partisan. You can anticipate the journalists' critical questions, but if you think that you are going to encounter particularly difficult ques-tions, take some specialist training in interview-control techniques.

Some journalists deliberately use rude and abrasive techniques to put their subject off balance, or it may be that the journalist knows something unpleasant which they are determined to make as much of as possible. The worst thing is to respond to rudeness or aggressive interviewing with aggression. It does not make the journalist any more polite, and will probably make them worse. In broadcast inter-views the audience will usually be on the side of the interviewee not the interviewer and there is no need to point out that the interviewer is being rude. The audience will know that and be more sympathetic towards you.

All your responses should put the positive aspects first, so that anything negative which is revealed later comes in context and perspective. Don't restate an opposing view in your answer and don't be defensive. If it is appropriate, don't be afraid to name drop and mention well-known users, customers or supporters. It helps rein-force the image of your product.

If the interviewer makes a mistake or a wrong assumption, correct it immediately. You will not be thought a 'smart-alec' but will gain respect for getting things clear, and it will help you feel in control of the situation.

Try not to allow yourself to be stunned into silence. If the inter-viewer says something outrageous and surprising, say so, then return to your messages.

It is unhelpful to say, 'You are not a very good journalist to ask a question like that', or, 'That's unbelievably rude and unjustified.' The journalist is likely to feel pleasure at your response, not embarrass-ment or regret.

If the interviewer tries to cut you off in mid-response, but you really want to finish, then you should try to do so. Say, 'Please let me finish', and then complete your sentence. Don't just say 'Yes' or 'No' – flesh out your answers but don't ramble. When you are finished, stop.

If the question is clearly far away from the subject, and irrelevant if provocative, say, 'That's not what we are discussing here. What we are talking about is . . .' or 'That's not relevant. What is important is . . .'.

Avoid saying, 'Before I answer that, let me tell you . . .', which is irritating to the listeners and viewers. Try to answer the journalist's question, or acknowledge it and give some response, before you attempt to move the conversation on to your agenda.

Don't stonewall, don't refuse outright to answer a question, don't allow the interviewer's hostility to provoke you. Stay calm, give some answer to the journalist's questions and then try to move on to your messages.

Don't argue with the interviewer, or contradict them. You can disagree if they make an incorrect point. Say, 'No, that's not true, the truth is . . .' but do not start arguing.

If you are asked a direct question that you want to avoid, do not just switch direct to your message. Say 'Yes' or 'No' in response to the question, otherwise you will get a reputation for avoidance. Say, 'Yes, but please remember that . . .' or 'No, but that's not the whole picture. You also have to consider . . .'.

If the journalist says, 'Surely, the truth is that . . .' make sure that you firmly put the truth as you see it. Don't allow the journalist to make a statement about the truth without you putting your version of the truth.

Sometimes a journalist might agree not to ask you about a topic, and then, on air, ask you about it. You can make it clear to the audience that the interviewer has broken the agreement by saying something like, 'We agreed not to discuss that, but since you have raised it . . .' and then give some response. Again, don't stonewall or refuse, but you can gain some audience sympathy by being polite.

On and off the record

On and off the record is a thorny issue. The simple answer to the question, 'When can something be off the record?' is: Never.

To be really safe, you should never say anything to a journalist that you do not want to see in print or hear broadcast. However, as you get to know a journalist and the relationship develops it is sometimes in the interests of both of you that things can be said which are not printed or broadcast. The keywords are relationships and trust.

Even if you do trust the journalist, the best maxim is still to say as little off the record as you can. The journalist does not want to hear things which cannot be used. It can be frustrating for the journalist to be told a lot of information off the record, and the more they are told the more tempting it is to use at least some of it.

There may be times when you want the journalist to know something but which you don't want attributed to you. You may have heard something about a competitor that you want the journalist to know, but it would be bad form to have you attributed as the source. Or you may have a new version of your product in the pipeline, and you think the journalist should know that so they are ready to review it when it is available, but you do not want it publicised because you have a stockroom full of the current version and it would ruin sales for the rest of the quarter.

If you want to go off the record mention it to the journalist before you say it, not after you have made the comment. Going off the record is an agreement between the two of you and it is a matter of trust. This agreement needs to be established before the words are spoken. It is no good telling a journalist something and then saying, 'That was off the record, alright?' because the journalist is not under any obligation to comply. Say, 'Can this be off the record?' and wait for them to say 'Yes' before continuing. They may want to clarify the situation, and say, 'Does that mean that you don't want me to use it at all, or just not attribute it to you?' You may ask them to hold on to the information until a later date, or they may use the information but not name you as the source, or the journalist may use the information as background facts but not refer to it directly.

Journalists know that off the record information can be incredibly useful. It means they can start working on a story before it becomes official, and they can possibly get a better piece than their rivals. Most journalists respect the relationship with trusted contacts and will not abuse their trust by printing something which has been given to them off the record. However, there are some journalists who put career before all else, and will do anything to get a scoop or better angle on a story, and will stop at nothing to get what they want. They will agree to something being off the record and then print it anyway. As you get to know a journalist better, you may feel confident enough to go off the record. Journalists know that they sometimes need off the record information and will generally respect their contacts. You can never, however, rely on it.

Do not attempt to go off the record in a studio or any place where there is recording equipment around. If the journalist agrees to go off the record, nothing you say should be written down or recorded and you should expect the journalist not to use it directly, although there is no right or law which can reinforce that. It is a personal agreement between the two of you, and you have no legal right to sue if the journalist subsequently prints or broadcasts what you have said. Most journalists will go to extraordinary lengths to protect a source who has put themselves on the line to pass on some information, while others just treat off the record information as a chance to get a scoop.

What not to say

There are a few cardinal rules which can take years to learn – but this book tells them to you in a few pages.

If you avoid saying the following things you will look more professional and experienced – if you say them the journalist will be annoyed or think you are crass.

- Never thank the journalist for a piece which has appeared or been broadcast. It makes the journalist think that it was not critical enough and they were too soft on you. The journalist is not there primarily to promote you or your product, but to satisfy their reader, listener or viewer. You can, however, compliment them generally on the professionalism of the piece.

- Never say 'No comment' because it looks so bad. It implies that you have something to hide and is a tacit acceptance of what the journalist is saying. Better to adopt some avoidance tactics than say it. If you do say 'No comment' the journalist is unlikely to leave the matter alone. They can say, 'Why will you not comment?' and keep on until they get some reply.

- Do not ask when the piece is going to appear, or if you do ask, do not be surprised if the journalist says they don't know. The journalist will know the deadline, but is unlikely to know definitely when it will be broadcast or printed.

- Do not ask to see the copy or hear the tape before it is used. If you are talking to a journalist you have to trust their professionalism to get it right. Asking to see copy or hear a tape indicates that you don't trust them. It also appears as though you think you have the power to change anything, which is *not* the case. Once you've spoken to a journalist, you have to trust them. They cannot be made to change anything that you don't like.

- Don't ask to be sent a cutting. If you know which publication it is for, make sure that you read it or use a cuttings agency. The journalists are too busy to send cuttings or issues to people they quote.

- Don't ask for your photograph or sample to be returned. Apart from the inconvenience and cost which will alienate the journalist, you should charge such costs to your promotion and marketing budget.

- Don't give any information which you do not want to see published or broadcast, or quoted back at you later. Don't start rambling. Stop when you have finished your statement and wait for the next question.

- Don't waffle. Keep your answers to the point, and long enough to keep the conversation going. You should aim to answer the journalist's question and get across some point of your own, and then stop.

- Don't continually be evasive or repeatedly dodge the journalist's questions in order to substitute the answer you want to see in print. The journalist may think that you are trying to hide something – and it's irritating for the listeners.

- Don't fob off the interviewer's questions and move too quickly on to your message every time. It has a negative effect, and people will want you to shut up.

- Do not lose your temper.

Ending the interview

As the interview comes to a close – and this can happen very rapidly, almost without warning – make sure you have the journalist's name and phone number. Using your Interview Check Sheet, make sure:

- you have the journalist's details and phone number
- you know the deadline
- you know what follow-up action has to be done
- you have conveyed your message.

As the journalist finishes, it is all right to say, 'Before you go, I'd just like to make sure that you know about . . .' and then proceed to tell them something about your product or company.

Practise and enjoy, develop confidence and be entertaining, and the journalist is likely to want to use you again.

Lastly, remember that journalists can be your best source of competitive information. They like to gossip, and are probably talking to your competitors. They can be a useful source of information to you, so don't be afraid to ask them what they know, or their views of the future. They'll probably be talking about you to your competitors some day!

Chapter summary

- Devise and print out some Interview Check Sheets to have available when you do a telephone interview. Write your messages on the top.
- Have your cue cards handy, with your snappy company and product messages.
- Mention your company name and product brand name as often as possible.
- Take control of the interview situation, and do not allow the journalist to lead the questioning.
- Give answers as passionately and colourfully as you can.
- Stop when you have finished your answer and wait for the next question.
- Correct any wrong statements immediately.
- Do not lie.
- Nothing is ever off the record (unless you know the journalist well, and even then . . .).
- Enjoy yourself – working with the media is fun.

CASE STUDIES

Case study 1: Product promotion to the lifestyle press

Cheered up by his success with Jane Marples, Paul tries to interest other journalists in talking to Karen. He updates the press releases, and has a version for all the angles on all the issues that Karen wants to comment on, plus some fresh releases on the KoolWay range. The company has made a couple of large sales – one abroad – and he believes that these are newsworthy stories.

He divides the list of journalists into groups according to their areas of interest and specialisation, and starts telephoning. He is nervous to start with, and quickly picks up that the journalists are not interested in talking about the weather. By the time he gets to the fifth call, he has got his routine sorted out: he calls, asks whether they have a few moments to talk to him about a story he wants to suggest, and then, if they say yes, he tells them briefly that his managing director, Karen Jamison, has some strong views, and gives a feel of those views.

Several journalists express interest but say that it doesn't fit in with anything they are doing at the moment. But a local radio station says that it is planning a feature on EMU, while a catering publication is planning a feature on staff shortages. Another says that it is doing a series on health and safety issues, and invites Paul to send along details of the KoolWay range. This he does, and sends some samples of the products too.

As soon as he comes off the phone he sends each journalist the relevant press release by fax, and sets up some telephone interviews. He tells them that Karen will call at a certain time, and tries to make sure that she does. Sometimes the journalists' lines are busy, but Paul just perseveres until Karen gets through. One of the journalists does not appear to have any questions prepared, and just waits for Karen to speak. She finds this disconcerting, but asks him a few questions about what he is working on and other viewpoints that he has come across, and eventually she is able to add to those comments and give her own as well.

Paul also decides to start planning another press event, but smaller than the press conference. Karen is extremely reluctant, saying, 'We've had some good success with the telephone interviews, why don't we continue with those?' Paul agrees that they have been successful, but says that he feels they need to meet some of the journalists face to face and build on the relationships.

He decides on a press lunch, and sits down to think through the angles and stories which will attract the journalists and make sure they will attend.

- **Comment**: Paul is getting the idea now. His approach is more structured and he understands better what the journalists want.

Case study 2: Product promotion to the computer press

The SoftMicro breakfast seminar is booked to be held at a Central London hotel near to several of the key publishing houses, so that the journalists will not have to travel far. It is a popular location, where the food and hospitality are relaxed but of good quality. Richard doesn't want somewhere too formal or expensive, which he thinks will give the wrong impression of the company. 'We are not a big firm and they won't want to see us spending money extravagantly.'

The breakfast is scheduled to be served as a running buffet between 8.30 and 10 a.m., for the duration of the seminar. The idea is that journalists can wander around during the presentations and discussions, helping themselves to food and drink.

Two weeks before the event, Sasha sends out 60 invitations to journalists who are fairly new to the job, and some to established freelances who might be interested in the debate. She follows up a few days before, and this time Joe trains her before she calls anyone, and then supervises her calls. He assumes that it was her inexperience which alienated the journalists and led them to promise to come and then not turn up. This time, she calls and gets straight to the point. She is businesslike and straightforward, reminding the journalists of the event and the topics to be covered. She gets 20 confirmations.

The room for the event is set up with a large round table, with Professor Higgins, two teachers who use KiddieLearn 2, and Richard and Jessica, seated at intervals around it. There is room for three or four journalists between each of them. A large AV screen linked to a portable computer displays KiddieLearn 2 so that everyone can see it.

Journalists start to arrive at 8.30, and for the first fifteen minutes spend time just standing around chatting with everyone. At 8.50, Joe calls the meeting together and invites everyone to take their seats.

There is an agenda, which starts with a statement from the Professor along the lines of 'Computer-based training (CBT) can be bad for students.' This radical position, apparently at odds with the one which he could be expected to take, proves very interesting for the journalists and a lively debate quickly develops, with Joe acting as chairperson.

The journalists ask questions about the use of CBT, and the teachers give their experiences of CBT in action. Most journalists make notes as the session continues. Some journalists come in late and sit down quietly, catching up with what's going on, while some others leave when they have to get going to their offices.

At several points the AV equipment is used, with Richard or one of the teachers showing how KiddieLearn 2 tailors itself to each individual child, and how it is virtually impossible for a child to cheat by skipping sections. There is much debate about the philosophy of using computers in place of teachers, and the Professor is forced to admit that his statement needs to be qualified – 'Computer-based training can be bad for children if it is not used in close collaboration with teachers and parents.'

Over the next few weeks there are several features which raise many of the issues discussed at the seminar. Obviously, the journalists have gone back to their offices and suggested to the feature editors that they run features on these topics. There is even one front-page news story which leads with the Professor's statements, and then quotes several other leading educational pundits.

By now, Richard is relaxed with the press and pleased with Jessica. Jessica feels that she has learned from Joe, but she is happy to leave the planning of one more event to him. By now she realises the value of professional PR, which is to act as a buffer between the company and the press. Also, Joe knows many of the journalists personally because he used to be one himself, and understands how to pitch things to them and not to waste their time.

The cuttings list for SoftMicro and KiddieLearn 2 is looking very healthy.

- **Comment**: Sasha has learned fast, and the seminar is a great success. By working to satisfy the journalists' agenda, SoftMicro is getting the editorial coverage it wants.

Case study 3: Diary of a freelance journalist

Some days you just can't get going. I've just had two phone calls from junior PR agency people wanting to know whether I'd got the press release, and another wanting to know if I needed a photograph. When will they get it? If I want something, I'll call. In none of the instances can I remember which press release they were talking about. It's very hard not to be rude when you are busy working on something with a deadline approaching and someone calls up with a stupid question like that.

I've also been trying to speak to a certain MD about a story about faulty products, and he appears to be avoiding me. Can't blame him really – there is a rumour that the company is about to be involved in a management sell-out to a large holding company, and this is probably the last thing he needs. The newspaper is going to run the story though, and I have managed to talk to several of his competitors. The longer he avoids me, the more it looks like there is truth behind the faulty products story. They are manufactured in Mexico, so he's probably waiting until after they get to work this afternoon, our time, before speaking about it. I'll give him until late afternoon, and then I'm going to have to file the story.

Later
The MD was waiting for his Mexican manager to get into the factory, and I was telephoned by both on a conference call at 5 p.m. Basically, they blamed faulty raw materials and admitted that their inventory quality-control system was not as good as it should have been. They also said that they were offering compensation to anyone with faulty products, as well as automatic replacement. I will, of course, be putting all that in the story. He was lucky, though, that the story had not been filed earlier in the day.

Next day
I've been looking forward to today for a few weeks – an overnight trip to Paris as the guest of a computer hardware firm. Apparently we leave London around lunchtime, and I have to leave home at breakfast time in order to make the rendezvous at Waterloo Station EuroStar Check-In. I hope I get some good stories out of the trip – it means a day and a half out of my working week. And I hope we have some fun too.

Two days later
The trip to Paris was a disaster! Despite having an excellent bunch of journalists, the organising company managed to screw up. The problem is basically that some PR companies who organise these trips, and/or the companies they work for, expect to have your full attention the whole time. The journalists know that there is no such thing as a free lunch, and we expect a seminar, press conference or something similar, and we know that we are expected to write about the story if we possibly can, but this was a classic disaster.

First, on the train, the PR person (I'll call him Robert) insisted on walking up and down the carriage telling us about the product and introducing the client personnel. He should have waited or introduced us more subtly. Luckily I was sitting next to an old friend I haven't seen for five years since we both went freelance, so I was able to ignore Robert and just have a good old chinwag.

Then, when we got to the hotel, we found that our rooms were the smallest and grottiest of a cheap dive by the side of a motorway. There was no minibar, and the facilities were decidedly third rate. We cheered up at the prospect of a dinner at a nice restaurant, but again everything was decidedly cheapskate and tacky. Still, when we got back to the hotel we sat up late in the bar and got stuck into the Cognac, and put everything on Robert's bill.

Next morning there was the expected formal presentation – but it was more than formal, it was stiff. There was no really strong story either. It lasted for two hours, we all had hangovers, and it was as boring as it can get. If only they had been a bit more sensible – spent a bit more on the accommodation and meal, and a bit less on the AV equipment. When will they learn that we don't have to be *sold* to? We know the deal. If we can possibly mention the product, if the product warrants it, and if it is relevant to our audience, we will.

We had a couple of hours 'free' after the press conference to do some shopping, but the hotel was so far from the shopping centres that we had to take taxis – at our own expense – and then we had to buy our own lunches. It's not that I want to seem ungrateful, but . . . what was the name of the company? Strange, I can't remember . . .

- **Comment**: Sometimes, journalists like Suzie give the press a bad name, but she only abuses those marketing and PR people who set themselves up for it. She has no respect for professionals who don't understand what she wants or why she goes to events. She went on the Paris trip expecting a good story and it was a waste of her time, and as a freelance that's costly as well as very annoying. Freelances gain a lot from just chatting to other freelances, and don't need to be 'sold to' the whole time. If only the organisers had thought through the event from the journalists' perspective, Suzie would probably remember their name and be writing about them.

CHAPTER SEVEN

Radio, TV and the Internet

Introduction

Broadcast media are more effective than print in terms of impact, and it is important to understand how they work. Research has shown that people who read magazines and newspapers can have trouble remembering the names of products and people, but are better at recalling them later if they hear them on radio or see the faces on television.

Any plan to promote your product to the media must include radio and TV. Media are a four-legged stool and print journalism is only one of those 'legs', especially these days with the upsurge of digital broadcasting. This so-called 'digital revolution' will have three outcomes which will affect anyone thinking about promoting a product in the media: first, it will allow more channels, and thereby more opportunities for editorial exposure; second, it will offer higher-quality pictures and sound; and third, it will eventually allow viewers and listeners to interact with the promotion itself.

Radio and TV journalists have always been more voracious than print journalists and need more material, which gets consumed more hungrily. They are continually looking for stories and for good spokespersons, and are possibly even more likely than print journalists to be interested in your product or your views.

Whether you are dealing with radio, TV or print journalists, you are dealing with people following essentially the same agenda. Just bear in mind what you have already learned about making your story newsworthy and developing your message.

One big difference between broadcast and print media is that generally broadcast journalists are keener than print journalists for you to give a good answer. There is more collaboration between the journalist and the interviewee and so there is often more conferring before the interview about the questions and answers. It is rarely their intention to reduce you to a gibbering wreck, because they need you to speak interestingly and intelligently. A silence on TV – and especially on radio – is a disaster for the journalist, so they will be keen to keep the conversation flowing all the time. At worst, this may lead the broadcast journalist to use bullying techniques, pushing for an answer to their question, but it also means that they will be more inclined to help you than a print journalist, who is quite happy to sit there in an uncomfortable silence which you eventually feel compelled to fill.

Internet journalism

There are all types of publications on the Internet and the number is growing. Web-sites also include product reviews and case studies. (You may consider creating your own web-site and promoting your product that way, for which there are special marketing techniques which are outside the remit of this book but which you should bear in mind.)

If you are being interviewed by a journalist for a feature or item for Internet publishing, the fundamental rules are the same: the journalist will have the same objectives of seeking to entertain, educate and inform; will not be seeking to overtly publicise your product for you; and will have the Internet user in mind.

The main difference between Internet publishing and print, radio or TV is that it can be an amalgamation of all three. It can include written words, with quotations, appraisals, reviews and recommendations, but it can also include audio and video. People accessing the pages will also be able to respond interactively.

The same guidelines for approaching print journalists apply to Internet journalists. If you are to be interviewed by an Internet journalist, establish first whether the publication is words only – in which case you treat it like a print interview – or whether there will be audio or video – in which case you use the principles given here for radio and TV interviews.

Before the TV or radio interview

As with print interviews, spend time getting your messages clear in your mind. Anticipate any predictable, difficult questions the journalist might ask and have your responses ready. You can take cue cards to the studio, although be very discreet about using them on television – it can look as though you don't know your stuff if you have to resort to prompt cards.

Before the interview you should also have a clear idea:

- what the interview is going to be about
- what angle the journalist will take

- who else will be involved and/or who else the journalist is talking to
- whether it will be live or pre-recorded for later broadcast
- what form the final broadcast will take (straight one-to-one interview, as part of a report, part of a documentary, etc.)
- how long the final interview will be
- how long the final programme will be
- who the interviewer is
- what the first question will be.

Unlike most print interviews, you can find out all these things beforehand. This knowledge allows you to have your messages and appropriate responses prepared in a polished, concise and snappy style.

Finding out in advance who else is appearing on the same pro-gramme gives you an indication of the line of questioning, the angle of the piece and how much opportunity you will have to put your points across. It also allows you to prepare with specific research on the others.

It is all right to discuss the interview with the journalist and ask, for example, 'What angle do you intend to take?' Unlike print inter-views, when you are more likely to be working in the dark, you can understand the background, motivation and approach of the inter-view. Also, if you know where the idea for the story came from and who initiated it, you can get a good indication of the journalist's probable agenda.

But, like print interviews, don't ask the journalist to give you a list of questions in advance. For one thing, they probably don't have a clear one prepared. The way that interviews work involves questions leading one from another, and the journalist probably doesn't know exactly what the questions will be. There is also no guarantee that the journalist will stick to the list. To ask to be told all the questions in advance makes you look inexperienced.

While you may not know the exact questions, you can find out the line of questioning, which is the general drift of the interview as it is expected to proceed. Of course, there is no rule that says the inter-view has to stick to the predicted line and there may be some surprise questions, or the others in the discussion may take the conversation in an unexpected direction. There is nothing you can do about that, except to be as prepared as possible by doing background research, anticipating difficult questions and preparing your responses.

Sometimes a broadcast journalist will even invite you to make suggestions before the interview so that the questions asked best enable you to deliver your answers. It is worth having a few model questions written out on a piece of paper to be given to the inter-viewer in case this happens, although do not be surprised if they remain unused.

Ask the journalist in advance whether any further material will be helpful, such as tape-recordings, stills photographs, maps, models, reports, statistics or other visuals, which could be used in the broad-cast. For a radio journalist, you should provide a written document in advance which sets out all the facts and statistics you have. One way to make sure that you get the questions you want is to prepare the journalist as well as possible, although obviously you will have no control over the questioning or the angle when the time comes.

In the studio

You can do several things to minimise the risk of being flustered for the interview and to maximise the likelihood of delivering a satisfac-tory performance.

You should make sure you arrive early, so that you have time to relax and feel familiar with the surroundings. Avoid any temptation to have an alcoholic drink before the interview. Some television stu-dios have a 'Green Room', mainly used by people when they have finished being interviewed, although sometimes also offered to those waiting for interview. There is often alcohol available in the Green Room – deny any temptation to have 'just the one to steady your nerves'. Even a very small amount of alcohol can have a dramatic effect on the way your voice sounds in a broadcast, and can slow your mental processes. Save the alcohol for afterwards.

Try to talk to the interviewer before the interview if that is poss-ible, although sometimes you will only talk to a researcher or an assistant. Some journalists prefer not to meet the interviewees be-forehand, to create a greater 'frisson'. During the interview, ignore the microphone, the dials, displays, sliders, knobs and camera, and just concentrate on the interviewer. The levels of stress and tension will rise just before going on air – ignore them.

It doesn't matter what you wear for radio but many find that it helps to be dressed for business if you are talking about business. Dress for the occasion but be comfortable. Your hand movements and facial expressions cannot be seen on radio but can, somehow, be felt by the listeners, so smile as much as possible and wave your hands around as much as you like. At the same time be careful not to describe something entirely with hand movements, saying 'this big' or 'this small', and be sure to explain everything verbally.

Be succinct and aim for sound-bites. Unless the programme is a specialist one, assume that the audience is wide and diverse and keep technical talk and jargon to a minimum.

Avoid 'ums' and 'ers' and do not tap the table or rustle paper. Remove any bleepers, mobile telephones or digital wrist-watches. Mention the name of your product and your company as often as possible.

Have your messages written out and placed in front of you if you are on radio. Aim to get them across, but do not entirely ignore the interviewer's questions. Nothing is more irritating for the listener than when people being interviewed completely ignore the question and just give a prepared response. Aim to answer the question *and* convey your message.

Whether there is a live audience, a panel or just you and the interviewer, pay attention solely to the interviewer. Do not worry about lighting or sound levels. Leave all that to the experts. You just talk in a normal voice and unless someone tells you to speak up or speak nearer the microphone, just talk normally and ignore the gadgets. Try to forget they are there – just focus on the interviewer and concentrate on your answers.

Before the interview starts, the technicians may ask you to do a sound check. You should just start speaking in your normal voice without leaning forward towards the mike or shouting. The usual tradition is to relate what you had for breakfast or how you got to the studio until they tell you to stop. So if you come into the studio and hear someone telling the technicians what they had for breakfast, you'll know that they're just doing a sound check!

Once the TV interview starts, either look at the interviewer or look steadily at the centre of the camera lens if you are in a remote studio and imagine that a person you know and love is on the other side, watching you. Talk to that person and do not think of the hundreds of people who might be watching – for all you know, everyone has switched off!

On television, sit slightly forward in the chair and be careful not to look sideways, to the floor or to the ceiling. All these eye movements make you look shifty and unreliable. Keep your gaze constant and do not glance away. Look straight at the interviewer, not at the camera, and keep still.

It is the interviewer's job to fill any gaps so you shouldn't worry about any silences. If you have an anecdote that you plan to tell on air, do not tell the journalist before the recording or broadcast. It will be much more spontaneous if the journalist has not heard it before.

Do not think that anything you say in the Green Room will not be broadcast. There are plenty of examples of politicians thinking that they were out of recording range and speaking too candidly. Behave as though you are on the record and being recorded the whole time. Always assume that the interview is still going on from the moment you enter the building until you are walking down the road after-wards. Nothing is ever off the record, and everything could poten-tially be on the air.

At the end, summarise your points. If the interview is to be edited, this helps ensure that your main messages are selected for any trailer.

The mobile broadcast journalist

It is common these days for a broadcast journalist to come to you rather than for you to go to a studio. Today's small, high-quality voice recorders are capable of broadcast quality and the cameras that TV journalists use are equally miniaturised and high quality. TV journalists still come as a team of at least two – there needs to be at least one to operate the camera as well as the journalist in front of it.

Mobile crews are far more likely to spring an interview on you, to shove a microphone in your face or a camera up close, and demand an answer to a question. This is known as 'doorstepping' and you don't have to give in to it. You could say, 'That's a very good ques-tion and I'd like to answer it when I've had a chance to consult with X', 'The final meeting is not until next week and it would be unfair for me to comment until then' or 'I have to discuss the matter with my colleagues before I can make a comment to the press, but please get back to me in a couple of days.' You are not, strictly speaking, being evasive because you are offering to give them another interview at a later stage, but you are avoiding the issue in the short term. Never say 'No comment' but give a positive reason why you can't talk at that time.

Remote TV studios

TV stations increasingly use remote studios – sometimes a car or van, if not an office. The interviews are conducted over the telephone and the camera is often operated by remote control. These set-ups can be disconcerting and pose some unique problems for the inexperienced interviewee but do not allow the situation to faze you. You will find the TV journalist and technicians extremely helpful.

If you are in a remote studio, you may not be able to see the interviewer, although sometimes there is a monitor. Misunderstandings can easily happen and it is difficult to catch every nuance of what is going on in the main studio. The best way to regard it is as a telephone interview, with the extra dimension that they can see you but you can't see them.

When dealing with an interview in a remote studio:

- look at the camera
- don't fiddle with the earpiece
- even when you are not being addressed you will be on air, so maintain the illusion of eye contact
- when the light is on, you are on air.

An interview in a remote studio requires a certain amount of play-acting. You have to give the impression that you can see the interviewer, so keep smiling and reacting as though you were in a face-to-face situation.

Remote radio studios are often physically even more uncomfortable than remote TV studios. They are sometimes just a box like a photo-booth containing recording equipment and a microphone. Behave as you would in a telephone interview and just concentrate on the interviewer, the questions and your messages.

Radio and TV phone-ins

The quality of telephone recordings means that they are usually only used for brief news comment or for specific phone-in programmes. You need to get to the point immediately and don't waste time on pleasantries. Answer the questions, try to get your message across and then stop and wait for a question.

Avoid thinking of your interviewer as the 'enemy' 'grilling' you or you are bound to sound defensive. Rather, regard the interview as an excellent opportunity to promote yourself and your product, and the interviewer as a friend trying to help you, and you will be fine.

Going live

Both recorded and live broadcasts have advantages and disadvantages. In a live broadcast you may run the risk of not saying the 'right' thing but at least no one will edit your words. Live interviews cannot be distorted, with quotes being taken out of context. However, you risk the interviewer talking about topics that you don't want to discuss and you may not have a chance to put across your message.

If a programme is pre-recorded you can stop and say, 'I'll start that bit again', and immediately go back to the beginning of your answer, confident that the editor will remove the offending piece. Do not restart half-way through a sentence, but go back to the beginning of your reply. Stop, pause, recover and restart. Your words are also more effective the first time you say them, so try not to stop an interview unless you have to. Perhaps have a colleague sitting nearby, who can signal to you if you are getting into trouble.

You will have no control over what is edited out of a pre-recorded interview, and an hour's interview may be edited down to a few minutes – without your key messages. A pre-recorded interview can be reduced to almost nothing at all. So, try to summarise your comments and views near the beginning or end. This can help the producer to decide what will be left in and what taken out. Repeat your message and give good, short sound-bites to increase the chance of them being included.

(Even live broadcasts often use a delay system to allow them to deal with cranks. A live interview is actually broadcast several seconds after it has taken place to allow the producer to hit the 'cut' button if necessary.)

If your interview is going to be broadcast live there is no opportunity to edit the results, but your words will benefit from the obvious immediacy and you can inject more passion and interest into your answers. Even if the interview is being recorded you are unlikely to have the opportunity to influence the editing, so only say things that you want broadcast. Do not say something stupid in the expectation that it will be cut.

Clothes and make-up

If the interview is for a business audience you should be in business clothing, even for radio.

- Dress as you would for a job interview and avoid overly casual clothes. If you don't look serious you won't be taken seriously, and it is better to overdress than underdress.

- Avoid stripes on television.

- Avoid loud colours. Apart from looking bad, it distracts the viewer from you and what you are saying.

- Avoid small checks, brown or bright white.

- Do not have bare arms or wear an off-the-shoulder dress.

- Do not wear bright jewellery.

- Remove badges, motifs or brooches.

- Button your jacket.

- Pull your jacket down sharply at the back and sit on the hem, if possible. This prevents it becoming unattractively hunched up over your shoulders and round the back of your neck. Good posture will help create a good impression.

Everyone who appears on television will need make-up. You will get just a few minutes with the make-up artist before you go on and they will put on some foundation and powder, possibly some eye make-up and some lipstick. If you think you need make-up, ask for it.

Women sometimes insist on doing their own make-up, but you should be guided by the professionals who know what works and what doesn't on television. Some men object to being made-up but you only notice make-up on television when it is not there. People without make-up appear pale and insignificant with shiny faces. The make-up will not be obvious on camera, so just hold your face up and allow the make-up person to do what they want. TV make-up often appears garish or over-dramatic in the flesh so you should remember to wipe it off afterwards – it will come off easily with water and a towel, or just a handkerchief.

Once made-up, avoid touching your face or hair. One professional trick is to use a small amount of Vaseline on your teeth because it helps you smile more easily. Nerves can cause a dry mouth which can create difficulty in relaxing and smiling on camera. Remember that if you dry up and don't know what to say, the journalist will help you – so relax.

Voice

A good delivery requires clarity, good pitch, even pace, animation and emphasis. You can control and alter all these, even the pitch. Try to limber up before an interview with facial exercises, and warm up your vocal chords by making a noise like a didgeridoo – sounds strange, but it works!

Both radio and TV favour rich, fruity and deep voices – in other words, most men's voices, and women should try to lower theirs slightly without losing naturalness. Open your mouth wide when you speak and don't mumble through your teeth. Practise using a microphone – don't suddenly drop the tone of your voice during an interview. Don't move closer to the microphone to answer the questions – the sound engineer will monitor and adjust the sound levels.

Be lively, bright, positive and confident. Be expressive and passionate and allow your enthusiasm to come through.

Avoid 'ums', 'ers' and unnecessary pauses, and don't fake an accent. Think about the speed of your speech – it is easy to start speaking too fast. If you find yourself gabbling, make yourself slow down. Remember that you can hear a smile – smile on radio and the telephone as well as on TV and in person.

Lastly, it is not your voice that gives you authority – it is the content of what you say. Your voice helps, but however good your voice, people will not listen if you are talking rubbish.

The questions

Unless you are a politician, the television or radio interviewer is unlikely to be setting out to trap you or get you to make a fool of yourself. They will want the interview to go well, and for the viewer or listener to be entertained and informed.

The benefit of a studio interview is that you are more likely to be given an idea of the questions you will be asked in advance, but often the most you can hope for is an idea of what the first question will be. TV and radio interviewers are sometimes better briefed than print journalists because they have researchers to help them.

One key difference between interviews on radio or TV and in print is that the viewer or listener is more likely to hear the question which leads to the answer. In print, the question is usually omitted. This means that broadcast journalists are part of the interview in a way that print journalists are not.

Think of the interview as just a chat between friends. Imagine the interviewer as someone to whom you are going to explain your new product, and let all your enthusiasm and fire show through. Do not be afraid of going 'over the top' – both television and radio like enthusiastic people: just think of Peter Snow and Patrick Moore. Quiet, shy, grey people come across as wet and pathetic, but enthusiasm makes good radio and television.

Don't avoid questions and do not bluff or lie. Keep your answers short, do not ramble, but say more than just 'yes' or 'no' answers. Aim to be interesting by modulating your voice. Rehearse as much as possible before the interview and practise on friends and family, standing up in front of them and telling them all about the product as though they were strangers, and then getting them to ask you questions about it, which you have to answer to their satisfaction. If you practise sufficiently, you will find that when the interview comes you will go into 'auto-pilot' mode, giving out prepared answers and explanations.

Have respect for the interviewer, but do not be deferential or sycophantic. Avoid familiarity with the interviewer – they may seem familiar to you because you see or hear them all the time, but you are a stranger to them.

Remember that they are professionals with a different agenda from yours – they are not your friends. Treat every question seriously, and do not scorn or sneer if the interviewer asks something crass or obvious.

You will find that the interviewer uses your name – do the same in return. You will appear to be in control. On both radio and TV, look at the interviewer the whole time and adopt a composed position, with legs closed.

Avoid quoting numbers, which can have an off-putting effect on air. People are looking for essential truth and immediate accessibility, and having to think about numbers slows them down.

If you are good at telling them, throw in a few anecdotes – they usually make very good radio and television, provided they are interesting and/or amusing and not too long.

You will find that broadcast journalists ask questions which are more precise and follow on from each other in a more regulated way than print journalists, who can allow their questions to ramble. In a broadcast, a rambling interviewer looks and sounds ignorant. Broadcast questions are more succinct, and your answers should be too.

The unexpected

Radio interviews are altogether more friendly, print interviews are easier to control, while TV is more difficult. But in all three, the unexpected can catch you unawares.

Most interviews start with easy questions to relax you, but sometimes the journalist will sneak in a tricky question when you are not expecting it. Keep your cool. If something unexpected happens don't be tempted to make an unscripted, off-the-cuff remark or joke to hide your nerves or confusion. Do not attempt unscripted humour – it is dangerous, and more often than not embarrassing.

Don't bluff, lie or deny things which are true. Better to tell the truth, explain and apologise.

If the interviewer starts asking you about something you have not prepared for, you should say something like, 'Well, that is not the subject that I was asked here to speak about but I am happy to give you my views off the top of my head', thereby making it clear to the viewer or listener that the interviewer has tricked you but you are willing to do your best to answer the questions. Do not refuse outright to talk about a topic.

Try not to be flustered into a response you will regret. If you find yourself in territory you have not prepared for, make your comments short and lively, and use phrases like 'to the best of my knowledge' or 'as far as I can remember', so keeping the audience aware that you have not been given a chance to prepare.

If the interviewer says something inaccurate or unfair, do not let it pass out of politeness. The viewer or listener will respect you more if you politely point out the inaccuracy. Don't be afraid to assert yourself if you know you are right, and correct mistakes or false assumptions or statements immediately. Allowing them to stand uncorrected is taken as implicit agreement.

Remember that if the interviewer is too aggressive, the audience's sympathy will be with you. If you are arrogant, abrasive or too knowledgeable, the audience's sympathy will be with the journalist. *Never lose your temper*. The journalist will love it if you lose control and your credibility will vanish. Stay cool and collected even if you can't be calm. Whatever you do, don't walk out. It may be tempting, but it does you no good. Better to handle the situation with aplomb, or even to mishandle it, than walk out.

Remember it's not over until you are down the road. Do not think that the journalist appearing to end the interview means that it is over and you can relax and go off the record. The journalist is always working, even in apparently informal situations.

Chapter summary

- Radio and TV offer more opportunities than ever before and are more effective than print for spreading messages.

- Radio and TV journalists want the interview to 'work'. They don't want silences.

- Anticipate any tricky questions and prepare your responses.

- Concentrate on the interviewer; ignore the technology.

- Relax and breathe deeply several times just before you go on air. Drop your shoulders.

- Be emotional. It's better than being unemotional – that's unmemorable.

- The audience's sympathy will always be with you, unless you are arrogant or aggressive.

- Be concise.

- Mention the name of your company and product as often as you can.

- At the end, summarise your points, especially for pre-recorded interviews.

- Don't lose your temper.

- It's not over until you are out of the studio or the recording crew has left.

CASE STUDIES

Case study 1: Product promotion to the lifestyle press

By now Paul is getting to know some of the journalists quite well. However, a couple of times he calls for a chat, to find that they are not interested in talking to him. One tells him why: 'You haven't got a story. I'm working, I need an angle.' Paul is surprised at this, thinking that the journalist would be as keen to develop the friend- ship. 'I don't mean to be rude, Paul,' says the journalist, 'but I am busy. Our relationship is a working one and I'm happy to speak to you if there is a story, but please don't waste my time.' After that, Paul is more cautious about contacting a journalist unless he has a specific story or angle.

An opportunity arises when one of BettaProds' competitors, SupaProds, launches a range of kitchenware with claims similar to those for BettaProds' KoolWay range. SupaProds' range, however, is distinctly inferior, and much cheaper. Paul is cautious about being seen to speak too critically of a BettaProds competitor, but feels that some statement to the press is called for.

First he drafts a press release, saying that Karen is disturbed by customers possibly being misled by the SupaProds marketing cam- paign, and pointing out that the KoolWay range of product is defi- nitely superior. There is also a quote from a respected expert in health and safety matters, saying that one can not economise where safety is concerned.

Paul sends the press release to around 150 journalists, spread- ing his net to include all kinds of lifestyle and general consumer press journalists. He receives ten phone calls enquiring about the story, and they all ask to be sent a photograph of Karen.

At the same time Paul is planning his press lunch. He sends out his invitations – to 50 key journalists that he feels are writing for the most important titles and programmes – and also sets an agenda for the lunch. He states on the invitation that the main topic for debate will be whether safety can be compromised by cost, and says that there will be independent analysts and pundits attending.

A week before the event is due, he rings around to see who will attend and is pleased that 40 give definite or provisional confirma- tion. He has to increase the size of his reservation at the restaurant. He has chosen a popular central London venue, serving trendy Italian/American food. He wanted to have a private room, but with that number of journalists it is impossible, and he has to settle for tables in the main restaurant.

The day before he does another quick ring around of those who said they would, or probably would, attend, and the number is reduced to 30 definites. He is irritated, because if he'd known it was 30 he would have booked a room because they can hold that number. Now it's too late because all the private rooms have been taken.

On the day of the event, Paul has 30 press packs delivered to the restaurant in the morning, and makes sure that Karen and the analysts and experts arrive in good time. They collect in the bar, where they mingle with the other restaurant customers. Gradually Paul spots one or two of the journalists, but doesn't know what they all look like so isn't sure if he is missing some others.

The lunch is due to start at 1p.m. and by 12.45 there are eight journalists drinking with Karen in the bar. Paul is keeping a lookout for the rest, but the restaurant is busy and it is hard to find them. At 1.15 Karen and the journalists, by then 14, go to the tables. The restaurant has reserved 30 places across six large tables, so they look rather silly. They sit at two tables, squashing eight people on each. The restaurant manager opens up the other four tables to the public.

The restaurant seems to get busier and busier, and there is no chance of a serious discussion or debate about the topic Paul suggested. He just decides to enjoy himself and starts drinking seriously, quickly getting quite drunk. Several of the journalists decide to join him, and by the time the lunch is over most of the party are too drunk to go back to work. They decide to take the rest of the afternoon off and continue to sit at the tables, which are a bit less crowded since some of the journalists left halfway through the meal, for the rest of the afternoon, putting all the booze and cigars on BettaProds' bill.

At 3.30 Karen excused herself and went back to the office.

Next morning she has a meeting with Paul, when she fires him. 'It was a fiasco,' she says, 'and it cost us a lot of money.' 'But I was building relationships,' he says, 'and I'm sure it was worthwhile.' 'It's not the sort of relationships I want,' says Karen. 'Now clear your desk, and don't come back.'

- **Comment**: It looks like Paul is going to have a career change, and perhaps it is just as well. He does not appear to be suited to PR, although he tried hard to make it work. Despite the efforts of several journalists to explain to him where he was going wrong, he seemed unable to grasp their agenda.

Case study 2: Product promotion to the computer press

Jessica continues to learn much from Joe Probe about how to work with the press, and over the next few weeks several journalists call her wanting views on educational or CBT issues and topics broadly connected with the IT industry. One wanted Richard to comment on the effect Bill Gates and Microsoft were having on the computing industry; another wanted his views on the general shortage of specialist IT skills and programmers.

Richard finds that he is receiving significantly more telephone calls from advertising sales staff, usually those working for the same magazines and radio and TV stations as the journalists. He realises that he can play the advertising and editorial teams off against each other, if he agrees to take advertising on condition that he gets an editorial mention. When he says that, a journalist seems to call back within the next few days.

He mentions this to Joe, who warns against trying to leverage any link between advertising and editorial. 'The journalists don't like the media sales lot,' he says. But the next time Richard is speaking to Anne Gables, a staff writer with *What Computers Today In Your Education System?* magazine, he can't resist asking whether his advertisement for KiddieLearn 2 can be sited next to the feature she is writing on CBT. Immediately she goes cold on the phone. 'I've no idea about that,' she says. When the piece comes out he is disappointed to find that he is not quoted after all.

Richard is irritated by this. Surely, after all, Anne realises that she wouldn't have a job if people like him didn't buy advertising. He gives Anne a call. 'I thought I had some fairly good views and opinions,' he says. 'I'm surprised you didn't quote me.' Anne is distant and vague. 'Oh,' she says, 'I spoke to a lot of people and I really can't remember. I had enough comments for the feature, thanks anyway. Perhaps next time.'

Joe is not surprised when Richard mentions the incident to him. 'I told you, journalists don't like media sales,' he says. 'But they depend on advertising,' Richard protests. 'It's a controlled circulation title.' Joe explains that, to the journalists, that doesn't matter. 'They have to feel they're independent. There's the commercial reality and then there's the way that most journalists on controlled titles work.' Joe goes on to explain that although there is often some cross-fertilisation between the media sales team and the journalists, it is rarely overt. 'Journalists are sometimes given a list of people that the publisher or advertising team would like them to speak to and quote while they're writing the feature, but there's almost never any compulsion for them to do so. Sometimes the advertising sales team are given a list of the names of the people quoted, but they rarely see copy and the editor, if any good, will never let the copy be changed.'

'So I'm powerless to influence the editorial, despite the size of my advertising spend with the title,' ponders Richard. 'Right,' says Joe.

- **Comment**: Jessica looks like having a long career in PR and marketing. She has listened to the experts and to the journalists themselves, and has learned and absorbed what she has been told. She and Richard have also learned that you cannot control a journalist, and even if you do everything right, you still cannot be sure that you will get the column inches.

Case study 3: Diary of a freelance journalist

Went to a great press lunch today. It was in my favourite West End restaurant, and some of my favourite friends were there. It was organised by that rather silly young man from BettaProds, but I've no idea why or what he was telling us about. It was a shame, because I tried out the BettaProds products last night and I was really surprised and impressed. They do an excellent job, and although it's hard to see how, the saucepans really do manage to cook the food properly while keeping the sides of the saucepan cool enough to touch.

I went to the press lunch hoping to talk to Karen Jamison at BettaProds, but I couldn't get near her. The restaurant was crowded and noisy, and once you got seated in one place you couldn't move. I didn't mind too much and just spent the time having a good chat about the industry and technologies, and other matters, with some old pals. The trouble with being freelance is that it is easy to lose touch with people, so the lunch was a good opportunity to rekindle some old friendships. There was also a commissioning editor there, John Carlton, who I haven't seen for a while, and we had a quick chat about some features I'd like to do. I must give him a call tomorrow to follow up.

Next day
Called Karen Jamison and had a chat about future developments of KoolWay. One of my journo friends was saying over lunch that the BettaProds competitors are catching up fast with the technology while BettaProds has not been investing sufficiently in R&D, and I ask Karen about that. She is defensive, which makes me think that there is something in the story. I give the SupaProds marcoms

[marketing communications] person a call, and she says she'll get the MD to call me back. Hasn't returned my call yet, though.

I also ring James Carlton and talk about some future features. He asks me to fax over a list of suggestions, which I do, and then we talk about them over the phone. We agree a series of six features over the next six issues, and talk about subject, word counts and deadlines. It's good for me to have work in the pipeline like that – I can keep the features in the back of my mind and start working on them in between other features – and it's good for him to have the features worked out. His advertising sales team will be pleased too, because they have a list of features which they can sell advertising space against. James is a strong and mature editor who doesn't take any pressure from the advertising team, but I have worked for publications that give a list of names alongside the commission, and request that you quote them. I always make it clear that I will if I can, but that the commission is not dependent on it. Otherwise I will end up just writing PR puff instead of independent editorial. It works out fine if the people on the list are worth quoting and have strong views and opinions, but if they just spout the company line and keep pushing their product information, I won't quote them.

- **Comment**: Here you can get a better feel for the way a freelance works. They are self-employed and continually have to have an eye on their billing and future work. Most freelances are dedicated professionals like Suzie, who like to deal with professional marketing and PR people.

Chapter Eight

Following up

Introduction

Making contact, having an interview, sending a press release or just having lunch with a journalist is only part of the story. You then have to follow up. Journalists are resistant to time-wasting follow-ups but this chapter will show you how to follow up without being a 'chaser'.

The problem is that the media generally dislike follow-ups. If you have unsuccessfully pitched an idea or once they have run a story, as far as they are concerned it is dead and gone – finished. You therefore have to be subtle, and remember the rule:

- **DON'T follow up** without a very good reason: *you must have something to add.*

Product promotion is not a one-off business, it is a long-term practice. If you are trying to promote a product to the press, it is a waste of your initial effort just to make one or two pitches and then, if you are not successful, simply let the matter drop. Once you have made contact with a journalist and have the beginnings of a relationship, you must try to keep it going if you can, although the onus is firmly on you to build and maintain momentum. You need to keep a regular flow of newsworthy stories coming through, all the while keeping the angle controversial and opinionated.

Journalists usually have a well-developed air of prickly hostility which protects them from the most irritating, thick-skinned or determined approaches. Unless you have something interesting to say, which you genuinely think the journalist is going to be keen to hear about, *don't waste their time*. Certainly don't just ring up to pass the time of day. Journalists remember those who make pointless, time-wasting calls. You need to be sensitive and aware of the journalist's deadlines and pressures, and should not bother them unless you have a good reason to contact them.

Human nature dictates that journalists generally prefer to deal with someone they already know (provided previous encounters were pleasant, of course) so, once you have made an initial contact, had a drink or met at an event, subsequent attempts at communication should be easier.

Following up the press release

If anyone suggests that you 'just call up to see if the press release has arrived', they are teasing you. Whatever you do – *don't do it*. Calling to follow up the press release is one of the initiation rites PR agencies inflict on novices, comparable to sending the new young lad in the builder's firm along to the ironmongers to ask for a bubble for the spirit level, or to ask for a long weight. Sometimes inexperienced PR people who are told to ring up journalists on such an errand get a moderately polite response but more often the reply is abrupt and to the point.

There are few things which irritate a journalist more than the question 'Did you get our press release?', so much so that it's a joke in many editorial offices. This is understandable if you remember that journalists often get hundreds of press releases each week. If everyone who sends a press release rang to check whether it had arrived, the journalist would deal with nothing else all day.

However, there are other ways of following up a release, most of which journalists are wise to, such as: 'We are having trouble with our post and we just wanted to make sure that the press release had arrived all right – and by the way, what did you think of it?'

Some PR people use other tricks, such as to omit an important piece of information like the price of the product, and then call up after the release should have arrived to volunteer the missing information. Unfortunately, most journalists see this trick coming and those who try to use it will also be given a rough time.

If the story is a good one, and if the journalist has read the press release and is interested by it, they will follow it up whether or not you call them. Calling them to see if it has arrived or to see whether it is useful is unlikely to encourage them to read it or use it. Your intention may be to draw the journalist's attention to the press release but just following up with a querying call is not, generally speaking, the way to do it.

If it is a really good, strong story, one strategy is to telephone the journalist a few days before you send the release to warn them that it's coming. This is something which should be reserved for outstandingly newsworthy stories and not used for every release. If the journalist is alerted they can look out for the release when it arrives, but if they don't call you back you must assume that they are not interested for some reason.

It is also a bad idea to ring the journalist and ask, 'Could you send me a copy of the issue which mentions our product in it?' or even, 'Are you going to use the story?' Even if the journalist is going to use the story, they are unlikely to want to tell you. Every call like that distracts the journalist's attention and is irritating. You have to have a definite, valid purpose to the call.

Remember the rule once again:

- **DON'T follow up** without a very good reason: *you must have something to add.*

Revamping the press release

If your original press release didn't attract much interest, you could try a completely new angle, create a new story and generate a new release. Don't just send the old one again, but if you can find an original angle which was not emphasised before, then rewrite and resend.

Journalists are not interested in plugging your product for you, but if you can find an interesting angle which provides a good hook, they will possibly consider the story. For example, perhaps the technique of production is unusual, perhaps the sales are bringing extra jobs, or there has been a high-value sale to a high-profile customer.

It's no good trying to dress up something which is not there, or completely inventing a story which will not stand up to investigation. But there is also no point in just resending the original press release with the date changed: if a journalist runs the story the second time around and then discovers that it is not news, your credibility will be seriously damaged.

Following up after the press conference

Following up after a press conference is a little easier than after a press release because you have a valid reason for the call. You can legitimately telephone and make sure that the journalist got everything they wanted, spoke to everyone they wished to speak to and got all the pictures they were after at the event. You have a credible opportunity to discuss the launch and perhaps set up further interviews or send more information in the post. You still need to be sensitive – some journalists dislike being contacted post-interview. They believe that you have had your opportunity and there is no point in continuing the interview. But others sometimes welcome a chance to quickly go over the key points, or they may want a photograph or a sample of the product. These are all valid reasons for you to call.

Whatever you do, if you speak to a journalist after you have tried to interest them in a story, don't even hint at your advertising spend (see Chapter 1 for the differences between advertising and editorial). It makes you look very inexperienced and is liable to antagonise and irritate the journalist. It implies that they have no editorial integrity and that the editorial and advertising departments are linked. Even if they are, do not mention it to the journalist.

Checking attribution

The whole point of talking to a journalist is to get your name and/or your product name in editorial, so it makes sense that, having given a journalist an interview, you want to follow up to make sure that your name and the product are spelled right and mentioned as frequently as possible throughout the piece. Sometimes it is also appropriate for a contact name and phone number to appear at the end of the piece, and it is valid for you therefore to call to make sure that any such name and number are the right ones.

Strictly speaking, journalists should attribute any remark which is not their own to the person who made it, and give the source of any quote which they have used, but they do not always do so. The point of a call to follow up an interview is to make sure that your comments are attributed to you as much as possible.

Most journalists know that it gives a comment more weight and authority if it is attributed to an expert, so they are usually keen to do so. The journalist will probably want to attribute the quote if the statement is unusual or wild; or comes from someone highly respected or well known; or the person is particularly identified with the idea; or someone makes an attack on or criticism of another product or person.

When the piece appears, you may find that your quote is linked to verbs of expression such as the following:

- revealed
- asserted
- claimed
- explained.

You have no control over these. If you dislike the choice of words the journalist has used to attribute the quote to you (perhaps because 'claimed' has a ring of cynical doubt about it, and appears to dissociate the journalist from your remarks), there unfortunately is nothing you can do.

Over-use of attribution indicates that a journalist has been lazy or has doubts about a story. Effective attribution moves a story forward, and does not come between the journalist and the audience. But it is always good for you – as someone wishing to increase your media profile – to be attributed as the source of information as frequently as possible.

General follow-ups

Few journalists mind if you make regular calls to see if they are working on anything with which you can help. They may be looking for people to quote or for stories and, provided you don't try to turn a conversation into a push for your own product and that every now and again you *are* able to help, they will usually be fairly polite. A quick call every month or so (probably no more frequently or you become a nuisance) to establish whether you have or can get information or quotes which they might need is usually appreciated. This applies in particular if you have a continual stream of newsworthy stories connected with your product.

You can also call to comment on topical issues which are pertinent to your product or market area. Journalists usually welcome such calls, and not enough people make them. If there has been a news story from a competitor, or some other issue develops on which you have a view, then you can contact the journalist and tell them. It is quite possible that they are looking for comment, and may well welcome your call.

Remember that journalists depend on people contacting them with stories and, provided you don't become a pain or irritating, they will probably be happy to hear from you, if you have something for them.

But the fundamental message is: don't waste the journalists' time, and only call when you have something to say.

Features lists

You'll find a section on features lists in Chapter 5 which explains how extremely useful they are for people promoting products. Features lists warn you when a feature is being written, often tell you who is writing it, and allow you to provide timely information or views at exactly the time the journalists need them. Sometimes the advertising sales teams only get the features list after the journalists have written the copy, which means they are too late for you to contribute editorially, but if there is still time and the feature has not closed the journalists are often grateful for opinionated comments.

Generally speaking, you will find they are receptive to calls from people trying to promote products, provided you are willing to be opinionated and outspoken.

Become a source of information

Once you have established contact with a journalist, you should aim to become their pundit of choice. You want them to call you up every time they need a comment on your area of speciality. To do this you need to be reliable and controversial, but not necessarily in that order.

To become a contact whom the journalist calls when they need a quote or comment, you have to be:

- *reliable* – concerning the content of your comments. You must be accurate in what you tell them.
- *available* – the journalist wants someone who makes time to talk to them. Remember that there are often dozens of your competitors also wanting to promote their product to the press, and if you don't respond promptly, they will.
- *quotable* – delivering your views and opinions in short, snappy statements.
- *controversial and opinionated* – someone who delivers personal views with passion, conviction and wit, without too much regard for the consequences.
- *frank and honest* – if you don't have anything to say tell them. Hopefully, there will always be another opportunity.

By building yourself into a pundit or 'rent-a-quote' you will effectively and quickly raise your profile and that of your product. The process also has a snowballing effect – the more you do, the more other journalists want you to do. But if you have nothing to say, admit it and don't waste their time.

Creating opportunities

Sometimes you have to create opportunities by proactively nominating yourself and your product for review, comment or analysis. You have to keep an eye on the newspapers and magazines, watch the TV and listen to the radio, and if you see a slot which you could fill, contact the journalist or editor and suggest that you do it. For example, many magazines have personality profile pages – don't be shy, suggest that they do a profile on you. The knock-on effect will be promotion for your product.

If a story appears which you either disagree with or think that you should have been given a chance to comment on, again contact the journalist or editor and let them know your feelings. Too many people read, listen to or watch something and think, 'I could have done that', 'I don't agree with that' or 'That's not right', without doing anything about it. The journalist is likely to welcome controversial comment from someone who disagrees with an item that has appeared or been broadcast.

Radio phone-ins and letters pages are invitations for people to get in touch and proffer their views and experience. Provided there is some tenuous link with your product, take every opportunity you can find for raising your profile by getting your name, and that of your product, mentioned.

Letters pages in particular are often undersubscribed, and editors are pleased to have as many controversial letters as possible.

Thanking the journalist

One of the cardinal rules of press relations is never to openly thank the journalist for giving you some editorial. Some people think it is good manners to thank a journalist for a piece which mentions or quotes them. Instead, it makes the journalist concerned.

Why? Because if they are thanked by the person promoting the product, most journalists feel extremely uncomfortable and think that they haven't done a good enough job. Gratitude from the product promoters suggests that the journalist has written the piece 'for them' rather than taking an independent stance 'for the audience'. The journalist will think that they have not been critical enough on behalf of their customer – the reader, viewer or listener.

There are other, less overt ways to show your gratitude. Few journalists, for example, will complain at a general compliment about a piece. You could also call after the piece appears with some additional information, to extend the debate further but not to thank the journalist for the piece.

Editorial competitions and special offers

Many publications and some broadcast programmes like to run competitions for their listeners, viewers or readers, which can be sponsored. As someone promoting a product, you may consider becoming a sponsoring company.

For example, some consumer magazines like to run a weekly or monthly 'Person of the month' award, with a straightforward tie-breaker and a prize donated by a company attempting to promote their product. It boosts their circulation and if it doesn't cost them anything editors are usually keen to do it.

The golden rule is that you should not interfere with the judging process. Unless you are invited to be part of this process, leave it to the editorial team to find the winner – your role is just to provide the prize. You may sometimes ask for the names and addresses of all entrants, which can give you a mailing list of interested people and potential customers. Many editors also like to run special offers, for the same reason: it is a cheap way to boost sales.

You will need to negotiate both competitions and special offers with either the editor, publisher or producer. As part of the negotiation process, you should aim to get the competition or special offer mentioned as often as possible, and mentioned in pre-publicity if you can. It could be mentioned on the contents page, and you may be able to organise a cover flash which flags to the reader that there is a sponsored competition or special offer inside.

Product round-ups and reviews

Many trade and user publications run group tests, product comparisons and straightforward single reviews, and the resulting copy, providing it is favourable, makes excellent marketing and sales material. Call the editor or ask for the journalist handling the product reviews, and ask whether there is a suitable round-up scheduled. Sometimes the media sales team will know if there is a suitable review being planned.

Ask if you can deliver the product to their office, and ideally persuade them to let you set it up, install it or demonstrate how it works. This has two purposes: it makes sure that they use the product properly and give it a fair review, and secondly it gives you a chance to meet and talk to the journalists. Make sure that the product you send *works* before you send it, and make sure that the price and buyer contact details are included.

Don't ask for the survey results in advance – you are unlikely to be told, and it shows your inexperience. Do not be surprised if the media sales team pressures you into advertising near the review. On a high-quality magazine, the review will not be affected by whether you advertise or not. On a cheap publication there may be some influence over editorial, but ask yourself: if the editorial is not independent, will people really read it and believe it? Try not to allow yourself to be bullied, and do not believe that buying advertising affects the review.

Watching for new developments or issues

To maintain your profile with journalists and hopefully keep yourself and your product in the media, keep an eye on events inside your company which are newsworthy and outside your company – in the rest of your market or in the news in general – which you can comment on. Armed with these, you can contact the press again. First, write the press release, and then make contact with those journalists who you believe might be interested. Send the press release to everyone on your target list and phone those you particularly would like to pick it up.

Other opportunities

Once a piece about you or your product or service has appeared, you should try to keep the story alive by initiating debate about it. You could follow up with a letter to the editor or journalist, perhaps politely pointing out some element which was overlooked, or putting right any misunderstanding. By opening a debate you will keep public awareness of your product at a high level.

- Many publications welcome editorial contributions. For the editor, it means free copy (they would otherwise have to pay a journalist to write the words) and for you it can mean an opportunity to get your message across in the words you want to see. Provided they are not too over-the-top, many editors will print them verbatim, but remember that the editor still has a power of veto, so there is no point in getting carried away with the sales puff and hyperbole. Commission a freelance journalist to write it for you – it is more likely to be in the style and format which will be acceptable.

- Journalists are often looking for case studies, and editors are often keen to print case studies alongside their features, so, if you have some prepared, be ready to send them to the journalist.

- You may be invited to write a feature for contribution. Check the word length required and don't over-write (you are not doing them a favour by giving them more words – they will only have to cut it back to make it fit the page). Find out the deadline and whether they want pictures too. In the writing, take an independent view if you can, and take a broad perspective. If the copy is too like advertorial they may cut it or not use it.

- Check whether you will get the by-line (that is to say the line which says, 'by John Smith') and offer a photo of you to go with the feature. Such exposure is excellent value.

Keep an eye on several issues and programmes and become known as an independent expert on these. Hopefully, you will eventually be contacted by the journalist for your comments.

Developing the relationship

Journalists probably speak to your competitors, customers and manufacturers, and can probably tell you what your competitors are planning. They can be an extremely useful source of competitive information. Don't be afraid to ask them what they have heard about your competitors, or what they think about your competitors' products. Remember that they are probably talking about you too!

When talking to a journalist and in all your dealings, be neither too familiar nor too formal. One thing that sets a journalist's teeth on edge is sycophancy, and the sort of telephone call which sounds like someone trying to sell double glazing or life insurance. This approach seems to be the natural tendency for many inexperienced PR people to adopt – a 'salesy' tone and approach, which quickly results in the journalist giving them the brush-off. If the journalist is treated in a professional, businesslike way, the chances are that they will respond in a similar manner.

But you have to remember that the relationship is always going to be a mainly professional one, so however friendly you become with a journalist you should always treat them with some degree of respect. Even if you are meeting a journalist socially, for business calls you should always introduce yourself with your full name. Telephoning and saying, 'It's John here' or 'Hi, it's Sue' will reduce any respect that the journalist has for you. You don't know how many other people, or how many other Johns or Sues, the journalist is having to talk to. Always introduce yourself with your full name job title and company name – it's good business manners.

If you start seeing the journalist on a regular basis, you might want to start giving her or him some information or a lead on a story. If you have something to say which you know is reliable and might be of interest to the journalist then tell them. As you get to know the journalist better you can start to tell them things off the record and be fairly confident that they will respect your trust.

Creating 'reasons to respond'

Some professional marketing people believe that it is helpful for developing a long-term relationship with a journalist to create reasons and mechanisms for the journalist to contact you. These should not be too obvious or they become irritating. Some PR agencies frequently send out invitations without a critical element, such as the date or the time or location. Of course they risk not having anyone turn up because they can't be bothered to call up and ask, but it also leaves a reason for you to contact the journalist with the missing information.

Others do not send a photograph with the press release but put a note on it saying that photographs are available in the hope that the journalist will call, or to create an opportunity to call the journalist to offer a photograph. Again, this is a risky strategy.

Basically, if the story is strong and the product interesting, the journalist will want to follow up and get more information or arrange an interview. If the story is weak or non-existent, no amount of 'opportunities' or 'reasons' will persuade the journalist to follow up.

The best reason for a journalist to respond to you is if your story is so compelling and fascinating, and of such clear interest to the target audience, that the journalist wants to know more.

If the journalist follows up

It may be that the journalist calls you after receiving the press release or after an interview or press conference. They are unlikely to be calling for a chat.

- Determine the purpose of the call, and make sure that you satisfy their requirements, but also try to develop the call into other areas.
- Ask whether there is anything else that the journalist is working on that you can help them with.

- Ask if they are looking for comment on other issues, or whether there are product reviews coming up which you would like to be included in.
- Try to create further opportunities in which to mention your product.

You need to have an efficient system for dealing with enquiries from the press. It may be that they need more information, another copy of the press release, a photograph, or they want to check the spelling of a name. There are many reasons why a journalist may call you, and you need to respond promptly. You may not get a second chance – there are always plenty of other people wanting to talk to the media, and although the deadline may be some time away, the chances are that the journalist wants to finish the story as quickly as possible.

Exploiting media coverage

Once you have had some editorial exposure, either in the form of quotes or mentions of your product, you should try to cash in on your fame to a wider audience.

- You can use copies of the editorial in your marketing material.
- If your product is reviewed, ask for reprints to give to potential customers.
- Clip the editorial to the next press release.
- Send copies of the editorial to your existing clients, to reassure them that your product is the best.
- Circulate it among your colleagues.

Take care, however, not to fall foul of the copyright laws. You can't just cut out reviews and interviews and send them to your clients or potential clients. The copy belongs to the publication, and you need to ask permission, usually from the publisher, before using it. Some publishing houses charge for this, or provide a reprint service.

Chapter summary

- The press needs to be told that you are available for comment.
- Don't follow up unless you have a story or an angle.
- That story or angle has to be genuine and worthwhile.
- Don't ring up just to see if the press release has arrived.
- Don't revamp an old press release.

- You can call to check that the journalist has everything they need.
- Follow up features lists.
- Make sure you are prepared with a strong opinion and some facts.
- If a journalist calls you respond as fast as you can, even if the deadline is not immediate. If not, you'll find your competitors have seized the opportunity.
- Maximise any editorial coverage by using reprints for your marketing material.

CASE STUDIES

Case study 1: Product promotion to the lifestyle press

With Paul gone, Karen does not rush to fill the job of press manager immediately. She considers taking on an outside agency to help create media interest in the KoolWay range and get editorial inches for BettaProds. But she also starts considering that she could handle most of the press activity work herself. When Paul took over the job she was nervous of the press, but at the media training day she had learned a lot about the way journalists work and what they are looking for, and how to contact them and deal with an interview. So Karen decides that she will take the main responsibility for press relations on herself, supported by Delia, an office assistant.

Karen instructs Delia to take over the list of key magazines and journalists that Paul built, and update it. Delia calls everyone on the list and checks that the contact name is still correct, and asks when the news and feature copy deadlines are. She also asks to be sent a features list. For those publications which say that they do produce a features list, Delia calls the advertising sales team and gets them to send her one. Only a few of the publications do not have any forward features list.

Once she has the lists, Delia goes through them looking for opportunities and issues where Karen might be able to give a comment. Then Karen also scans them, looking for issues and topics which she had not previously considered.

There is a feature in a trade magazine, for example, on customer loyalty, and another on the problems of customers who pay late. There is a feature on factoring, which Karen hadn't even considered as something she could comment on, even though BettaProds uses a factoring agent to improve its cash flow.

There are also several product reviews and reports being planned by some consumer magazines, and Delia immediately contacts them and arranges to send some samples of the KoolWay products to the reviews editor in time to be included in the feature.

Karen clears a half-day a week from her diary, and uses the time to concentrate on contacting staff and freelance journalists who as she knows from the features lists, are writing about issues on which she has a view. She prepares for each call, having a crib sheet of her messages in front of her and an Interview Check Sheet for keeping a record of the conversation. She knows what the issue is that the journalist is writing about, and when she calls she has already thought through her views and tried to second-guess the journalist's questions.

On a typical day she calls five or six journalists, talking to each for about five or ten minutes about the issue at the heart of the feature and giving her views on the matter. The journalists particularly like it when she gets passionate and agitated about her topic, and the issue of women in the workplace is particularly close to her heart.

Every week she works through Delia's short-list or checks the features lists herself for likely opportunities. She gets Delia to send a photograph of herself to each publication or programme, and sometimes sends free samples of the products to any journalists who are unsure of the features and benefits of the KoolWay technology.

Delia keeps a careful record of every mention and quote, and after three months Karen assesses her performance by evaluating the number of quotes, categorised by the importance of the publication or programme and the priority that she was given in the piece. She costs out the equivalent price of advertising to achieve the same exposure, and quickly realises that her half-day a week has been about twenty times more cost-effective than if she had paid for equivalent advertising and used the time on her other responsibilities. In terms of her time, the editorial coverage would have cost two or three full-page advertisements per week.

There is also a huge intangible value, which is that the profile of BettaProds and KoolWay has been raised to become a household name. Karen is also emerging as a media personality, with strong, outspoken views on a variety of topics. She is becoming ubiquitous in the trade press, and is being asked to speak at conferences and on panels.

At the beginning of November she decides to hold a Christmas party for press and clients, but uses an agency to organise it. In the New Year Karen plans to take some key journalists to Ireland to see the factory where the KoolWay products are made and to show them the R&D department. The scientists there have made some significant developments and a new type of KoolWay product is due to be launched, and Karen believes that taking a group of the right journalists at the right time will create advance interest in the latest technology. She thinks that she will probably use an agency to organise that trip, but is determined to have a personal hand in the invitation list, and will continue to devote half a day a week to proactively contacting journalists.

- **Comment**: Karen realises that press relations and the process of promoting the BettaProds range in the press are largely a matter of common sense and good relations with individual journalists. She understands that she has to have strong views on issues and topics, and by delivering those to the journalists she is highly likely to get some editorial coverage. Karen also acknowledges that managing press relations takes time and is almost a full time job for Delia, but Delia is cheaper than a professional in-house PR person or an outside agency. With supervision, and by using an agency for specific tasks, Karen and Delia can manage the press between them.

Case study 2: Product promotion to the computer press

An independent American research agency launches a report which declares that, according to their findings, children who use computer-based training (CBT) methods suffer in the long run. They may learn the material, but they have little idea how to relate what they know to the real world, and their learning is unhealthily confined to a rigid formula of concepts which they may be able to repeat but do not really understand.

Within a two-hour period at SoftMicro, six publications, the local radio station and a national television journalist are on the telephone, wanting an interview or comment on the report. Richard is caught completely off-guard, and asks one of the journalists to fax him over a copy of the report. He will give an interview and have a comment, he says, once he has read it.

He calls Joe Probe, and Joe and Sasha immediately go to the SoftMicro offices. It takes an hour before the report is actually in Richard's hands, and then he sits down with Jessica, Joe and Sasha and they read it through in detail. On the left side of a flip-chart Joe lists all the issues raised by the report and next to each puts the SoftMicro reaction, comment and statement. He also puts the predictable journalistic reaction to that comment, and the SoftMicro response to that. Richard also calls Professor Higgins and talks through the report and the SoftMicro reactions to each of its findings.

An hour later Richard is calling back all the journalists and some others who he thought should know his views, giving them the SoftMicro position on each of the issues raised by the American report. Sometimes he is in agreement and sometimes in complete contradiction; sometimes he gives a qualified remark. He also suggests that the report cannot really be compared with the situation in the UK, because here CBT is used in a more controlled environment than in the USA, where students are encouraged to work at their own pace at home in addition to their classroom work. Professor Higgins agrees that CBT can be harmful if not used properly, and suggests that in some schools it is used as a lazy way to teach children. But that is not the recommended way, and he continually states that CBT has to be used as a supplement to – not a replacement for – traditional teaching techniques.

The first radio reports are broadcast on a national news magazine programme early that evening, when the American report is announced and Richard's comments on it are quoted. All the next day's national newspapers carry a piece on the report, with Richard's views alongside photographs of himself and Professor Higgins. KiddieLearn 2 is mentioned many times as a valuable aid to learning when used in conjunction with properly trained teacher supervision.

Richard and Jessica are extremely pleased. A potential disaster for KiddieLearn – a report which criticises CBT technology – has been turned into a positive campaign for SoftMicro, and KiddieLearn 2 has been given some first-class publicity initiated by another party. The report has been turned into a good thing for Richard and SoftMicro.

- **Comment**: Richard and Jessica are seeing the benefits of taking control of their press relations. Joe Probe, the PR professional, has contributed some invaluable input from which Richard and Jessica have learned much.

Case study 3: Diary of a freelance journalist

It's been a tough couple of weeks, with plenty of work but all the deadlines seemed to come at once. I've also had to do some long case studies for a couple of PR companies, which involved detailed telephone conversations with the clients and their customers, and I've been commissioned to write a White Paper on domestic health and safety which is going to take six weeks or so, fitted around my other work.

I see that BettaProds has a new PR person. She rang me wanting to know my deadlines, which of course do not have a pattern as I am freelance, and the features I'm working on. I send her my latest features list and ask about the SupaProds range. I've been invited to the launch of that next week. They've already sent me a full range of the products, which is unusual. You usually have to go to the press event to get the freebies, but in this case it means I can test out the products before the conference. It also means that I might pass on the conference.

I am sent a report by e-mail from an American research agency which makes some fairly bold claims about CBT, and I call Richard Devine and SoftMicro for comment. He hasn't seen the report so I fax it over to him. He then calls me back and gives me his views. I also talk to Professor Higgins, and a headmaster that I know.

I then call the news editor of the national daily that I write for, and suggest it as a news story. He agrees, and we decide on a rate – £80 for 200 words. They'll probably run it on page 4 or 5. He also suggests that I talk to the editor of their educational supplement, and I call her and talk the story through. She wants a news feature for the next issue, and needs the copy for tomorrow. The rate is £200 for 800 words, but I'll be able to use the same research so both pieces should be fairly easy to write.

My post is rather getting out of control again. For the past three days I've been sorting through and pulling out important-looking envelopes and leaving the press releases and magazines for another day. I'll have to find time over the weekend to catch up.

I got a phone call from a young PR man that I met at a press conference two weeks ago. He introduced himself as 'Steven'. Now I like to hear from interesting young men, and we had quite a long and varied chat over lunch after the formal proceedings, but did he really expect me to remember him? 'Steven who?' I said, and then he gave his full name and company. 'Ah yes, now I remember.' My memory of a charming young man is replaced by a vision of an arrogant PR novice. And I have no idea which product he is promoting, or why he called this morning.

I also got some software to review without any indication of who it is from. Perhaps it is part of a teaser campaign. I can't be bothered to load it unless I believe that the time will be well spent. I'll put the disks to one side until I get some idea what it is and who it's from.

I've been working nine- and ten-hour days this week. If I get any more time-wasting calls from PR people today, I think I will start to get rude.

Saturday

I spent this morning sorting through my pile of four days' worth of press releases. I counted them – 240. Of that lot I held back 30 and the rest immediately went into the bin. Or rather, onto my pile of scrap paper because I hate to waste trees and I will use the back for notes and copies of print-outs. Of those 30 I saved, I can use five immediately as leads for spokespeople for features which are already under way. They've given me names for contacts, ideas to add to the features and a couple of other viewpoints which I hadn't considered. One had a very useful report which I will probably start one feature with. Statistics and facts and figures always make very good hooks and beginnings.

Of the remaining press releases I'll have another look on Monday, but I think several are possible leads for news stories. I'll call a couple of commissioning editors on Monday and talk through some news and feature ideas. The rest are information which I can use in features which I'm writing over the next six months. I'll just file the press releases, and then when I come to write the features I'll have several contacts to use right away. One of the press releases in particular is centred on someone's view over a topical issue, and that will be a good start to the feature.

I also need to come up with some novel feature ideas for a couple of new magazines which are launching in the New Year. I need to start talking to the commissioning editors soon, to try and get a piece in the launch issues. That's always a good place to get a by-line. The trouble is that the magazines are competing, and I expect the editors will want me to be exclusive. I'll have to guess which magazine I think will be most prestigious, and contact them first.

- **Comment**: You can see how many different tasks a freelance journalist has to tackle. The job is a balance of office management skills, intelligent reaction to information and proactive selling and promotion of themselves. You can also understand how journalists grow impatient with PR and marketing people who waste time, and why you should be straightforward and business-like. If you have a good newsworthy story the journalist will be interested, but if you haven't it's better not to bother.

CHAPTER NINE

Damage limitation

Introduction

You are unlikely to have to manage a full-scale crisis or implement a disaster management strategy, but you may have to limit the damage caused by adverse publicity or a misquote.

At worst, your product may turn out to be dangerous, or there may be an accident which is blamed on your product. You have no control over what is printed or said in the media and have to leave a lot to trust. Sometimes that trust is broken, either accidentally or intentionally. You need to know how to deal with the situation, and if you think you are facing that kind of scenario, you should perhaps consult a PR consultant specialising in crisis management.

Failure to respond quickly and efficiently to wrong assumptions or statements which are damaging can lead to an uncontrollable situation which then degenerates into an uncontrollable crisis. However, a complaint needs to be handled carefully to avoid alienating the journalists, with whom you will probably want to deal again in the future.

One thing is sure – if there is a crisis with your product you have to deal with it, either alone or with professional help. Complaining about bad media coverage is also a vital part of the process of getting good media coverage. If you try to ignore a problem, either in the coverage you have received or with the product in the market, or cover it up, it will only get worse. The trick is to try and turn a situation around to your positive advantage.

Never go to an interview with the intention of covering up. If you are invited to an interview and you feel that you are not going to be able to be honest, it is better to decline the interview even though you would accept under any other circumstances.

The key principles are the following:

- Don't attempt to cover up.
- Don't tell lies.
- Don't avoid difficulties – deal with them.
- Say little, smile a lot and grab those photo opportunities.

You may feel guilt, embarrassment, regret, pain or despair, but on no account should you let them show. It is also important to keep looking

169

good. Without appearing smug, complacement or that you think that you are untouchable, it is important to given an impression of confidence. Say as little as possible, and when you do, accentuate the positive.

If there is a crisis with your product, or something that you have said being misquoted, get expert help as quickly as possible. There are crisis management experts among the Appendix listing of PR agencies at the back of this book – pick up the phone and call one.

Product problems

If you are being questioned and criticised for difficulties with your product, you should admit the problem and accept the reality. The worst thing you can do is lie. Be straight, and show remorse.

You can limit the damage by offering to put the situation right as far as you can. You can be sorry, apologetic and emotional without admitting liability. 'It's an awful thing that has happened, but it's really not our fault' is the sort of comment that you can make.

You should be reassuring that you will do everything within your power to make sure that the situation does not happen again. And then, of course, make sure that it doesn't happen again.

Reasons why you might want to complain

Journalists almost invariably set out to produce a story which is accurate and fair. But it doesn't always turn out that way.

There are several possible reasons why you may be unhappy with the treatment given to your interview.

You may feel that your words have been distorted. However, it is unlikely to be exactly what you said. It is probably far better, far more succinct and accurate. You'll probably say to yourself, 'Did I say that?' with pleasant surprise. You probably used 'ums' and 'ers', jumped all over the place in your answer and repeated yourself. A waffly, verbose quote is not going to make good copy. It is the journalist's responsibility to edit and sub what you say – also known as paraphrasing. This does not mean that the journalist can put words into your mouth, but they do have a certain degree of freedom to make your quotes appeal to the reader by being readable and arresting. But if you believe that the presentation of your quotes is unflattering or negatively inaccurate, it can be corrected.

It may be that your product is criticised, in your view unfairly. The journalist is obliged to give you the right of reply under the voluntary

Code of Practice. This is not a legal obligation, but any respectable journalist will give you the chance to write a letter for publication. The journalist is often also given the chance to respond to your letter of complaint, and you are unlikely to have the right of reply to that comment.

At worst, the journalist may take the opportunity to blast and abuse you or your product, in some way. The journalist is in a position of power and if there is a personal vendetta then there may be some unfair and inaccurate reporting.

What to do

The strategy for dealing with trouble is:

- Evaluate and appreciate the situation.
- Define your objectives and achievable targets.
- Decide on your complaint procedure and who you will contact.
- Make contact and communicate your problem.
- Assess the results.
- Only escalate the complaint if absolutely necessary.
- Learn from the experience.
- Reassess your message, and rewrite if necessary.

If you feel that you have been genuinely and unfairly treated, and your product sales have suffered as a direct result of a journalist's personal feelings, you can ultimately report the matter to the Press Council.

However, it is wise to do nothing for the first 24 hours after the piece appears. It is very easy to make a kneejerk reaction to something which is actually only a minor error and does not really have any long-term ramifications. You need to be pragmatic, and realise that drawing attention to the problem can cause more publicity than just letting sleeping dogs lie. Sometimes it is better to take the view that the damage is done and it is best to move on.

If you feel that you have been seriously misquoted to the point where it is damaging, or the piece is factually wrong and the results are likely to seriously affect the sales of your product, your first call should be to the journalist. He or she is likely to react in one of two ways: either to agree that there has been a mistake (and they might blame the sub-editor or other external factors) and offer some way of putting the record straight, or they will deny it. If the journalist says that you did, in fact, say the words printed or broadcast, then you have to judge whether you need to take the matter further, and how much further you are prepared to go to get satisfaction. It may be that you decide that it was a minor mistake which will not have any real impact, and it is best left. By getting an apology printed, or having a letter to the editor published, you are possibly drawing attention to the mistake for people who have otherwise missed it – but on the other hand you are extending your publicity opportunity.

It is crucial to be absolutely accurate when you are making your complaint. You must be able to pinpoint exactly the facts that are wrong. It is usually better to overlook minor inaccuracies, although it is often worth just mentioning it to the journalist so that they know to be more careful next time.

At all times it is best to take a reasonable standpoint. Remember that you are dealing with someone that you don't want to upset, someone who could be very useful – or very damaging – in future. Consider very carefully before you escalate your complaint. Complaining takes time and energy which can probably be more usefully spent elsewhere.

If you are seriously unhappy with the response you receive from the journalist, your next contact should be with the editor, but be aware that you are going over the head of someone with whom you might want to deal again in the future. If the editor does not give you satisfaction you have the right to go to the producer or publisher, and ultimately you can go to court, but none of those actions is likely to bring you much positive publicity. A libel action can draw much adverse coverage which you would probably rather be without, so you need to decide in advance how far you want to take the matter.

It is not advisable to threaten to stop your advertising, or to actually pull your advertising. This will not prevent the journalist writing about you and, if the journalist is particularly perverse, may encourage them to continue to report negatively on your product. The object is to make a friend of the journalist, not an enemy.

Threatening to stop advertising

The threat to withhold or stop advertising can have varied results. You certainly risk alienating the editorial team, and it may or may not have any effect on editorial coverage.

Journalists on publications where there is little dependence on advertising for revenue, and/or where there is clear separation between advertising and editorial, will not care whether you stop advertising. In fact, many journalists actually relish a threat to pull the advertising because it is seen as an indicator of their independence.

However, on many titles the advertising is critical to the existence of the publication and journalists are aware that it is the advertising which pays their salaries. Editors are less likely to care about advertising but the advertising manager and the publisher will be upset by any prospect of a drop in revenue. To publishers, and to some weak editors, the threat of the removal of advertising spend will make them retract and apologise.

You need to assess the publication and its journalists before deciding what to do. Generally speaking, threatening to remove your advertising is a strategy which can misfire, and is not recommended.

Damage repair

An unhappy experience can cast a shadow over your future relations with the press, and it is important to deal with the situation, put it behind you and move on. You are going to have to continue to deal with the press, even with the journalist who caused you trouble.

You need to take a view on whether the relations between yourself and that journalist have reached such a low that nothing can be done to improve the situation. If so, get someone else to deal with that journalist on your behalf.

Otherwise, if your relationship with the journalist was previously good and you felt that you were on basically good terms, perhaps take the journalist out for lunch or for a drink to close a door on the matter. Try not to leave it unresolved, or continue with a hostile feeling.

Spin doctors

'Spin doctor' is a new term for a marketing executive or media relations manager, or a PR professional employed to put a positive on- and off-the-record angle on a story to journalists. They can be used before or after a product launch or interview, not just in times of crisis.

In reality, spin doctors are PR people skilful at being economical with the truth, and are used to give off-the-record information which the journalists are not expected to attribute but which helps their copy to be better informed and more fleshed out. They can expand and explain a message more broadly, sometimes by giving background or sensitive information which you may not want to be attributed to you. They can kill a negative story and create a good one, although sometimes they lay a false scent to make sure they send the press pack off in the wrong direction and, by the time they eventually come back, the story has gone cold. Consequently, journalists don't like them much.

If you call in a PR professional to help you out of a crisis situation, do not allow them to try and 'spin a cover-up'. If things have gone wrong, admit it. If you attempt a cover-up, you will be found out sooner or later: things will be far worse and your credibility shattered. The use of spin doctors, trying to put a positive gloss on a negative situation, can quickly fly out of control. You risk alienating the press, who can see through most attempts at spin doctoring.

Rights of reply

All journalists have an obligation to give a right of reply to someone who has been criticised, and this is usually done within the original piece. Your right of reply extends to responding after the piece has appeared, in several ways – such as a letter for publication, a disclaimer or correction, or an agreed statement.

You also have the right of silence. Although it can look bad and appear as an admission of guilt, you can always refuse to talk to the press or issue a statement without further comment. In some situations, this can be the best strategy.

Letter for publication

The most common way of dealing with mistakes is by writing a letter to the editor for publication. The journalist or editor may invite you to do so when you tell them about the inaccuracy of the piece, or you may write a letter instead of telephoning. Sometimes the publication will print your letter followed by a response or explanation, or an apology if that is appropriate.

The advantage of writing a letter for publication is that it is an opportunity to keep the story 'alive' for longer than the original coverage, and it gives you fresh mentions. Try to keep your letter short and to the point, otherwise it is likely to be cut and may possibly lose its effectiveness.

Disclaimers and corrections

If offence has been unintentionally caused because of a mistake or confusion – for example, if captions were transposed or the wrong names used in a feature – then the editor may offer to run a disclaimer which explains what has happened and apologises for any offence caused. A *disclaimer* is a printed statement explaining that the person/company named is not the person/company mentioned in a previously published story. It is used to mitigate unintentional offence caused through confusion of identity. A *correction* is used where the offence has been caused by a straightforward mistake of fact. This is usually a brief printed statement putting the matter right and perhaps including an apology.

The disclaimer or correction should be given adequate and comparable prominence appropriate to the damage which may have been caused, although you have no control over where the editor chooses to place the box containing the words.

Agreed statement

If the situation is extremely serious, perhaps because significant damage has been caused by an error, and if counsel has been consulted, the editor and lawyer may get together to agree the words of a statement. Sometimes part of this agreement is the prominence given to the correction and apology, and sometimes the location and prominence are left to the editor's discretion. If you are discussing an agreed statement, try and make sure that you get a size, site and prominence which you feel happy with.

Damages

If the mistake or misquote causes significant damage to your reputation or business, and you have grounds for a legal suit, the publishing house may want to settle out of court with a combination of an agreed statement or correction and a sum of money. If such an agreement is not forthcoming, or if the publisher or producer contests the claim or the amount, then you are free to let the action proceed to the courts.

Press Complaints Commission

In cases where there is a refusal to correct or make a satisfactory attempt to set the record straight, or there is alleged intrusion or bad taste, you can contact the Press Complaints Commission who will investigate.

The Commission is a self-regulatory body set up in 1991 to deal with complaints against the press as one of the recommendations of the Committee of Privacy and Related Matters chaired by Sir David Calcutt QC. One of its objectives is to make the press more culpable, although it has no real power.

Libel and litigation

Libel is when someone's reputation is damaged by something which appears in writing or print. Slander is when something defamatory is said or broadcast.

Libel is notoriously difficult to define, but the three best-known definitions are as follows:

- a statement concerning a person which exposes them to hatred, ridicule or contempt which cause them to be shunned or avoided or which has a tendency to injure them in their office, profession or trade
- a false statement about a person to their discredit
- a statement which tends to lower the plaintiff in the estimation of right-thinking peers.

The most common form of libel is when something is written which is true. Just because it is true does not mean that it is not libellous. The truth can be defamatory and can result in heavy damages. Another danger area lies in personal stories told by a third party. There is still a risk of libel action being upheld if the words are libellous, even though they are reported.

Institutions and companies cannot be libelled. All libel cases are made against individuals, which is why it is the editor of a magazine or the producer of a broadcast programme who will be deemed to be liable and will appear in court.

If you feel that your character or livelihood have been damaged because of statements made by a journalist, you can sue for libel. Most of these cases either fail or attract so much publicity that the action has a negative effect. The law is so vague that it is often based on past cases or made up as it goes along.

The editor might contest your claim and maintain that the statements or quotes were true and accurate, or say that the story 'was told in good faith and without malice and in the public interest'.

Threats of libel are common – in fact some journalists do not feel that they are doing a good job unless they attract a few libel threats a year. It means that they are upsetting people by printing things that they do not want printed, and this pleases some journalists. However, many publishers will step in when libel is threatened, to protect the title. It is, however, the editor who appears in the dock to represent the publication, if it ever comes to court regardless of who actually wrote the words, or whether they appear in the editorial or advertising pages.

Sometimes libel threats are settled out of court, especially if the publication's lawyers believe that there is a case to answer and they might lose.

If you are aware that something which is potentially damaging is going to appear, you can try to stop publication by serving a writ on the editor threatening legal action.

Chapter summary

- If there is trouble on the horizon, get professional help.
- Don't lie.
- Admit to any problems, apologise but don't admit liability.
- Express regret.
- Be reassuring that it will not happen again.
- If you are misquoted, consider whether it really matters before reacting.
- Write a letter for publication.
- Contact the journalist you spoke to, and be reasonable.
- Only go above the journalist's head to the editor if really necessary.
- Only go to the publisher if you really have to.
- Don't threaten to stop advertising – the journalists won't care.
- Put the incident behind you. Learn from it and move on.

CASE STUDIES

Case study 1: Product promotion to the lifestyle press

The first that Karen knows about a problem with the latest version of the KoolWay technology and the new KoolChild range is when a journalist calls and asks her to comment on the report that a child has been badly burned. She admits that she knows nothing about it, and asks the journalist their source. She is told that a child has suffered third-degree burns on both hands while it was using an insulated toddler plate in the KoolChild range, made of the KoolWay technology. The range has been in the shops for four weeks and Karen was feeling pleased that the trips to the Irish factory and reviews in the press had created considerable market demand, and the products were practically walking off the shelves.

Karen decides to get professional help, and contacts Flash PR, the agency which she has been using for logistical tasks and to help organise events. They are not under a retainer or contract, but are working on a job-by-job basis. The managing director, Gillian Flash, negotiates a fee based on an hourly rate for managing the crisis, and is in Karen's office within an hour.

Gillian finds out more about the incident, in which a toddler was apparently using a BettaProds suction-base junior plate, which is stuck to the table or high chair of the child and keeps hot food at a constant warm temperature for far longer than an ordinary plate. The range had been selling well, and Gillian warns Karen that they might have to issue a product recall notice, if it transpires that the plate was faulty. Gillian goes to the hospital where the child has been admitted, and sees the mother.

The mother explains that the food was perhaps a little too warm when it was put onto the plate, but says that the plate had warmed up instead of remaining cool, and the child had burned itself when it touched the plate. A journalist from a local newspaper and another from a consumer advice publication are also at the hospital, insisting on a comment from Karen. Karen says to them, 'It is a most unfortunate incident and we are extremely sorry that the child has been injured. However, it would seem that the mother did not use the plate according to instructions. We are going to take the plate away for examination and will then be issuing a statement.' The journalists continue to push for more explanation from Karen, but she and Gillian are firm about not making any further comment for the time being. 'I will talk to you again when we have examined the plate,' says Karen, 'but we do not have any comment to make at the moment other than to say how sorry we are that the child has been injured.'

Back at the labs, BettaProds' scientists have a close look at the plate and it is immediately apparent that it is a SupaProds plate. Their competitors have made a plate which looks similar enough to the BettaProds product to be confused with it. Gillian tells Karen to contact her solicitor immediately, and he issues an injunction and starts proceedings straight away against SupaProds.

Gillian writes a press release stating the situation and reassuring BettaProds' customers that the KoolWay products and the KoolChild range are safe. She arranges for a press event, and invites journalists to see a demonstration conducted by independent experts of the inferior SupaProds plate compared with a KoolChild plate.

Fifteen journalists turn up to the event, and the story features on the front pages of several publications, on the local radio news, and in several consumer radio programmes over the next few weeks. The SupaProds plate is withdrawn from the market, while the BettaProds plate and the KoolWay range have received widespread positive publicity. There are features which explain how the technology was developed, give other potential applications, and Karen sees sales rise rapidly. She also receives enquiries from other manufacturers wanting to license the KoolWay technology for their products.

Three months later Karen hears that SupaProds has gone into receivership.

- **Comment**: Rightly, Karen decides to call in an expert when things look tough. Without expert help, her negative situation could have turned out very badly for her and the company, but the PR agency is able to turn things around without alienating the journalists.

Case study 2: Product promotion to the computer press

After ten months of working on the SoftMicro account, Sasha has learned much and is back in control of the KiddieLearn 2 campaign. Joe is almost completely hands-off, and Sasha works closely with Jessica and Richard.

They have monthly meetings at which they review the results of the past few weeks and plan their future activity. Generally, Richard is pleased with Sasha and Probe PR but begins to feel that he would like to bring the PR work back in-house. It is partly a matter of cost, and partly because Jessica is keen to take it over again. Consequently, SoftMicro gives Probe PR two months' notice, and Jessica assumes the PR role again.

Jessica's plan for the next 12 months includes promoting Professor Higgins as well as Richard as educational software pundits and experts, and she works hard at keeping in touch with the key journalists to look for and create opportunities for the two men to be quoted. Often they are quoted commenting on issues which are not immediately associated with KiddieLearn 2, such as the role of supply teachers, educational standards and the issue of free versus fee-paying education. The Professor is particularly good at being able to deliver a snappy quote off the cuff, and consequently appears more than Richard, but they both have a rising media profile which Jessica is proud of. The product is mentioned occasionally but not every time, but nevertheless sales are rising fast.

Jessica decides to hold another event at a school so that journalists can see KiddieLearn 2 in use, but this time selects a school which is near to the journalists' offices. She arranges to meet them at a well-known location, and makes it clear on the invitation that journalists will be able to talk about many of the topics in the educational news today, such as falling teacher numbers, dropping school standards, university charges, and so forth. She invites 20 key journalists and this time gets 18 acceptances two days before, and 17 turn up on the day. Each has been sent a map of the venue, and is expecting to have some newsworthy copy as a result of the event.

Professor Higgins is at hand again, along with some independent educational experts and the Minister for Education. Although Jessica invited the Minister she had not really expected her to come, and she is particularly pleased that the Minister decided to find time to attend at the last minute. Regrettably there was not enough time to flag the Minister's attendance on the invitations, but still, the journalists who are there are able to get fairly long interviews, and the Minister makes some comments which are reported on several front pages next day.

This creates a debate in educational circles, and some other software vendors and CBT specialists join in. Some are critical of the KiddieLearn 2 approach, but Jessica is able to brief Richard to make some robust comments in defence of SoftMicro and the product.

Richard is also able to let it be known that KiddieLearn 3 is nearly at beta stage and will be ready for early review soon. Jessica is unconvinced that it is a good idea to announce KiddieLearn 3 until it is actually ready, and thinks that they should be careful about making the software available for review too soon. Richard disagrees, saying that the journalists know what to look for and that SoftMicro can point out what is still being finalised.

Richard arranges for six of the most important journalists to have an early beta version of KiddieLearn 3, but is then dismayed to see two reports criticising the software, even though he had made it clear that the development is unfinished. On his behalf, Jessica immediately writes letters for publication pointing out that the review copies were early beta versions but it is too late – the damage has been done and sales drop off.

It takes Jessica six months to recover the situation, by which time the fully finished version of the software is launched and she personally delivers a copy to the key journalists and explains the problems with the early beta version. She estimates that it will be a full 12 months before confidence is fully restored, but suspects that the damage to sales caused by the negative reviews cannot ever wholly be put right. Some people will always remember.

- **Comment**: Although the problem of the negative reviews of the beta version will never go away, Jessica has probably done as much as she can to restore confidence.

Case study 3: Diary of a freelance journalist

Tuesday morning
I had a bad day yesterday.

First an editor rang and wasn't happy with a feature I'd delivered three weeks ago. This happens so rarely – I think this is only the third time in five years of freelancing that I've had a commissioning editor come back and say it doesn't meet the brief. In this case it is plainly a matter of style. The magazine house style indicates that the sub prefers reported speech and first-person opinion rather than direct quotes, which I had admittedly packed the feature with. It is a title that I really want to work with in future, so I have to grovel and drop everything else and dig out the file and my notes and rework the copy. I takes me most of the morning to get it right and resend it electronically.

Then I get a call from an editor who ran a piece of mine in his last issue, saying that he'd had several telephone calls from readers claiming inaccuracy. This is far more serious. I say I'll turn out the original copy and he faxes me the page as it appeared, and I say I'll get back to him. I get on the phone to the person who gave me the original comments, and I find he's left his job. No one knows where he is – gone abroad with a nervous breakdown, someone says. Great.

I get back to the editor and explain the situation, which was that I quoted my source in good faith and had no reason to believe that he didn't know what he was talking about. It seems unlikely that there will be any writ for libel, but the magazine will have to print a correction in the next issue, which the editor is not pleased about, and I'm unlikely to get any work again from that source.

I also had two 1,300-word features to finish. Luckily I had started both last week so I was able to meet the deadlines.

Wednesday

An opinion piece to finish today, and a press release to write for an agency that I do some regular work for. They also want me to spend a few hours with one of their clients doing some media training. I explain that media training is a specialist thing, and I can do it but I need a full day with their client plus a half-day beforehand to prepare properly. The cost is £1,000 a day for groups of up to five people. I send over some references that they can telephone to get some comments from people I've trained in the past.

Thursday

If I do a long day today I'll try and take tomorrow afternoon off, to make a long weekend. Well, there have to be some benefits from being self-employed! I started at 8 and I'll probably finish at 6. That's a long time to be hunched over the computer.

I spend some time in the morning setting up some interviews for a new feature I've been commissioned to do, for the new lifestyle publication. I want to do some personality profile journalism, and spend some time considering who would make good subjects. I also call the features editor on the Sunday supplement that I sometimes write for, suggesting a series of profiles.

I finish at 6.30, having written around 3,000 words today. I'll have to spend some time tomorrow morning going over it all, subbing it and polishing the copy before I send it off.

- **Comment**: From this case study hopefully you have gained a clearer idea of the pressures and difficulties freelances face. It's not an easy life, which is why good PR and marketing is so important. Journalists like Suzie know that good PR can help them do their jobs more efficiently.

Chapter Ten

The role of professional PR agencies

Introduction

You should now have the confidence and ability to get mentioned editorially – all you need is some experience. This chapter talks about the people you should contact if you still feel unsure, or do not have the time to devote to the task. PR professionals do nothing else but work with journalists on behalf of clients to get positive editorial coverage.

Theirs is a strange role: you might pay them but they work with the press. For this reason PR people are not always liked by all parties because their loyalties are often divided and confused. Regrettably, the PR industry has traditionally attracted a certain dishonest, syco-phantic, empty-headed type which irritates journalists. But for every three or four like that there is one excellent PR professional. They are invaluable, and good journalists will work with PR people to help them get good stories. If, despite all the advice and hints and tips in the preceding chapters about how to work with journalists, you are still reluctant to make direct contact with the press, PR professionals are there to help you.

(Note: although PR, strictly speaking, stands for Public Relations, in this context it stands for Press Relations.)

How journalists regard PRs

The relationship between journalists and PRs is often fraught and full of antagonism. Many journalists dislike PRs intensely, but realise that they need them. At worst, journalists think PR people are crass, guilty of misrepresentation and generally irritating. But a good rela-tionship between a PR person and journalists is extremely valuable and productive, if it can be achieved.

The good PRs are those who know the two cardinal rules:

- Do not waste journalists' time.
- Do not tell them lies.

Unfortunately, because their client is paying them to enhance information, they are often guilty of hype or soft-selling. Sometimes it is not even 'soft' selling – some PRs are guilty of heavy-duty pressure and attempt to spread propaganda, which quickly creates resistance and antipathy among journalists.

The best PRs try to build good working relationships with journalists, entertaining them and only calling when they have something genuinely interesting. They know that the relationship is symbiotic and two-way.

What journalists hate most about PRs

A classic PR mistake is to be too familiar. Just because you have one meeting or conversation with a journalist, do not think that you are best buddies. Journalists are meeting lots of people all the time. They should not telephone and introduce themselves with just a first name – use a surname too. Journalists are not lifelong friends if you have only met once or twice. It is important to keep a professional distance between you.

PR people frequently think it is part of their job to make overblown exaggerations about the company, product or people they are representing. On the contrary, such grandiose claims can be counterproductive. Journalists have sensitive antennae which alert them when they are being told exaggerated or untrue things about a product, and then they switch off.

All PR people should know the press days and deadlines of various publications and freelances, but a surprising number ignore that information and still contact journalists on press day. Find out which days to avoid – and avoid them!

In-house versus agency

There are pros and cons to using an agency or doing your media relations yourself or using someone employed in-house.

An agency can offer far greater skills and expertise, but may lack the loyalty of an in-house person. Agency personnel are often young, full of bright ideas but lacking experience, although they can often draw on wider experience within the agency as a whole. However, you may be competing with other agency clients for your account manager's time. These may be better known and pay more, so guess who takes second place? However, you can fire an agency more easily than an in-house person. External costs are easier to quantify and monitor while in-house costs can easily get absorbed into other activities and budgets. On the other hand, an in-house person can enjoy greater trust and company knowledge than an agency person, who is always regarded as an outsider.

It's a partnership

A cynic will say that the relationship between PR agency and client is a straightforward business one. They have a service and you are buying. But for success you need to have more than that. It has to be a partnership in which both sides trust each other.

Sometimes the agency may tell you things you don't want to hear, but you have to respect their experience. For PR people to work successfully they need to have the confidence of the journalists, and that means delivering what the journalists want and not wasting their time. So if your PR person advises you not to hold a press conference, or not to send a press release every three days, they are acting in your best interests.

A good, professional PR person will have the ear of the key journalists, and that relationship is critical to them. They will not want to jeopardise it. Still, for the relationship between client and agency to work there has to be a high degree of trust, openness and mutual respect. If both sides understand each other and appreciate each other's goals, they will be able to work together in the long term.

Some clients believe that it is healthy to keep chopping and changing agencies, but it is probably only a good idea to change agencies – or at least get others in to pitch for your account – if you believe the incumbent is becoming stale or not giving you the attention you expect. It does happen that agencies become complacent, or have other, newer clients to which they give more time. On the other hand, by sticking with an agency you will develop the strong bonds and long-term understanding necessary to work together effectively on a press campaign.

One common complaint is that when an agency pitches for a client's business you get to meet the principals, but after that you never see them again and the account is managed by less experienced 'executives'. If this happens, do not stand for it. You are, after all, the customer. When the agency first pitches for the business, insist on meeting the staff who will be handling your account and make it clear that if there are staff changes you reserve the right to move to another agency.

Successful partnerships with PR agencies depend on personal relationships between the client and the account handlers, and on the
client having a clear and realistic idea of what is achievable. Recruit
the agency at an early stage of the product launch, not as a last-
minute afterthought.

A good PR strategy involves more than just getting as many mentions in the press as possible. There should also be references to business objectives. Remember that, ultimately, the press is not your
audience – it is the conduit to them. While the press is an extremely
influential factor in the marketing process, you should also engage in
some promotional activity to reach your customers directly.

What PR agencies offer

Despite accusations of being shallow, superficial and cosmetic, good
PR professionals perform an essential function in the relations between the press and members of the public. Many editors and journalists rely on good PRs for the smooth running of their publications.
Although PRs also have a function to cover up, distract attention and
neutralise criticism, they provide invaluable help in oiling the wheels
of the publicity machine, bringing products and people to journalists'
attention and achieving media mentions. They can also be blamed
when things go wrong!

PR professionals will help select the key titles and journalists that
you need to approach. There should be several lists, divided by a
grading of 'critical', 'important' and 'less important' or something
similar. The agency's primary objective is to help you win the hearts
and minds of the journalists, so that they think of you and your
product favourably.

They will plan your media campaign for you and monitor the
results. Measuring PR effectiveness is a thorny topic: some people
doubt whether it can be done in a tangible way, while others believe
that it can be done and that it is essential to do so.

They will also help you develop the messages that you want to
convey to the press to build a positive image and reputation. At its
worst, PR is a process of hype. PRs can select the right journalists for
one-to-one meetings or lunches, brief them to make sure they know
in advance what your product does and who you are, and fill them in
on any controversial issues to ensure that they ask the right questions
so that they can get a story out of the interview. They will sit in on
interviews to help you get your messages across and make sure the
journalist has a clear, accurate understanding of your product.

PR professionals can also help you develop your messages and anticipate any difficult or obvious questions that the journalists might ask. Even better, they will help you rehearse your replies to difficult questions.

They will be able to give you media training for your meetings with journalists, or will know someone who can.

They are there to help you if you are getting out of your depth. It is easier for the PR person to ask the journalist to stop an interview which is going wrong. This is not to be recommended, however, as it gives a bad impression to the journalist, but if it saves you from some negative publicity it will be worthwhile.

Part of an agency's job is to keep close tabs on the members of the press. All agencies keep detailed files on all journalists to track and monitor their work and careers. They know details of their private and family lives, as well as possessing analyses of their preferences, biases, attitudes and obsessions. They know whether a journalist is likely to be fair, independent, difficult or biased. So, if you are telephoned by a journalist you don't know, your first reaction could be to delay the journalist by five minutes ('I'm just going into a meeting, I'll call you right back') and then call your PR agency and ask them what they know about the journalist. They should be able to give you a quick snapshot of his or her to help you in the interview. Then call the journalist back.

PRs also spend a lot of time monitoring features lists and will alert you when a feature is being written which offers you the opportunity to be quoted. As well as obvious features covering your specialist area, you need to think laterally and have a view on topics which are not your core business.

They work closely with journalists and offer them a source of stories and information. Sometimes they seem closer to the journalists than they do to you, the client. Many journalists rely heavily on PRs to provide background information, ideas for features or contacts for quotes, and a good PR will have a close relationship with key members of the press.

They will take over the tiresome task of following up after events, making sure the journalist has everything they need. They can particularly come into their own in a crisis situation, or if you have to deal with any problems.

Selecting the right agency

The first step is probably to ask a friend or colleague who has used a PR agency for their recommendations. Alternatively, contact the

Public Relations Consultants Association, which has a computerised referral scheme called Preview that helps match people and their products with the right agency.

You should definitely ask journalists which agencies they like to deal with. If you are thinking of hiring an agency or an individual, call a journalist and ask their comments on your candidate: they usually like to be asked because they would rather be working with PR people they like and respect, and so rarely mind anyone asking their advice about who is good and who should be avoided.

Short-list those agencies which (a) have a high percentage of ex-journalists on their staff and (b) are highly regarded by the journalists you want to target.

Asking the agencies to pitch

To select the right agencies, arrange for two or three to pitch to you, demonstrating what they can do. This is a two-stage process. First, you have to brief them with what you want and how much you want to pay. You have to tell them your expectations and experiences and must be frank about any problems.

When they return with the pitch presentation, you can expect them to tell you what they will do, on what time-scale and for how much. If you ask more than four or five agencies to pitch, you cannot expect them all to give you their full attention. It can be counter-productive to ask too many to pitch. Just ask two or three, and make it clear to them that it is a competitive situation, but not an unrealistic one.

Look for an agency which indicates that it intends to learn your business. Also, look for one which promises continuity of account handlers. It is better to choose based on the individual account handlers, not the overall agency. Pick one with a track record for getting good publicity, and talk to their past and present clients.

Agencies which have former journalists on the staff are almost always the best.

Many agencies charge to pitch. This growing trend is realistic and avoids time-wasting. If the agency is going to invest the necessary amount of time in the briefing, preparation and presentation, and make the process worthwhile, it is fair to expect to pay them. At worst, some people take the agency's ideas without using the agency. Usually, the pitch fee is deducted from the first bill.

Getting the most out of your PR agency

Here are a few golden rules to help achieve a happy marriage between you, the client, and your PR agency. The first step is to be clear about your motives for hiring the agency in the first place. You also need to be clear that what you are buying is their time, expertise and access to resources which you would not otherwise have.

Then, once you have appointed an agency:

- Spend time fully briefing your new agency.
- Agree measurable objectives.
- Agree a time-scale.
- Agree points of contact.
- Have regular reviews, at least quarterly.
- If it is agreed that changes are necessary, make sure they happen.
- And finally, respect your agency's views and accept its advice. You have chosen them because they are the experts at communicating your message to the press – if they advise you not to have a press conference, listen to them.

The biggest single reason for a breakdown of relationship between agency and client is false and unrealistic expectations. Sometimes agencies create false expectations in their pitch. False expectations can be avoided by careful briefings, discussions and the setting of agreed objectives.

To work with an agency long term, you need to:

- believe in your product or service
- motivate the PR team
- give feedback
- recognise good work
- monitor the workload and expectations
- measure performance according to mutually agreed milestones
- recognise the ultimate impotence of PR people to control journalists.

Monitoring your agency

Evaluation of agency performance is always a thorny issue. Many PR clients ask, 'What do they *do* all day?' but, as any PR person will confirm, there are many other tasks to be done as well as dealing directly with the press.

They have to monitor the press and create opportunities for you. Keeping track of the individual journalists and all the publications and programmes is a full-time job, as well as monitoring the forward features lists and proactively seeking media opportunities for you. And then there is all the backroom account management work, such as planning a media campaign, thinking up ideas for stories and writing press releases and case studies.

Make sure the agency is well co-ordinated internally. Larger agencies especially can become very disorganised, and journalists sometimes have to endure several calls each day from different people within the same agency. Make sure there is a smooth system for contacting the press – and that it works. Again, check with the journalists that your agency is performing well. For the relationship to work you need to be happy that you are getting value for money and there needs to be some measure of the objectives, so that the agency is accountable for its activities. Sometimes simple column inches of media coverage, and frequency of mentions, can be counted. Often a PR agency's work is more subtle, and much effort can go into background PR activity which may not have an immediate or measurable effect. You need to agree some quantifiable targets with the agency at the outset, but exactly what these are varies according to your product and your media requirements. You can only measure the effectiveness of a media campaign when you have an appraisal, strategy and plan to start from, against which measurement can be made.

Regular reviews and appraisals are essential for an effective long-term relationship. Review questions can include:

- Does the agency reach the right audience?
- Are you improving your performance against your competitors as a result of the PR (and are your competitors being properly tracked)?
- Have your strengths and weaknesses changed since using the agency (i.e. fewer weaknesses)?
- Does the PR investment deliver value for money?

Remember, monitoring and measuring the agency's performance is only the first stage – then you need to act upon your observations and effect improvements and changes as necessary.

Measuring PR effectiveness

It is extremely difficult to measure the effectiveness of your PR agency, but you need to have some kind of yardstick. There is a saying that if you can't measure it, you can't manage it, which certainly applies to PR agencies. Without some kind of measure you can easily begin to feel dissatisfied with their performance.

PR Week recommends that 10 per cent of every PR budget should be spent on research, pre-planning and evaluation of the campaign. Its 'best practice guidelines' suggest that better planning and evaluation are crucial to successful media relations and product promotion. Campaigns should be planned and measured against business objectives as well as media impact.

The techniques to measure PR effectiveness are focus groups, opinion polls, customer surveys, media analysis and customer feedback.

Ultimately, PR is essentially uncontrollable because the journalists are uncontrollable. Press activity can be extremely random and it is hard to make it accountable and numeric. And the interpretation of the results of press coverage may not be in the form of orders. There are three basic options:

- *column inches*, a crude but reassuring and visible yardstick
- *weighted measurement*, in which column inches are measured against the cost of getting the coverage, taking into account various factors like how many people read the publication and whether they are the target audience
- *all-in*, in which some measurement of intangibles and long-term press benefits to a favourable view and mention of the product, are taken into account.

The criteria for measurement need to be agreed, but you can suggest to the agency that they define their own, and without some kind of measurement you will not engage their services. If you can't agree a timetable and targets, you should ask yourself whether it is better not to use the agency.

It is easy to say that editorial coverage gives good value for money, but to ensure that that statement makes sense you need to have a way of evaluating column inches. Not every encounter with a journalist or every interview will lead directly to press coverage, so you need some way to evaluate those encounters too. Sometimes a press campaign will lead only to a raised awareness of your product and not to immediate sales. These are known as 'soft benefits' or 'intangibles' and are crucial to raising brand awareness – but are extremely hard to measure and evaluate.

In evaluating your media coverage, you need to agree a methodology which is fair and fits with your objectives. Some companies are looking for the greatest number of column inches while others are equally concerned about raising the profile of the brand among journalists, without direct and overt media coverage in the short term.

There is no single correct approach, but the vital requirement is that all media appraisal is undertaken in a continuous, consistent and objective way.

Media mentions can be coded for evaluation purposes, according to the following criteria:

- the size and impact of the headline
- the overall size of the story and the power of the hook
- the position in the paper, programme or schedule
- the strength of the content and the editorial focus, compared with stories surrounding it
- the prominence of the story.

You need to determine the value of every mention according to how much a comparable advertisement would cost. This needs to be set against the cost of obtaining the mention, using this formula:

$$\frac{\text{The total value of the mentions in terms of the cost of comparable advertising}}{\text{The total value of sales generated by the publicity activity}}$$

This figure needs to be set against and compared with the outcome of this formula:

$$\frac{\text{The total value of sales generated by the publicity activity}}{\text{The total cost of the activity}}$$

However, this approach, known as 'return on investment', does not take into account the intangible benefits of effective press relations.

Some believe that the only way to continuously track the market's perception of you, and how much of that is down to your media activity, is to undertake continuous market research. This is expensive and usually impractical.

Most PR agencies offer a media evaluation service, which is usually based on quantitative and qualitative elements. The first element counts the number of mentions, the column inches and the number of publications and programmes, while the second attempts to evaluate the tone of the comment, the degree of understanding of the press and reader or listener, the context of the mention and whether it was mentioned alone or with competing products. Some mentions are trivial and primitive, while others may be brief but extremely valuable because of their timing or placing.

You have to remind yourself that you have no control over what the journalist does with the information you give them. Your responsibilities end when you have delivered the message in the most effective way you can, and you cannot influence how the message is delivered to the potential customers. The journalist may or may not use the photographs you supply, or they may get the caption wrong, or transpose the caption with another. You cannot control the page on which the story appears, or whatever else is on the page.

You should compare your mentions and all press exposure with the original messages you were trying to put across and your original objectives. Don't forget to track your competitors' media efforts, attempting to learn how much time and money they are spending on working with journalists, how much exposure they are getting as a result and the tone of it.

Use software programs to track and report on the media coverage, correlating that with sales leads and actual sales, and to compare with competitors' activities.

Chapter summary

- Journalists don't love PR people, but know they have to live with them.
- The best PRs are often ex-journalists.
- However, few journalists would be seen dead taking on a PR role.
- The worst PR people are sycophantic, creepy, over-familiar and incompetent.
- The best PR people are business-like, know not to waste a journalist's time, and know what the journalist needs.
- The best PR people value their relationship with the media more highly than their relationship with the client.
- When selecting a PR person, check with a journalist whether the candidate is well regarded.
- Agency people are easier to fire.
- You have to tell your PR what you want, and push them until they deliver.
- Listen to your PR – they know the media better than you do.
- A good PR person will be respected by the leading journalist.
- Agree your expectations at the outset, and monitor the relationship regularly.

CASE STUDIES

Case study 1: Product promotion to the lifestyle press

BettaProds is doing so well that Karen decides that she should take the company to the stock market. Although she may lose some control and be answerable to shareholders, a flotation would raise enough capital to expand their R&D department and work on development of new innovations in the KoolWay technology.

Quietly, she prepares the company for flotation. Unfortunately she inadvisedly discusses her plans with Jane Marples, who by now has become a personal friend. Two days later, her scheme is in the financial press and she is besieged by journalists. More worryingly, she is approached by two large companies who want to buy BettaProds. Moreover, the staff, who feel that she should have discussed her plans with them before talking to the press, are extremely aggrieved.

Karen realises she's made a big mistake. She is tempted to call Jane and let her know her feelings, but does not want to alienate a journalist working for key titles. Anyway, Karen recognises that it was her fault for talking to Jane in the first place. She cannot remember whether there was an agreement for the conversation to be off the record, but anyway it's too late now. She just makes a mental note to avoid seeing Jane in an informal setting again.

She calls a staff meeting and honestly tells them of her mistake, and brings them up to date on the situation. She is more worried by the attempts to buy out her company, and calls in her accountant and solicitor to help deal with the situation.

Karen falls back on her routine of dealing with the press for half a day a week, and gradually talks to all the key journalists about what is going on at BettaProds. She learns to keep quiet about things which are sensitive. Her rule becomes: if she doesn't want to see it reported, she doesn't say it. She spends more time commenting on wider topical issues, and her confidence with the press is rebuilt. She is more cautious, but has a better understanding of the boundaries.

- **Comment**: BettaProds' continued success is almost certainly due largely to the marketing and press relations. However, Karen has made the mistake of believing that a journalist can ever be off duty. Although Jane Marples probably regrets breaking the confidence, it is likely that she felt that it was her responsibility to broadcast the news. Journalists' primary obligation is to their audience.

Case study 2: Product promotion to the computer press

Jessica has spent much time promoting Professor Higgins and Richard to the press, but one day a journalist calls and asks *her* to comment on the launch of a new product which, according to the claims of the developers, is the same as or better than KiddieLearn.

Jessica is surprised that they want her to comment and not the Professor or Richard, and is rightly cautious, saying, 'If I can see a copy of the product I'd be able to comment.' She is sent a version, loads it and realises that it is a poor imitation of KiddieLearn but makes the same claims. As far as she can see, there is little comparison. She calls Richard and Professor Higgins to tell them, then initiates a full-scale press campaign to distance SoftMicro from the imitation, which is made by a small English software house called RightBadly.

Richard consults a lawyer who says that there is no copyright infringement and, although the product is similar, no law has been broken. Jessica writes a press release damning the competing product, pointing out its failings and faults and suggesting that the competitor is attempting to steal business from SoftMicro by imitating its products. She also says that it would seem that RightBadly has taken some code from the SoftMicro product, because there are similarities which RightBadly could not possibly have developed in their own development labs. She sends the press release out, and next day it is reported in the trade and educational press. 'SoftMicro accuses RightBadly of theft' screams the headline.

The day after, Richard receives a writ from RightBadly's solicitors suing them for libel. They also send writs to the publications who have printed the story, accusing them of libel.

Richard calls Joe Probe at Probe PR and asks him to take over the matter immediately. Joe is initially annoyed with Jessica for creating the situation, but then, after consulting with SoftMicro's solicitor, immediately draws up a press release of apology and encourages Richard to apologise through the press. 'It was an unfortunate clerical mix-up,' he says. 'We do not think that RightBadly has behaved illegally, although we are unhappy that it is making claims that its product is similar to ours when there is clearly no comparison.' The RightBadly solicitors are reluctant to let the matter pass, and push the publications to print retractions and a statement and apology from Richard and the respective editors.

Joe encourages the editors in question, plus others involved in the educational and computing press, to run comparisons of the two products so that readers can judge for themselves. This idea is quickly seized upon, and three publications do so. The outcome and verdicts are predictable – the SoftMicro product is demonstrably better. 'The problem was the accusation that they had imitated our code,' says Richard. 'If we had just maintained a dignified distance and said that it was inferior we would have been all right.' Joe agrees, but adds that the results of the head-to-head test are fairly convincing.

Six months later RightBadly drops its educational range, sales of which barely picked up at all after the results of the comparative tests were published. They were dropped by their distributors, and SoftMicro was clearly seen as the market leader.

- **Comment**: Again, you can see what can go wrong when someone misjudges the press, or does not understand their primary responsibility. Jessica has learned the hard way. Joe has again rescued the situation, and SoftMicro has emerged from the incident looking good.

Case study 3: Diary of a freelance journalist

I've been invited on a six-day trip to America by a software company, and it is very tempting to accept. Starting in New York and then spending some time in California, it will be all expenses paid and all the best hotels, and I should learn some interesting facts about the company and its products. But the question is, will I get a week's worth of features out of it? I'm self-employed so I can't afford to go unless I can be sure that I'm going to get some good stories. But then again, I was thinking that I haven't had a holiday this year, and I could regard it as time off. If I get a story, all well and good, but it's not a disaster if I don't. It would also mean that I can relax on the trip and not be too obsessed with working. I've found that a more relaxed approach can often lead to the best stories. Some of my colleagues routinely spend most of the time they are on trips in the bar, and they can get better stories than the rest of us who religiously attend every seminar and talk to every executive that's sat in front of us.

Two months later
I went on the trip, and had a great time. I treated it like a working holiday, and actually stayed on after the six days and saw some friends in California, and the PR kindly arranged to change my return flight. I went to some seminars but not all, and only used my notepad occasionally. But I met a lot of interesting people and got

involved with some fascinating conversations about the way the software industry is evolving, the way products are developing and whether they actually deliver what people need.

When I got back I was able to write three features almost immediately for the various magazines that I write for regularly.

I've also been invited by a TV programme to appear on a panel to discuss the Year 2000 problem, giving an independent view on the way the industry is coping and whether the government is doing enough. I'm looking forward to that very much. The researcher I spoke to said they are particularly keen to find female pundits to talk about the topic, and there is a good chance that I will get similar work in future.

- **Comment**: The marketing manager of the firm which took Suzie to America is probably regarding the expense as wasted, but she had a good time and will remember the company positively. She got a lot out of it and there will probably be long-term benefits to the company which sponsored the trip. You have to be pragmatic when dealing with the press.

Appendix 1

Myths and facts

Press releases don't work.
Yes, they do. It's true that journalists get hundreds each week (sometimes hundreds every day) but they are an essential way to get your message across. Many get 'filed' immediately in the waste-bin, but many others lead to ideas for features, directly to stories or provide background research. Just make sure every press release has a credible story.

Journalists get their best stories by following their hunches. Pushing your product does not produce stories.
No. Most of their best stories come from leads given by people like you. Sometimes you don't mean to – often the best leads are given accidentally. Pushing your product might lead directly to a story, or to a story which you didn't realise was there.

I should ring up and ask whether the press release has arrived/ whether it is going to be used/when it is going to be used.
Only call to ask those questions if you are a masochist who likes people being abusive on the phone. All those questions are definitely OUT.

I should check with every journalist whether they want to receive press releases or not.
No, just send them if you think the journalist is working in your target market area.

If I put 'Embargo' at the top of the press release, the journalist will think it is something special.
No, the journalist will evaluate it in the same way as they look at all press releases – in about 10 seconds. And they will not necessarily respect an embargo if they really want to use the story.

I should send a photograph with every press release.
Only if you want to waste your budget. Send photographs only to those who might use them, such as staff writers and editors.

Freelances are unlikely to use photographs. They can always ask for them if they want one. But some magazines choose their top stories according to which has the best picture, so make sure the publications get the pix.

I don't understand the technology, but I'm sure the journalist will.
No. If you can't understand it, don't send it. Don't assume the journalist has highly technical knowledge – chances are they don't, even if they are working on a technical publication.

I can make my press release eight pages long. That will make fascinating reading.
No. Only the headline and first paragraph are crucial, the rest is for quotes and brief background information. Keep a two-page limit to your press releases. If the journalist is interested they will call you for more information. Putting it on the press release will not encourage the journalist to use the story.

If I send my press release by fax it will catch the journalist's eye.
Only if that is the way the journalist has requested to receive press releases. Otherwise, faxed press releases cost the journalist money to receive and are a nuisance.

In these days of high technology, I can send my press release by e-mail.
Only if that is the way the journalist has requested to receive press releases. Otherwise, they may not read their e-mail regularly, and it costs them to download it. The advantage of e-mailed press releases is that they can be stored electronically and searched on keywords, but not many journalists like doing it.

I have a great idea. I'll send the journalist three or four teaser press releases before the real one, so that they know it's coming.
No, you will only irritate the journalist. If you've got a story – tell them. Don't try to tease.

I must follow up every day.
No, but you should follow up regularly. Follow up after a press release is sent, to check whether the journalist has all the information they need. Follow up a week or so later to see if there is anything more they want. Don't keep pursuing a story which the journalist is obviously not interested in.

If I ask the journalist when a piece is going to appear and which page it will be on, I can place my advertisement next to it.
No. First, the journalist is extremely unlikely to know exactly when and where the piece will appear, and second they will probably not want to tell you even if they do know. Journalists like to keep advertising and editorial apart, for fear of the publication looking too advertising-led.

If you mention to the journalist how much you are spending on advertising, it affects the amount of space they give your product mention and the quality of the report.
No, at least on any publication or programme which is respected. If they do, you should ask yourself, 'Do I really want to advertise here?' Many journalists react extremely negatively to any suggestion that they might write differently if there is a worthwhile advertising budget.

If you send a bunch of flowers or bottle of champagne with the press release, the journalist will use the story.
No. They will probably welcome the gift, but if the journalist is any good, it won't make a jot of difference to whether the story is used, or to the degree of prominence it is given.

If I tell the journalist something confidential which might get me in a lot of trouble, they will protect me and not reveal me as the source of their information.
You can't rely on it, in the same way that talking off the record is a matter of trust and a verbal agreement between you and the journalist without any legal support. It is a fundamental principle of journalism that journalists should be able to protect their sources, and not be forced to divulge them, and they will usually do so even when faced with prison or fines. Unfortunately, some judges have decided that it is in the public interest that a journalist's protection of the identity of their sources is less important than the right of companies to discipline its staff for speaking out to the press. Despite a landmark ruling in the European Court of Human Rights in 1996, UK courts are still deciding that the vital watchdog role of the press can and should be undermined by forcing the journalists to reveal their sources. So a journalist may be forced to reveal their sources, even if they don't want to.

If I tell the journalist about my fascinating new product, they will be enthralled.
Unlikely, but possible. It is more likely that you will have to spell out the benefits and implications, so the journalist can see clearly the story and its relevance to their readers.

If I don't give the journalist some of the sales information, they won't understand what my product can do.
Give the journalist the information, but cut out the sales talk. You are not selling to the journalist and they can detect when you are moving into hype. Keep it businesslike and straight. Many journalists find marketing speak highly offensive.

But my product *is* the best/largest/cheapest/first.
Only make those claims if you can back them up with independent research and analysis. If you have such data and statistics, use them.

If I send my press release to as many journalists as I can find, surely I stand a better chance of some of them using it.
If you want to waste your budget then send everything to everyone, including photographs and sample products. If you want a campaign which gives good return on investment, target your mailing and make sure that you only send photos to those who might use them.

I don't need to read every single magazine – if I just contact the journalist they can judge whether the story is suitable.
If you want to impress a journalist, be intimately familiar with their publication – every section, every type of story and all their deadlines. If you want to irritate and give a poor impression, just ring up convinced that your story is suitable, even though you have no awareness of the contents and audience.

While I'm talking to the journalist I can ask whether there is anything else they are working on that I can help them with.
Yes. Chances are, there is.

The magazine has just come out and, despite taking the journalist out for lunch, I'm not mentioned. I think I'll complain, and perhaps even stop my advertising.
It's not necessarily the journalist's fault. They submit the copy to the editor who passes it to the sub-editor, and either may have removed that section of the piece. So perhaps the journalist did not use your quotes – perhaps they were not interesting or controversial enough. Or perhaps the journalist did, but the mention was removed at another stage. It may be that the space for the feature was reduced, so something had to be cut.

By all means call the journalist and ask why, but only to learn from the experience, not to complain. And pulling your advertising? No, it will not change the situation and you will be cutting off your nose to spite your face. And it will not change the journalist's actions the next time. Anyway, you can't expect to be quoted every time.

Freelances keep changing job. They are not as important as staff writers.
No. Freelances are *more* important. They write for more titles, they are more experienced and they are more likely to be career professionals. A relationship with a freelance should be viewed as a long-term one. Make sure they are well briefed and kept updated on your product.

Journalists are mainly stuck at their word processors. They don't get out much. They don't meet many people.
Some do, some don't. But you can be sure they are talking to your competitors and probably have a wide grasp of the market. If you have a story to tell, take the journalist out for lunch and talk to them about your competitors.

Freelances have plenty of time to come to lunch and go on long trips.
No. For freelances, time is money. While they probably appreciate hospitality as much as or more than staffers, they have to justify time spent away from the word processor far more acutely than staffers.

Freelances aren't going to need White Papers or case studies.
They may not use them verbatim, but the chances are they will find them invaluable for background information. If you have any such material, send it to the freelance.

All journalists are different.
Yes. Different in the way they work, their deadlines, subject-matter, preferred angles, audiences and specialisations. Create a database detailing each one's preferences, including how they prefer to receive information. Note all kinds of snippets about their family, hobbies, likes and dislikes. You never know when it will be useful.

An agency has several people working on my account, and they can all have relationships with the key media.
No. Only one person should deal with each journalist. It is irritating for a journalist to be rung several times in a day by different people within an agency, with no one knowing what the others are doing.

Journalists only ring up a few people for quotes. They have their favourite contacts, and nothing can change that.
Yes, journalists do have contacts they know they can rely on to say something quotable, but you should be aiming to join that group. Be

outspoken, opinionated, able to take a broad overview, and able to back up any claims with facts.

I was so pleased with the piece the journalist wrote that I think I'll telephone and thank them.
No. If you do that, the journalist will start wondering whether they did a critical enough job. The journalist is not there to please you but to satisfy their readers, viewers or listeners. Thanking them is not good form. You could compliment them on the piece in a general way ('That was a damned fine piece you wrote . . .') but do not thank them directly for the publicity they gave you.

I love gossiping with journalists. They really know everything that is happening.
Yes, most journalists like to gossip, but it is dangerous practice. They are not obliged not to quote you, however informal the situation might be.

Surely the journalist is off duty some time?
As far as you are concerned, *no*. Always regard a journalist as working, unless they are truly personal friends.

A journalist needs me as much as I need them.
Yes. They rely on people like you for their stories and, provided you have a story, they will be pleased to hear from you or meet you. They are not relying on you for your advertising, though. That is a separate department. They are relying on you for comments and information.

I sent the journalist a sample of the product. They haven't reviewed it or mentioned it so I think I will ask for it back.
No. The best thing can be if the journalist is using your product on a regular basis. You gave it to them – leave it with them. Asking for it back looks cheap and tacky. And if they were going to mention it, they won't after you've asked for it back.

The journalist hasn't mentioned the product I sent them – should I call and ask them why?
No. You could perhaps call to make sure it's working properly and they have all they need, but don't hassle them about when any mention might appear. If it does, it does – if it doesn't, it doesn't. Your asking won't make any difference.

Editors want to be wined and dined.
Probably, but only if you are good company and don't expect anything in return. Otherwise, it is a waste of time. Remember that

editors are not necessarily the ones who will be writing about your product, anyway. It may be better to spend your hospitality budget on the poor journalists who are badly paid. Just don't expect anything back and you might get it.

My company has a new version of my product and we are very proud of it. If I hold a press conference, the media will report it.
If you simply hold a press conference to announce a new version it is unlikely many – if any – will turn up. Those who do are unlikely to write about it unless it has radical implications for their readers, viewers and listeners. Don't bother. Think of another less stressful, more effective way of getting the news of your product upgrade to the media, and make sure you have a strong angle already thought through.

To get a journalist's attention I have to be outrageous.
You have to have a good story and some interesting views and opinions. Create a lot of noise or use novelty marketing techniques and you are more likely to irritate.

Publicity is a matter of luck.
A bit, but more important are experience and timing. There are so many things that you have to get right and so many ways that you can get it wrong, that some luck does have to come into it. You have no control over what the journalist will report, and no control over what else might happen to affect the story, but you can do a lot to give yourself a good chance of getting some good publicity.

The press is out to get everyone.
Up to a point. Some are on a witch-hunt, and some enjoy giving bad publicity to those who have irritated them. But mainly they are looking for good stories for their audience, and that means being critical and independent. If that means not giving you an easy ride, your comment is true. But rarely is that their primary objective.

Appendix 2

Sources of further information

Media directories and media analysis

Advance Themetree. Forthcoming features list. 0171 287 3008

Benn's media directory. Lists all newspapers and magazines in the UK. 01732 362666

Blue Book of Broadcasting. Gives details of UK radio and TV stations. 0171 490 1442

Brad. Media contacts for journalists. 0171 505 8273

Contact. Directory for journalists and PR people. 0282 841 3970

Contact. The Press and Public Relations Handbook. Listing of agencies. 0171 413 4086

Crystal Plan. Media database of journalists and publications. 01332 824781

Editors. Listing of newspapers and magazines and the journalists who work for them, with forthcoming features. 0171 251 9000

First pages. Source of information for journalists. 01275 333455

FeaturesExec. Electronic features lists. 0171 978 6296

Hollis. Press and PR Annual listing of news controls and information sources for journalists. 0181 977 7711

Impacon. Media analysis. 0181 579 0911

Impact. Media analysis and evaluation. 0171 353 2320

Institute of Public Relations. 0171 253 5151

M2 Presswire. Web-based press release distribution service. 01203 634700; Web: www.presswire.net; e-mail: info@presswire.net

The Media Boffin Agency. Contact agency for expert speakers and independent specialists with views. 0700 780978

MediaSpec. List of journalists. 01344 291910

National Union of Journalists. Journalists' trade union. 0171 278 7916

PIMS. Press release distribution service. 0171 354 7058

Pims UK Media Directory. List of newspapers and magazines. 0171 226 1000

PRnet. Electronic information and press releases for journalists. 01604 672004 or 0171 553 6830

PR Planner. Names of editors and journalists, with up-and-coming features. 0181 882 0155

Public Relations Consultants Association (PRCA). Professional association. 0171 223 6026

Two-Ten Communications, London. Media directories and listings of publications and journalists. 0171 490 8111

Willings Press Guide. List of magazines and newspapers. 01342 326972

Writers & Artists Yearbook. A&C Black, London. 0171 242 0946

Press cuttings services

CIS Information Services: 0171 583 7167
CXT: 0171 378 8139
Durrants Press Service: 0171 588 3671
International Press Cuttings Bureau: 0171 708 2113
PIMS: 0171 226 1000
Portfolio Metrica: 0171 240 6959
Romeike & Curtice: 0181 882 0155

Books on writing and journalism

The Elements of Style. William Strunk and E.B. White: Allyn & Bacon, USA, 1979.

Waterhouse on Newspaper Style. Keith Waterhouse: Viking, London, 1989.

English our English (and how to sing it). Keith Waterhouse: Viking, London, 1991.

Useful reference

Fowlers Modern English Usage, edited by R.W. Burchfield: Oxford University Press. ISBN 0–19–869126–2.

Rogets Thesaurus, Longman or Penguin. New edition prepared by Betty Kirkpatrick MA. ISBN 0–582–89363–1.

The Writers Handbook, Macmillan, published annually.

UK Marketing Source Book. Directory with marketing and business information sources and including UK government organisations, Chambers of Commerce, libraries, online database hosts and consumer organisations. NCT Publications, PO Box 69, Henley on Thames, Oxon RG9 1GB. 01491 411000

Writers & Artists Yearbook, A&C Black, London. ISBN 0–7136–4721–3.

Books on media relations

Hitting the Headlines. Stephen White, Peter Evans, Chris Mihill and Maryon Tyson: The British Psychological Society, Leicester.
How to Handle Media Interviews. Andrew Boyd: Mercury.
Making the Most of the Media. Michael Barratt: Kogan Page, London, 1996.
Media Interview Techniques. Peter Tidman and H. Lloyd Slater: McGraw-Hill.
Surviving the Media Jungle. Diana Ross: Pitman.
Your Message & the Media. Linda Fairbrother: Nicholas Brealey Publishing.

Periodicals

Press Gazette (weekly).
PR Planner (regularly updated directory).
PR Week (weekly).
Willings Press Guide.

Other useful numbers

Institute of Trade Mark Agents: 0181 686 2052

APPENDIX 3

Writing and delivering press releases

Introduction

The importance of effective press releases can never be underestimated, and this appendix shows you how to create one. Press releases are the primary method of informing a journalist about your product or alerting them to the fact that you have some important views which you wish to air. They are a message to the journalist, calling 'Over here, I've got something to say.' Most are thrown in the bin, but nevertheless they are the backbone of your media campaign.

The successful press release is one which arrives at the right place at the right time with the right story. The trick is just to get them written well and delivered accurately. The key to success is unknown but the key to failure is trying to please everybody.

Constructing the press release

The primary purpose of a press release is to inform, not to entertain. They need to have all the right information in the right order, with the right emphasis on information and relevance, in as short a space as possible.

Press releases are similar to news stories – they should come straight to the point and deliver the most interesting part of the story first, following on with more information, quotes and background, and ending with contact names and phone numbers.

The introduction or first paragraph is the most crucial – journalists only scan the headline and first paragraph and if you haven't caught their attention, then they will bin your release.

Publications often get tens – if not hundreds – of press releases each day, and you have to make sure that the point of yours is immediately obvious.

The first few sentences have to answer the questions 'Who' 'What' 'Where' 'When' 'Why' and 'How':

- Who is the story about?
- What is the story about?
- Where is your product available, or where is the event being held?
- When is it happening?
- Why is it interesting, or why is it happening?
- How does it work?

Do not overload the first paragraph by trying to answer all those questions at once. Select the most important – probably 'Who' and 'What'.

When the journalist reads the press release, they will be asking, 'So?' You have to make the relevance immediately apparent. The journalist will also ask:

- Why is this story going to interest our readers?
- What has happened?
- Where did it/will it happen?
- When did it/will it occur?
- Who is involved, which company or individual?

Concentrate on the facts in descending order of importance and present the story in a clear, digestible form. Only put one idea in each sentence and do not express yourself negatively.

You should tailor several versions of the press release to suit several types of journalist and audience, for example trade, consumer and local press. Finally, it is important to make sure your press release really contains newsworthy information, and is not just a sales letter dressed up.

Practical rules

The release should be double-spaced. The second (and last) page can contain a paragraph of background information which can be single-spaced.

Two pages are ideal. One is probably not enough and three are too many. Staple the two sheets together at the top left corner. Only put information on one side. Give all contact names, numbers, e-mail addresses at the end. Just put one line on the front page with the contact name and phone number, in case the two pages become separated. Put a date at the start and end.

Find the main hook for this particular story, expand on that in the first couple of paragraphs, put in a quote. On the second page give some background to the product and your company, with contact details for further information. Swamping the journalist with too much information can be counter-productive.

Use letterheaded notepaper. Having special paper printed with the words 'Press Release' is a waste of money, but it is useful to use spot colour or printed photographs to catch the eye. You can use colour in the printing, but preferably use plain white paper because coloured paper is distracting, not eyecatching.

Be brief, pithy and keep it simple. Give a headline which grabs and a standfirst which explains. Give the relevance immediately, in the headline.

If you send out a press release and then find that there is a mistake, correct it quickly. Telephone or fax with the correction.

Quotes

All press releases should contain at least one quote. They make a story come alive and personalise a narrative. A busy journalist writing a story may use a quote direct from the release without bothering to call.

Quotes can add depth to a story, personalise it, add humour and can convey strong opinions which would look out of place in a straight narrative. Quotes should be used to express opinion, and can start 'I think . . .' or 'In my view . . .', but they should not be just trite comments, such as 'This product has changed my life.'

Quotes should appear on the front page of the press release, supporting the statements or news in the opening paragraphs. Preferably use more than one sentence in the quote, so that if several publications use it they may use different words by picking different sentences from the quote. If the same quote appears in several publications, the effect is diminished.

Attribute the quote to someone fairly senior, relevant to the topic of the press release, and available for further comment if the journalist calls. The person quoted should be trained to be receptive and helpful, and must understand the journalist's agenda. A quote can be from a company representative, a customer or an independent expert.

Do not use indirect reported speech, such as 'Mr Jones said that the product will revolutionise the way that roads are built and people use them.' Better to say: '"The product will revolutionise the way roads are built and people use them," said Mr Jones.' It has much more impact. Sometimes journalists turn direct speech into indirect speech so that it fits in better with the style of the piece, but let the journalist decide. It is better for you to provide direct-speech quotes.

Expert opinion

Independent expert opinion is extremely valuable and carries significant weight, and should be included in the press release if possible.

If a recognised and respected expert will say to the press that your product is innovative, good value, or just plain interesting, you have a unique opportunity to make your press release a little bit different. You should use the commendation near the top of the press release. You can also use it on other marketing material.

It is worth giving free samples of your product to respected specialists, and asking them if they would mind their name being used as a reference or for accreditation.

Some journalists use a specialist's name as the main hook for the story, and will almost certainly want to talk to them, so make sure that they are prepared to talk to a journalist who calls. There is nothing worse for a journalist or more embarrassing for the person promoting the product, than if a journalist calls an expert whose name has been used in the press release, only to be met with a blank wall or negative response. Make sure that your expert is primed, and knows that they have been quoted and a journalist might call, and what to say if that happens.

Headlines and cross-heads

The headline and standfirst of a press release are crucial for catching the journalist's attention, but do not expect your headline to be used in print. It is there to catch the eye of the journalist. The captions and headlines in a newspaper or magazine are all conceived and written by the sub-editor.

Explain in the headline and standfirst what the product is and what the implications of it are. So do not just say, 'Wonderful Product Launched' but add, 'Wonderful Product Launched which will Revolutionise your Life'. Some *benefit* needs to be mentioned in the standfirst which puts the product in context and explains why the journalist should be interested in following up the story.

Generally, cross-heads (small headlines throughout the text) are not used in press releases. Some press releases highlight key words, and that can be effective.

Photographs

Photographs are essential. The old cliché of a picture being worth a thousand words is still true. People remember pictures and faces far more easily than they remember words and copy. Many editors choose stories according to the quality of the pictures, or give better prominence to a story with a good picture. Even though photography is susceptible to tricks, fakery, manipulation and misrepresentation, most people believe that a photograph cannot lie. They carry great weight.

Photographs should be lively, interesting and attention-grabbing. Have a selection of black-and-white and colour shots, some very plain and some unusual. But do not send a photograph with every press release – that is a waste of your budget because a lot of journalists will throw them straight into the bin. You should be selective, sending photographs to editors or others wanting them.

Have some shots prepared in advance of your meeting or interview with any journalists. All press packs should also contain photographs.

Use a professional photographer. It is false economy to think that you can take the photographs yourself, or have an amateur do it: taking photographs which are suitable for publication is a professional job and you should get a professional to do it. Don't just go to the high street photographer who usually does weddings. Ideally, use a press photographer to shoot the sort of pictures that will look good in print. Let the professional press photographer do it his or her way. They will avoid the plain, bland photographs which usually accompany press releases. A good picture has an image which is sharp and unfussy. An 'arty' shot is less likely to be used, although something a little unusual may catch the art editor's eye. If you have a corporate logo or brand name, have some shots with that clearly visible. Also have some without the logo or company name in the background.

Don't forget to stick a label on the back saying who or what is in the picture, the job title of the person, if any, and a contact phone number if the journalist needs more information.

Embargoes

An embargo is a request to a journalist not to use information before a certain date. Generally, journalists don't like them – by requesting an embargo you are trying to stop the journalist doing what comes naturally to them.

Embargoes used to be fairly common and were respected by journalists. These days they are more often used as a marketing device to make the journalist think that the information is particularly new or valuable (and they are wise to the trick).

The only embargoes which have any legal support are those issued by the Government (D-notices): otherwise embargoes are strictly a request, not a right. Generally, most journalists dislike and ignore them. Some dailies and weeklies respect embargoes, and if everyone else does too, it can help to get a story written in good time before the next issue. But they can't be sure that their competition titles will respect the embargo.

If you have a story which is particularly sensitive and you don't want the information made available to the public before a certain date, then don't send it out. A journalist is under no obligation to recognise or conform to the restrictions of an embargo. The only times when it is sensible to put an embargo date or time on a press release, and hope that the journalists will respect it, is if a story is being announced in different time zones and you want it to appear simultaneously.

Imposing an embargo may mean that some journalists might break it while others respect it; those who respect it will then feel aggrieved that they missed the story while their competitors went ahead and published. So, as a rule, don't impose embargoes.

Writing well

It should go without saying that, because your press release will be read by journalists, it needs to be carefully written.

- There must be no typos or literals (spelling mistakes).
- You must not repeat yourself.
- The sentences must be properly constructed.
- You must avoid clichés.
- The punctuation must be correct, with apostrophes in the right places.
- It must be written in an active, tight style or 'voice' by being direct and positive, and making definite assertions. Avoid tame, colourless language.
- Put the most important piece of information – what the press release is about – at the top. Flesh out the information as you move through it, with the background information at the end.
- Vary the length and construction of your sentences, keeping them short but avoiding jerkiness.
- Be concise but not abrupt. Too many short sentences are difficult to read, but long sentences fail to hold the reader's attention.

- Avoid repetition by keeping similar information grouped to-gether, and avoid repeating the same point by using different words.
- Avoid empty meaningless phrases or 'weasel' words.
- Avoid self-praise.
- Avoid exaggeration.
- Avoid rhetoric, marketing puff and jargon particularly in quotes.
- Avoid gobbledygook, and translate whatever you want to say into the simplest words.
- Flatter your readers by not talking down to them, but do not baffle them.

If you are unsure of your own writing ability, employ a professional to help. Press release writing is one of the services which professional PR agencies offer, and many freelance journalists will also write releases.

There are style books available for guidance, such as Strunk and White's *The Elements of Style*.

The following are clichés and 'puff words' to avoid:

credibility gap
doing battle
hit out at
industry leading
leading edge
point of no return
shock move
significant development
sign of the times
the world's first ever
unique paradigm
vital clues
world beating
world class
world shattering

The following words are so widely used that they could be con-sidered clichés now, although journalists still use them – they are part of a journalist's jargon. Given that journalists are looking for con-flict, controversy and something dramatic, you could be excused for including them:

accuse
act
axe
blame

boost
challenge
confront
demand
deny
exclusive
fairy-tale
fight
hit
horror
jibe
probe
refuse
reject
shock
slump
smashed
viable
warn

Typical gobbledygook phrases are these (followed by their 'translation' in brackets):

at the present time (now)
at this moment in time (now)
despite the fact that (although)
due to the fact that (because)
effect a saving (save)
in spite of the fact that (although)
in the course of (during)
in view of the fact that (because)
prior to (before)
take delivery of (receive)

Call a spade a spade, and a cat a cat, not 'a feline creature', nor a bird 'a feathered friend'.

Avoid foreign or little-used words. Do not use rendezvous for meeting, or fracas for fight. Do not garnish your press release with 'de rigueur', 'bête noir' or other French or Latin phrases.

Avoid long words when short ones will do:

adjacent to (near)
approximately (about *or* roughly)
consequently (so)
demonstrate (show)

Avoid euphemisms:

rationalisation (job cuts)
restructuring (job cuts)

Avoid words like 'very', 'quite' or 'rather' – and especially the word 'nice' – which are virtually meaningless.

Avoid over-dramatic or superlative adjectives, such as these:

bare minimum
broad daylight
completely untrue
coveted title
hard-hitting report
heated argument
rather fine
really good
sweeping reforms
wholly truthful

and double adjectives, like these:

deep blue sea
fine, sunny day
full, unabridged account
long, tedious journey

An adjective must extend the noun, not prop it up. A sentence in which every noun is preceded by an adjective is tedious and clumsy. Adjectives can usually be removed without changing the meaning, and should be.

Avoid metaphors which are past their sell-by date, such as:

tip of the iceberg
tower of strength

When all the information is in the press release and you think it is finished, read it through one last time and cut it down. Sub it, reduce it, cut out all the waffle and flowery writing and get it to the barest minimum. *Then* it is finished.

At that stage, get it checked by someone else. You will be surprised how many press releases arrive with spelling mistakes, and many journalists reject a release immediately they see a typo. One person writing and checking a press release can fail to see obvious mistakes. This is why, on magazines and newspapers, there are sub-editors to read through everything before it is printed. It is no reflection on your writing skills. You must have someone who reads the release cold in order to identify mistakes to which you may be blind.

You should look out for the following:

- ambiguity
- mis-spelling
- grammar
- accuracy
- repetition
- puff
- obscurity
- tedium.

Delivering the press release

There are three main ways to deliver a press release:

- post (or 'snail mail')
- e-mail
- fax.

You can also put it on your web-site, and pass it to the various news distribution agencies who transmit news to the press.

Every journalist and the editorial office for each publication or programme will have a preference as to how they want to receive press releases. When you create a list of the journalists, publications and programmes that you want to target, you should also find out those preferences. Once you find out, respect their wishes – don't then just ignore them.

Your press release will be ignored if it is sent in a non-acceptable way. You will waste effort and budget. When sending press releases to a newspaper or programme, do not bother to send a copy to every individual on the 'flannel panel' (list of names of people working on the title). At most send two or three copies to named individuals, but a blanket mailing to everyone is a waste of effort and budget.

Press releases have to be timely, that is to say, arriving before a publication closes and at the same time as they are made available to other publications. Determine the best day for the greatest number of journalists (perhaps the day after the previous issue has closed, when the journalists are starting to look for new stories for the next issue) and send all the releases together. You might decide to send those being posted a day before those being faxed or e-mailed, so that they all arrive on the same day.

Post

In the USA most journalists prefer to receive press releases by e-mail but in the UK the preference is still for the post, or 'snail mail'. This may change, but at the moment most UK journalists still prefer to read information on paper, despite the time it takes to open envelopes.

The key to successfully sending press releases by post is your database. If your database is out of date, you waste money sending to people who have left, changed jobs or changed job titles. You must have a well-maintained mailing list, and this is not necessarily ob-tained by buying one – some of those for sale are among the worst maintained.

Your database should be regularly cleaned and updated, and you should limit the number of press releases you send to each publica-tion. As stated above, a blanket mailing is a waste of money – just select the most important one or two individuals.

Each publication has a different procedure for dealing with the post and the press releases, but often they are opened by one person, then passed to the editor or section editor. He or she will tag those which are most interesting and possibly pass those stories to a jour-nalist to follow up. The pile will then be circulated among the rest of the editorial team. Sometimes the person who opens the mail re-moves any duplicates, so there is no point in sending more than one copy. Mail addressed to specific individuals is often opened centrally, so there may be no point in sending press releases to individual journalists. However, there is no hard-and-fast rule to the procedure for opening press releases, and in some editorial offices individuals open their own mail as well as seeing the central pile.

E-mail

First, establish that the journalist likes to receive press releases by e-mail – many dislike it because it involves them printing out the information. However, it also means that they have the press release stored electronically if they want to cut and paste it directly into a document. Some journalists rarely read their e-mail, so sending a press release to them that way is a waste of time.

As with snail mail, you should target your e-mails carefully, mak-ing sure that you are reaching the right people as well as those who are receptive to e-mail. Wild, huge postings are not complimentary to the journalists, and just broadcasting information and news is like spraying with a hosepipe. You need to send e-mails individually or to small select groups.

Obviously, take care to make sure that the address you use is exactly right (one wrong letter or full stop and it will not go through). Don't send one e-mail to a multiple address list. When the journalist receives the e-mail they can see who else you have sent it to, and this can appear insulting – it also takes some time to scroll through the list. Send to each journalist individually.

Don't add electronic attachments, HTML or other encoded or compressed data, because you don't know what sort of system the journalist is using and it may appear as gobbledygook. Use a straightforward text file.

Structure your e-mail with a header, like a headline; a synopsis, like a standfirst; the body text; and contacts at the end. Think before writing your e-mail. Grammar and spelling mistakes are accepted in cyberspace but still look unprofessional.

Be courteous – and remember that humour which works face-to-face may not work electronically. Be relevant and selective – it is easy to irritate journalists with time wasting blanket mailings. Reply to e-mail messages straight away so that the sender knows you received it.

Fax

As a general rule, only use the fax if the message or press release is time-critical, or if the journalist specifies that they prefer to receive information that way. Many journalists dislike faxes because of the reams of paper they generate (which they have to provide).

The fax should ideally be used in conjunction with the phone, calling first to warn the journalist that the press release is on its way. Bear in mind that many journalists and publications receive hundreds of press releases each week, so they will not appreciate being called for such a purpose. For this reason, the fax is best used to support a telephone interview, as a way of sending background information, rather than a routine way to send a press release.

Don't send long faxes – press releases should be no more than two pages, in any case.

Web-sites

A web-site is commonly part of most marketing plans these days, and one of the functions of a web-site is to carry press releases and media information. Many organisations also have an area specifically for the press, giving details of spokespersons on specific areas, case studies and so forth.

Journalists may come across your site while researching, or access it specifically to find out more about your company and product. Make sure that your web-site address is included on your press release, and make sure that the press release and any secondary information is posted there. Journalists can 'pull' information off your web-site and use it to supplement your press release and an interview. Obviously, your web-site should be attractively designed and provide lots of product information, case studies and anything else which the journalist might need.

News distribution sources

There are several agencies which collect press releases and reprint them and distribute them to their customers. These include Two Ten, M2 Distribution and VNU Newswire. By sending your press releases to these agencies your release will automatically reach a wider audience.

Editorial charges (colour separation costs)

There is a growing, invidious trend for publications to attempt to charge those wanting to promote their products in the media as a covert way of charging for printing press releases. It is something which professional journalists and editors resist, but often pressure is brought to bear by the publisher or advertising sales manager.

The first you will know is when, a few days after the press release is sent, you receive a phone call from someone wanting to discuss the colour separation costs of using your product photograph, or making a straightforward suggestion that if you pay, your press release will be used. The understanding is that you 'pay or stay off the page'.

The practice began quietly a few years ago but has now spread to many trade and technical publications, and into certain areas of the consumer press. Unfortunately, it seriously undermines the established subbing process of the editorial department, with the result that the quality, content and style of the editorial pages suffer. In other words, press releases are often used in the form in which they are sent and the hyperbole and PR puff is not removed, making the resulting editorial pages look like little more than a collection of press releases (which they are).

Sometimes there is a promise of editorial coverage, but do not allow yourself to be conned. The resulting editorial has no integrity and little market value, and the process is hardly better than 'vanity publishing' when writers pay to have their work appear in print, regardless of its literary worth. So, resist and avoid editorial charges in whatever guise they appear, and stand firm to help protect the integrity of the media.

Press releases that fail

At a guess, about 95 per cent of press releases are thrown in the bin within 30 seconds of being opened. That's not a good result.

The most common reasons for press releases failing to interest a journalist are these:

- Headline confused, complicated, unclear.
- Standfirst too wordy without explaining the story.
- Too technical.
- Too boring.
- Layout too dense – unable to grasp the story at a glance.
- Layout with too much white space. If the story isn't in the first half-page, forget it.
- Printed with single-line spacing and on both sides of the page.
- Introduction too wordy – get straight to the point.
- No obvious angle or relevance.
- Inspires the 'So what?' reaction.
- Old news.

Appendix 4

Journalist's Codes of Practice

1. Journalist's Code of Practice, drawn up by the Editors' Code Committee and published by The Press Complaints Commission, 26 November 1997

All members of the Press have a duty to maintain the highest professional and ethical standards. This Code sets the benchmark for those standards. It both protects the rights of individuals and upholds the public's right to know.

The Code is the cornerstone of the system of self-regulation to which the industry has made a binding commitment. Editors and publishers must ensure that the Code is observed rigorously not only by their staff but also by anyone who contributes to their publications.

It is essential to the workings of an agreed code that it be honoured not only to the letter but in the full spirit. The Code should not be interpreted so narrowly as to compromise its commitment to respect the rights of the individual, nor so broadly that it prevents publication in the public interest.

Any publication which is criticised by the PCC under one of the following clauses is duty bound to print the adjudication which follows in full and with due prominence.

1. Accuracy
1. Newspapers and periodicals must take care not to publish inaccurate, misleading or distorted material including pictures.
2. Whenever it is recognised that a significant inaccuracy, misleading statement or distorted report has been published, it should be corrected promptly and with due prominence.
3. An apology should be published whenever appropriate.
4. Newspapers, whilst free to be partisan, must distinguish clearly between comment, conjecture and fact.
5. A newspaper or periodical should always report fairly and accurately the outcome of an action for defamation to which it has been a party.

2. Opportunity to reply

A fair opportunity for reply to inaccuracies should be given to individuals or organisations when reasonably called for.

3. Privacy

1. Everyone is entitled to respect for his or her private and family life, home, health and correspondence. A publication will be expected to justify intrusions into any individual's private life without consent.
2. The use of long-lens photography to take pictures of people in private places without their consent is unacceptable.

Note: Private places are public or private property where there is a reasonable expectation of privacy.

4. Harassment

1. Journalists and photographers must neither obtain nor seek to obtain information or pictures through intimidation, harassment or persistent pursuit.
2. They must not photograph individuals in private places without their consent; must not persist in telephoning, questioning, pursuing or photographing individuals after having been asked to desist; and must not follow them.
3. Editors must ensure that those working for them comply with these requirements and must not publish material from other sources which do not meet these requirements.

5. Intrusion into grief or shock

In cases involving personal grief or shock, enquiries must be carried out and approaches made with sympathy and discretion. Publication must be handled sensitively at such times, but this should not be interpreted as restricting the right to report judicial proceedings.

6. Children

1. Young people should be free to complete their time at school without unnecessary intrusion.
2. Journalists must not interview or photograph children under the age of 16 on subjects involving the welfare of the child or of any other child, in the absence of or without the consent of a parent or other adult who is responsible for the children.
3. Pupils must not be approached or photographed while at school without the permission of the school authorities.

4. There must be no payments to minors for material involving the welfare of children, nor payment to parents or guardians for material about their children or wards unless it is demonstrably in the child's interest.

5. Where material about the private life of a child is published, there must be justification for publication other than the fame, notoriety or position of his or her parents or guardian.

7. *Children in sex cases*

1. The Press must not, even where the law does not prohibit it, identify children under the age of 16 who are involved in cases concerning sexual offences, whether as victims or as witnesses or defendants.

2. In any press report of a case involving a social offence against a child – the child must not be identified, the adult may be identified, the word 'incest' must not be used where a child victim might be identified.

3. Care must be taken that nothing in the report implies the relationship between the accused and the child.

8. *Listening devices*

Journalists must not obtain or publish material obtained by clandestine listening devices or by intercepting private telephone conversations.

9. *Hospitals*

1. Journalists or photographers making enquiries at hospitals or similar institutions must identify themselves to a responsible official and obtain permission before entering non-public areas.

2. The restrictions on intruding into privacy are particularly relevant to enquiries about individuals in hospitals or similar institutions.

10. *Innocent relatives and friends*

The Press must avoid identifying relatives or friends of persons convicted or accused of crime without their consent.

11. *Misrepresentation*

1. Journalists must not generally obtain or seek to obtain information or pictures through misrepresentation or subterfuge.

2. Documents or photographs should be removed only with the consent of the owner.

3. Subterfuge can be justified only in the public interest and only when material cannot be obtained by any other means.

12. *Victims of sexual assault*

The Press should not identify victims of sexual assault or publish material likely to contribute to such identification and unless, by law, they are free to do so.

13. *Discrimination*

1. The Press must avoid prejudicial or pejorative reference to a person's race, colour, religion, sex or sexual orientation or to any physical or mental illness or handicap.
2. It must avoid publishing details of a person's race, colour, religion, sex or sexual orientation unless these are directly relevant to the story.

14. *Financial journalism*

1. Even where the law does not prohibit it, journalists must not use for their own profit financial information they receive in advance of its general publication, nor should they pass such information on to others.
2. They must not write about shares or securities in whose performance they know they or their close families have a significant financial interest, without disclosing the interest to the editor or financial editor.
3. They must not buy or sell, either directly or through nominees or agents, shares or securities about which they have written recently or about which they intend to write in the near future.

15. *Confidential sources*

Journalists have a moral obligation to protect confidential sources of information.

16. *Payment for articles*

1. Payments or offers of payment for stories or information must not be made directly or through agents to witnesses or potential witnesses in current criminal proceedings except where the material concerned ought to be published in the public interest and there is an over-riding need to make or promise to make a payment for this to be done. Journalists must take every possible step to ensure that no financial dealings have influence on the evidence that those witnesses may give.
2. Payment or offers of payment for stories, pictures or information must not be made directly or through agents to convicted or confessed criminals or their associates – who may include family, friends and colleagues – except where the material concerned

ought to be published in the public interest and payment is necessary for this to be done.

2. Journalist's Code of Conduct, published by the National Union of Journalists (NUJ)

1. A journalist has a duty to maintain the highest professional and ethical standards.
2. A journalist shall at all times defend the principle of the freedom of the press and other media in relation to the collection of information and the expression of comment and criticism. He/she shall strive to eliminate distortion, news suppression and censorship.
3. A journalist shall strive to ensure that the information he/she disseminates is fair and accurate, avoid the expression of comment and conjecture as a well-established fact and falsification by distortion, selection or misrepresentation.
4. A journalist shall rectify promptly any harmful inaccuracies, ensure that correction and apologies receive due prominence and afford the right of reply to persons criticised when the issue is of sufficient importance.
5. A journalist shall obtain information, photographs and illustrations only by straightforward means. The use of other means can only be justified by over-riding considerations of the public interest. The journalist is entitled to exercise a personal conscientious objection to the use of such means.
6. Subject to the justification by over-riding considerations of the public interest, a journalist shall do nothing which entails intrusion into grief and distress.
7. A journalist shall protect confidential sources of information.
8. A journalist shall not accept bribes nor shall he/she allow other inducements to influence the performance of his/her professional duties.
9. A journalist shall not lend him/herself to the distortion or suppression of the truth because of advertising or other considerations.
10. A journalist shall only mention a person's age, race, colour, creed, illegitimacy, disability, marital status, gender or sexual orientation if this information is strictly relevant. A journalist shall neither originate nor process material which encourages discrimination, ridicule, prejudice or hatred on any of the above-mentioned grounds.
11. A journalist shall not take private advantage of information gained in the course of his/her duties, before the information is public knowledge.

12. A journalist shall not by way of statement, voice or appearance endorse by advertisement any commercial product or service save for the promotion of his/her own work or of the medium by which he/she is employed.

Appendix 5

A selection of media relations agencies

There are thousands of PR agencies in the UK and this is merely a cross-section. They vary dramatically according to size, speciality, services, experience and competence. Inclusion in this listing is not a recommendation and should not be taken as approval or accreditation. All information is as supplied by the agencies. You are advised to follow the guidelines set out in Chapter 10 for selecting an agency.

Anderson Walker, London WC2E 8HN
Tel: 0171 836 5596
Fax: 0171 831 1058
E-mail: paragram@cix.co.uk
Contact: Peter Walker
Services: Media relations, management consultancy, technology marketing.
Top 3 current clients: JTS/Atari, Best Group Ltd, Channel Dynamics

Arrow Public Relations, Crowthorne, Berks. RG11 7AU
Tel: 01344 486000
Fax: 01344 487000
E-mail: ken-deeks@arrow.co.uk
Contact: Ken Deeks
Specialist areas: Telecommunications and IT.
Services: Media relations, message development, media training, development, market research.
Top 3 current clients: 3Com, BusinessObjects, Software AG

Barkers Communications, Birmingham B4 6JB
Tel: 0121 236 9501
Fax: 0121 233 4156
Contact: Dianne Page
Specialist areas: Consumer and business-to-business PR.

Barkers Communications, Glasgow, Scotland G2 4QY
Tel: 0141 284 5030
Fax: 0141 204 0033
Contact: Nevin McGhee

Specialist areas: Broad portfolio of corporate, consumer, financial and business to business.

Services: Media relations, employee communications, video production, product launches, full print and design services. Planning and management of events, public affairs and government relations.

Clients: Bank of Scotland, British Aerospace, Scottish & Newcastle, Royal Mail Scotland, Scottish Salmon Board, Shell UK Exploration and Production, Suntory

Biss Lancaster, London WC2H 9DG
Tel: 0171 497 3001
Fax: 0171 497 8915
Contact: Isabel Greenwood
Specialist areas: Financial institutions, food and drink manufacturers, healthcare, travel and leisure, plus others.
Services: Corporate and financial public relations, consumer and brands marketing, employee relations, issue and crisis management.

Bite Communications, London W6 9BD
Tel: 0181 741 1123
Fax: 0181 653 1324
E-mail: clivea/grantc@bitecomm.co.uk
Web: www.bitecomm.co.uk
Contact: Clive Armitage
Specialist areas: Consumer technology.
Services: Consultancy.
Top 3 current clients: Oracle, Apple, BT Internet Services

Bridson & Bridson, Banbury, Oxon. OX17 3RD
Tel: 01295 812843
Fax: 01293 812844
E-mail: info@bandb.co.uk
Web: www.bandb.co.uk
Contact name: David Bridson
Specialist areas: IT, business to business.
Services: Press and public relations, advertising – creative and media, brochure copy writing and production, newsletter editorial and production, print management, recruitment advertising, marketing communications, consultancy.
Top 3 current clients: Dan Technology, Reflex Magnetics, Internet Security Systems

Brodeur APlus Group, Slough, Berks. SL3 7PT
Tel: 01753 790700
Fax: 01753 790701

E-mail: asmith@aplus.co.uk
Web: www.aplusgroup.com
Contact: Andrew Smith
Specialist areas: Telecommunications, consumer electronics, IT.
Services: Strategic consultancy, media relations, product branding, web-site design and support, direct marketing, design and production of marketing literature.
Top 3 current clients: IBM, Nortel, NetObjects

Buffalo Communications, London SW6 6AW
Tel: 0171 385 0777
Fax: 0171 385 8662
E-mail: kerry.hallard@buffalo.co.uk
Web: www.buffalo.co.uk
Contact: Kerry Hallard, MD
Specialist area: IT.
Services: PR and media relations.
Top 3 current clients: ICL, Simply Computers, IBS Consulting

Burston Marsteller, London WC1A 2PX
Tel: 0171 831 6262
Fax: 0171 430 1033
Contact: Alison Canning
Specialist areas: Corporate, financial, hi-tech, internal, healthcare and consumer.
Services: Full-range public relations, training, new media, research and planning, audio-visual production.
Clients: Walls, Glaxo

Charles Barker, London W1V 6HX
Tel: 0171 494 1331
Fax: 0171 439 1071
Contact: Angela Heylin
Specialist areas: Most sectors including travel and leisure, financial services, education, business, industrial products, and fast-moving consumer goods (FMCG).
Services: Full-range public relations, plus corporate positioning, event organisation, employee communications, measurement and evaluation, media training, product launches, research projects, reports and sponsorship.

Charlwood House PR, London SW15 5EQ
Tel: 0181 878 8871
Fax: 0181 876 1770
E-mail: sstride@cix.co.uk

Contact: Sue Stride
Specialist areas: Water industry, IT.
Services: Full press and public relations.
Top 3 current clients: British Water, SST, Genesys Consultants

CHC, Keighley, West Yorks. BD20 9DW
Tel: 01535 637055
Fax: 01535 632320
E-mail: chc@dial.pipex.com
Contact: Chris Hermann
Specialist area: Technology.
Services: PR, corporate, event days, media buying.
Top 3 current clients: Sonopress, MTDS, Winnov

Citigate, London EC2A 1DS
Tel: 0171 282 8000
Fax: 0171 282 8060
Web: www.citigate.com
Contact: Suzy Frith
Specialist areas: Telecommunications, IT and environmental sectors.
Services: Strategic positioning, issues development, media training, media relations, copywriting, newsletter and brochure production, research programmes.
Top 3 current clients: CMG, JBA, Silicon Graphics

Click Information Terminology Ltd (Click IT), Odiham, Hants. RG29 1JF
Tel: 01256 701646
Fax: 01256 701647
E-mail: vholton@click.co.uk
Contact: Vince Holton
Specialist areas: IT, personal computer industry, mobile data, mobile computing.
Services: PR, advertising, media selection and buying, event management, marcoms.
Top 3 current clients: TDK Grey Cell, Com One UK, Hugh Symons Group

Cohn & Wolfe, London WC2H 7LJ
Tel: 0171 331 5300
Fax: 0171 331 9083
E-mail: martin-thomas@eu.cohnwolfe.com
Web: www.cohnwolfe.com
Contact: Martin Thomas
Specialist areas: Healthcare, sports and technology.

Services: Research and planning, corporate positioning, internal communications, sponsorship, promotions, event management, press relations, print production.
Top 3 current clients: Eli Lilly & Co, Visa International, Coca-Cola GB

CTC Public Relations, Theale, Reading, Berks. RG7 5AJ
Tel: 0118 930 4090
Fax: 0118 930 4124
E-mail: info@ctcpr.com
Contact: Jenny Levin
Specialist areas: Networking, IT.
Services: Full-service public relations, advertising, media buying, marcoms.
Top 3 current clients: Intergraph Software Solutions, PairGain Technologies, First Virtual Corporation

DPA, Guildford, Surrey GU4 8BJ
Tel: 01483 456666
Fax: 01483 456555
E-mail: dpapr@attmail.com
Contact: John Coulston
Specialist areas: Hi-tech.
Services: Full-service PR and total image management, media training.
Clients: Amdahl, GE Information Services, ICL, Mercury, Retix

Edelman, London SW1Y 4SP
Tel: 0171 344 1265
Fax: 0171 344 1295
Contact: Abel Hadden
Specialist areas: Medical, financial, business and corporate, consumer and trade.
Services: Full-service PR including issue and crisis management, community and employee relations, design, print and publishing, evaluation.

Eric Leach Marketing, Hounslow, Middx. TW3 3NN
Tel: 0181 570 2182
Fax: 0181 572 3162
E-mail: eric-leach@compuserve.com
Web: http://ourworld.compuserve.com/homepages/eric-leach
Specialist areas: Event creation, event management, public relations and marketing services.
Top 3 current clients: Popkin Software & Systems, Documentum, The Object Management Group

Firefly Communications, London SW6 6AW
Tel: 0171 381 4505
Fax: 0171 385 4768
E-mail: mmellor@firefly.co.uk
Web: www.firefly.co.uk
Contact: Mark Mellor
Specialist areas: Hi-tech.
Services: Strategic consultancy, media relations, writing, brand management, event management, crisis management, media evaluation, sponsorship, issue tracking, media training, speaker placement.
Top 3 current clients: Compaq, Novell, Reuters

Flapjack Communications, London W1H 3PJ
Tel: 0171 224 4554
Fax: 0171 935 4052
E-mail: info@flapjack.com
Web: www.flapjack.com
Contact name: Jacki Vause
Specialist areas: IT and Internet.
Services: Seminars, research, PR consultancy.
Top 3 current clients: Carerra, Netnames, Allaire

Freud Communications, London W1 4HQ
Tel: 0171 580 2626
Fax: 0171 636 2726
Contact: Matthew Freud or Nick Wiszowaty
Specialist areas: All areas.
Services: Full-service PR.
Clients: Pepsi-Cola, Sega, Pizza Hut, British Telecom

GCI Group, London SW3 5AN
Tel: 0171 351 2400
Fax: 0171 352 6244
E-mail: adrian@gcilon. demon.co.uk
Contact: Adrian Wheeler
Specialist areas: Financial, consumer, corporate, healthcare, IT.
Services: Media, marketing, sponsorship, crisis management, internal relations.
Top 3 current clients: Budweiser, Novartis, DTI Business Links

Goode International, Reading, Berks. RG8 0JS
Tel: 01491 873323
Fax: 01491 873188
E-mail: info@goodeint.com
Web: www.goodeint.com

Contact: Becky Payne
Specialist areas: Hi-tech industries.
Services: PR, media buying, media planning, telemarketing, design, direct mail.
Top 3 current clients: Norman Data Defence Systems, G&A Imaging, Majenix Corporation

Grant Butler Coomber, Richmond, Surrey TW9 1DT
Tel: 0181 332 7022
Fax: 0181 332 6540
Contact: Sue Grant or Jill Coomber
Specialist areas: Hi-tech, IT, food, travel, leisure, health, telecoms.
Services: Full-service PR.

Grayling, London WC1B 3RA
Tel: 0171 255 1100
Fax: 0171 631 0602
Contact: Nigel Kennedy
Specialist areas: All sectors.
Services: Full-service agency.

Harrison Cowley, Manchester M22 5WB
Tel: 0161 437 4474
Fax: 0161 437 6029
Contact: David Heal or Charles Kell
Specialist areas: All sectors.
Services: Full-service PR including marketing services and resources, event organisation, literature production and market research.
Clients: John Menzies, The National Lottery, BICC Cables, St Ivel, The Bank of Wales

Hartmann & Lotz Europe, Andover, Hants. SP10 1DP
Tel: 01264 323141
Fax: 01264 323251
E-mail: jeff.lea@haleurope.com
Web: www.haleurope.com
Contact: Jeff Lea, MD
Specialist areas: Electronics, IT, telecommunications.
Services: UK and international PR (offices in Paris and Munich).
Top 3 current clients: Hewlett Packard, Andrew Corporation, Xircom

Harvard Public Relations, Harmondsworth, Middx. UB7 0AW
Tel: 0181 759 0005
Fax: 0181 897 3242
E-mail: info@harvard.com

Web: www.harvard.co.uk
Contact: Keith Mason
Specialist areas: Computing, communications, consumer, electronics, engineering, healthcare, Internet and leisure.
Services: Media relations, public relations, issue and crisis management, newsletter writing and production, collateral design and production.
Top 3 current clients: Agfa, Hitachi, Nintendo

Herald Communications, London SW1P 1DH
Tel: 0171 331 1300
Fax: 0171 331 1400
E-mail: info@herald-pr.com
Web: www.herald-pr.com
Contact: Kate Messenger or Amanda Slayton
Specialist areas: Technology (business software, consumer electronics, networking, new media, post-production, telecomms), consumer (brown goods, home video, insurance, stationery, travel, tourism, white goods).
Services: Analyst communications, corporate publications, crisis management, exhibitions, media relations, media training, press conferences, industry round-tables, speech writing.
Top 3 current clients: Hewlett Packard, Motorola, Eidos

Hill & Knowlton, London WC1X 8SH
Tel: 0171 413 3000
Fax: 0171 413 3111
Contact: Michael Southgate
Specialist areas: Food and FMCG, healthcare, science and technology, business to business.
Services: Full-service agency, corporate and financial counselling, parliamentary and political liaison, EU relations, corporate brand marketing, speech writing, sponsorship, training, creative writing.
Clients: 3Com, Adidas, American Express, First Choice Holidays, RSPCA, Sugar Bureau, Turkey, Vauxhall, Wellcome.

Hobsbawm Macauley Communications, London W1V 3DB
Tel: 0171 734 0222
Fax: 0171 734 0333
E-mail: info@hmclondon.co.uk
Contact: Julia Hobsbawm or Sarah Macauley
Services: Consultancy, campaigns, event organisation.
Clients: Vanity Fair, Oxford University Press, Internet Publishing, The Labour Party

Holmes, London EC4A 3EB
Tel: 0171 353 0303
Fax: 0171 583 0841
E-mail: info@holmes.co.uk
Contact: George Hayles
Specialist areas: Corporate community affairs, business to business, IT, financial services, sports and leisure, consumer products and services.
Services: Public relations, media relations, graphic design, advertising, sales promotion and integrated marketing programmes.
Top 3 current clients: Sainsburys, PPP Healthcare, Microvitec

Infopress, London EC4Y 8AA
Tel: 0171 353 2320
Fax: 0171 583 9347
Contact: David Watson
Specialist areas: Business to business, consumer, financial services, healthcare, public sector, technology.
Services: Full-range PR including communications analysis and corporate counselling, and creative marketing support.
Clients: Abbey Life, Air Jet, Barbour, Glaxo-Wellcome, National Physical Laboratory, Priory Hospital, Wyeth-Lederie

Insight Marketing, Macclesfield, Cheshire SK10 2XA
Tel: 01625 500800
Fax: 01625 500900
E-mail: cwarham@insightmkt.com
Web: www.insightmkt.com
Contact: Chris Warham
Specialist areas: Hi-tech, business to business.
Services: PR, web design, publishing.
Top 3 current clients: Dell, Hewlett Packard, Siemens

International Marketing, London SW1V 4HA
Tel: 0171 834 4874
Fax: 0171 834 5955
E-mail: sg@international-marketing.co.uk
Web: www.international-marketing.co.uk
Contact name: Sally Goodsell
Specialist areas: Software marketing and PR in UK, Europe and USA.
Top 3 current clients: Siemens Nixdorf AG in Germany, Eidos Technologies in USA, Cambridge Positioning Systems.

The ITPR Partnership, London SW19 4NG
Tel: 0181 944 6688
Fax: 0181 944 0739

E-mail: itpr@dial.pipex.com
Contact: Bob Dearsley
Specialist areas: IT and business to business
Services: Full-service agency – consultancy, PR, advertising, advertorial, media buying, direct mail, event management.
Top 3 current clients: Great Plains Software, DataWorks Europe, Interforum/Utopia Technology Partners

JBA Public Relations, Epsom, Surrey KT17 4PX
Tel: 0181 394 2515
Fax: 01372 727578
E-mail: jba@jbapr.com
Contact: Amanda Sokell
Specialist area: All business-to-business communications.
Services: Media relations, event management, speaker programmes.
Top 3 current clients: British Telecom, Microsoft European Services, Toshiba Electronic Imaging Division

John Hill Associates, Sutton, Surrey SM2 5HD
Tel: 0181 643 7783
Fax: 0181 661 2322
E-mail: jha@cix.co.uk
Specialist areas: Consumer electronics and IT.
Services: All aspects of the PR mix.
Top 3 current clients: Fuji, Sundanna, UKCMG

Kinross & Render, London SW1V 1DX
Tel: 0171 592 3100
Fax: 0171 931 9640
E-mail: sara@kinross-and-render.co.uk
Web: www.kinross-and-render.co.uk
Contact: Sara Render
Specialist areas: Telecommunications, IT, healthcare, consumer and public sector businesses.
Services: Integrated public relations and marketing media relations, crisis relations, issues management, sponsorship, media buying, design and print, event management.
Top 3 current clients: Energis, Barclays, olsy uk

Leading Edge Communications, London EC1M 6EA
Tel: 0171 454 9360
Fax: 0171 454 9361
E-mail: mail@leadingedge.co.uk
Web: www.leadingedge.co.uk
Contact: Lesley Wright

Specialist areas: IT, business to business, Internet.
Services: Media relations, media training, production.
Top 3 current clients: Scitex, Mitsubishi, Metacreations

Leopard, Cambridge CB4 1EL
Tel: 01223 314545
Fax: 01223 324611
E-mail: francescab@leopard.co.uk
Contact: Francesca Brosan
Specialist areas: Business to business, electronics, telecommunications.
Services: Public relations, advertising and design.
Top 3 current clients: Philips Semiconductors, Wimpey Homes, Serenus International

Lesniak Jones Liddell, Bourne End, Bucks. SL8 5AJ
Tel: 01628 522222
Fax: 01628 525722
E-mail: 100451.216@compuserve.com
Web: www.ljl.co.uk
Contact: Richard Stockdill
Specialist areas: Electronics and IT.
Services: Full-service PR, media buying, design and marcoms.
Top 3 current clients: LSI Logic, Farnell, Cegelec

Lewis, London WC2B 5AA
Tel: 0171 831 4890
Fax: 0171 831 4889
E-mail: enquiries@lewispr.com
Web: www.lewispr.com
Contact: Chris Lewis
Specialist area: Technology.
Services: International media relations and marketing (offices in Paris, Munich and San Diego).
Top 3 current clients: The Dialog Corporation, ICL Sorbus, Sun Microsystems

Lexicon, London EC1M 5NR
Tel: 0171 490 2973
Fax: 0171 490 7257
E-mail: lexicon@cix.co.uk
Contact: Lynne Thomas-Bowman or Niall Murray
Specialist area: IT.
Services: Media relations, strategic counsel, event management.
Top 3 current clients: Psion Dacom, Info'Products, Storage Dimensions

LIFE PR (previously Lynne Franks PR), London W9 3RB
Tel: 0171 724 6777
Fax: 0171 724 8484
Contact: Samantha Royston
Specialist areas: All sectors.
Services: Full-service PR.

Marbles, Henley-on-Thames, Oxon. RG9 1UR
Tel: 01491 411789
Fax: 01491 413313
E-mail: central@marbles.co.uk
Web: www.marbles.co.uk
Contact: Jan Stannard or Sue Beard
Specialist areas: Technology, business to business, consumer, corporate.
Services: Strategic counselling, media relations, event management, speech preparation, media training, writing services, issues tracking, crisis management, customer relations, employee communications and communications audits. Also web-site design.
Top 3 current clients: Financial Times, AEG, Forrester Research

The Marketing Department, Chalfont St Giles, Bucks. HP8 4BG
Tel: 01494 764858
Fax: 01494 763646
E-mail: tom@themark.demon.co.uk
Contact: Tom Hohenberg
Specialist areas: IT hardware, software, communications, services.
Services: PR, media buying, creative for advertising, direct mail and literature.
Top 3 current clients: NEC Europe, Karma UK, Lynx Financial Systems

The Marketing Exchange, Burgess Hill, Sussex RH15 9DQ
Tel: 01444 258333
Fax: 01444 239725
E-mail: info@mexchange.demon.co.uk
Web: mexchange.demon.co.uk
Contact: Gill Warren or Steve Warren
Specialist areas: Small and medium businesses.
Services: Public/press relations, event management, sales incentive programmes, advertising, marketing materials, exhibitions, product launches, roadshows, press conferences.
Top 3 current clients: Cisco, Microsoft, VNU Business Publications

Marshall Jennings PR, Henley-on-Thames, Oxon. RG9 2AH
Tel: 01491 410323
Fax: 01491 410181

E-mail: mjpr@compuserve.com
Contact: Neil Marshall
Specialist areas: Electrical, electronics, IT, design, industrial.
Services: PR, advertising, marketing, direct mail.

MCC International, Alton, Hants. GU34 1QR
Tel: 01420 542598
Fax: 01420 542599
E-mail: info@mcc.co.uk
Web: www.mccint.co.uk/mccint/
Contact: Fiona Brewer
Services: Full press and public relations, high-level strategic marketing consultancy, direct marketing, advertising, design and direct mail.
Top 3 current clients: Cabletron, XcalleNet, GeoFox.

Media Crystal, Mackworth, Derbys. DE22 4NE
Tel: 01332 824781
Fax: 01332 824755
E-mail: admin@media-crystal.co.uk
Web: www.media-crystal.co.uk
Contact: John Allsopp
Specialist areas: Technology, business to business, international.
Services: Payment-by-results PR, direct marketing, Internet marketing.
Top 3 current clients: GemPlus, MicroPlanning International, XMA Ltd

Media Link, Pangbourne, Berks. RG8 7JW
Tel: 0118 984 3386
Fax: 0118 984 3010
E-mail: peter@medialink.co.uk
Web: www.medialink.demon.co.uk
Contact: Peter Linton
Specialist area: IT.
Services: Press relations, advertising, brochures, newsletters.

Mmd Marketing Communications, Old Isleworth, Middx. TW7 6BW
Tel: 01635 524526
Fax: 01635 573601
Contact: Chris Dobson
Specialist areas: Telecommunications, finance, IT, agriculture.
Services: Full-service agency (PR, advertising, events management, direct marketing etc.).
Top 3 current clients: Oki Systems, Lucent Technologies, Dictaphone

Moores Associates, Slough, Berks. SL1 6DQ
Tel: 01628 667701
Fax: 01628 602995
E-mail: bmoores@cix.co.uk
Contact: Bill Moores
Specialist areas: Computer software.
Services: Public relations, press relations, event management, in-house publications.
Top 3 current clients: Brio, MicroStrategy, Informatica

Motive Public Relations, Riseley, Berks. RG7 1QQ
Tel: 0118 988 0600
Fax: 0118 988 0601
E-mail: mail@motivepr.co.uk
Contact: Andrew Smith
Specialist area: IT.
Services: Media relations, media auditing.
Top 3 current clients: SSA, Ilion, IS Solutions

Noiseworks, Maidenhead, Berks. SL6 1PT
Tel: 01628 628080
Fax: 01628 779999
E-mail: noise@noiseworks.com
Web: www.noiseworks.com
Contact: James Hanson
Specialist areas: Corporate and consumer technology, online PR.
Services: Full range of international media relations.
Top 3 current clients: Lotus Development, Hewlett Packard, Bay Networks

Oast Communications, Westerham, Kent TN16 1TW
Tel: 01959 565626
Fax: 01959 565636
E-mail: info@oast.co.uk
Web: www.oast.co.uk
Contact: Richard Arkle
Specialist areas: IT, financial, manufacturing, telecoms and other vertical markets.
Services: Media relations, case studies, customer newsletters and magazines, brochures, White Papers, direct mail and event organisation.
Top 3 current clients: IBM, Sybase, Lawson Software

On Demand PR and Marketing, London SE26 6HA
Tel: 0181 676 9916
Fax: 0181 676 8826

E-mail: ondemand@dial.pipex.com
Contact: Julie Vindis
Specialist areas: Call centre technology and services.
Services: PR, marketing, corporate hospitality, photography.
Clients: Association of Computer Telephone Integration Users & Suppliers, Call Centre Management Association, Telecommunications Human Resource Association, Network Outsourcing Association

Paragon, London W1V 4LL
Tel: 0171 734 6030
Fax: 0171 437 6085
Contact: Julia Thorn
Specialist areas: All sectors.
Services: Full-service PR including crisis management and contract publishing.

Peter Rennison PR, Hemel Hempstead HP1 3AA
Tel: 01442 245030
Fax: 01442 235227
E-mail: pr@prpr.co.uk
Contact: Peter Rennison
Specialist areas: Building, design, IT.
Services: Media relations, product and corporate literature, newsletters and advertising.
Top 3 current clients: The Olivetti & Oracle Research Labs, Wick Hill, Lava Systems

Portfolio Communications, London WC2E 8AA
Tel: 0171 240 6959
Fax: 0171 240 4849
E-mail: markw@portmet.co.uk
Web: www.portmet.co.uk
Contact: Mark Westaby
Specialist areas: Financial services, paper and packaging, business to business, IT.
Services: Full-service public relations plus planning, research and evaluation.
Top 3 current clients: Tandem, Quantum, Dresdner Kleinwort Benson Finance.

Premier Marketing Services, Kenley, Surrey CR8 5JR
Tel: 0181 660 3152
Fax: 0181 660 3121
E-mail: gblay@cix.co.uk
Contact: Gerard Blay

Specialist areas: Computer software, telecommunications, CTI, management consultancy.
Services: Business-to-business marketing and PR consultancy.
Top 3 current clients: Learning Tree International, The Retic Group, Image Data Systems.

PR with Purpose, Esher, Surrey KT10 0AP
Tel: 0181 873 2186
Fax: 0181 873 2186
E-mail: pr@purpose.co.uk
Web: www.purpose.co.uk
Contact: Jennifer Perry
Specialist areas: Internet-related business, hi-tech.
Services: Strategic marketing consultancy, establishing in-house PR, full-service account management.
Top 3 current clients: NetLink, DisplayMate, Oki

Roger Staton Associates, Marlow, Bucks. SL7 3AN
Tel: 01628 487222
Fax: 01628 487223
E-mail: rstaton@cix.co.uk
Contact: Paul Kelly, MD
Specialist areas: Technology, computing, electronics, IT, telecommunications, electrical engineering, industrial plant and equipment, automation and control, AV equipment.
Services: Media relations programmes, marketing communications, company periodicals, crisis and issue management, sales support collateral material, direct marketing.
Top 3 current clients: Ericsson Group, PictureTel, Tellabs

Shandwick, London W1X 9DA
Tel: 0171 408 2232
Fax: 0171 493 8163
Specialist areas: All sectors.
Services: Full-service PR.

Shaw Public Relations, London N1 8QE
Tel: 0171 226 9177
Fax: 0171 359 6351
E-mail: geo@joshaw.co.uk
Contact: George Shaw
Specialist areas: IT, healthcare, media, business to business.
Services: Media relations, advertising, design.
Top 3 current clients: Elcom Group, Kingston Technology, Ethan Adams & Associates

Sheldon Communications, London WC1A 1LH
Tel: 0171 436 1553
Fax: 0171 436 7825
E-mail: dcunliffe@sheldon.compulink.co.uk
Web: www.compulink.co.uk/sheldon/welcome.htm
Contact: Peter Sheldon Green or David Cunliffe
Specialist areas: IT, corporate, business to business.
Services: Full-service PR consultancy.
Top 3 current clients: Mars Corp, Syquest, Financial Times Group

Sixth Sense Limited, Newbury, Berks. RG14 1JN
Tel: 01635 552694
Fax: 01635 551621
E-mail: sarah@sixthsense.co.uk
Contact: Sarah Chidgey
Specialist area: IT.

Stanton Associates, Windsor, Berks. SL4 3D
Tel: 01753 855901
Fax: 01753 853984
E-mail: cgs@cix.co.uk
Contact: Clare Stanton
Specialist area: IT.
Services: Media relations, copywriting, marketing consultancy.
Top 3 current clients: PRO-IV, ROCC Computers, Bourne River PR

Strategic Alliance International, Old Amersham, Bucks. HP7 0HT
Tel: 01494 434434
Fax: 01494 434224
E-mail: reception@sai.co.uk
Contact: Nick Flowerdew or Nigel Parker
Specialist areas: Technology, office, industrial.
Services: Press and analyst relations, business-to-business communications.
Top 3 clients: Hughes, Bell and Howell, Arbor

Tavistock Communications, London EC2R 7HX
Tel: 0171 600 2288
Fax: 0171 600 5084
E-mail: tavistock@compuserve.com
Web: www.tavistock.com
Contact: Jeremy Carey
Specialist areas: Financial and corporate.
Services: Media relations, media training, event management, corporate literature, consultancy support.

Top 3 current clients: Vodaphone Group, Hillier Parker, Cazenove Fund Management

UPA Group. Virtual agency located around UK
Tel: 01295 812843
01344 301022
01535 637055
0181 427 8992
01273 487617
E-mail: bandb@cix.co.uk
maggied@cix.co.uk
chc@cix.co.uk
shj@cix.co.uk
jml@cix.co.uk
Contact: David Bridson, Maggie Davies, Chris Hermann, Sonia Howell-Jones, Jane Lee
Specialist areas: Consumer technology
Services: Full service PR. Unique 'virtual' PR agency with independent businesses and collective services

Vousden Levick Publicity, London SE1 2LP
Tel: 0171 403 7500
Fax: 0171 403 6714
E-mail: paulv@vlp.co.uk
Web: www.vlp.co.uk
Contact: Paul Vousden, Managing Partner
Specialist areas: Business to business, especially automotive, construction, building products, IT and hotels.
Services: PR, advertising, marketing advice.
Top 3 current clients: Eastern Electricity, Hays Information Management, Varity Perkins

White Horse Associates, Teddington, Middx. TW11 8PY
Tel: 0181 255 2332
Fax: 0181 255 2345
E-mail: sian.davies@ukonline.co.uk
Contact: Sian Davies
Specialist area: Consumer-tech.
Services: Full range of PR disciplines, plus copywriting, print production, event management and media training.
Top 3 current clients: CD Imports, Technical Asset Management, Sofsource

Media trainers

Annie Gurton
01736 364787

David Tebbutt
0181 866 4400

Martin Banks
01582 429254

Media Counsellors
01344 874707

Media First
01635 872384

Media Interviews
01249 655275

Television & Radio Techniques
0800 783 6208

Television & Radio Training
0115 981 7787

The Vertex Group
0171 702 2490

Appendix 6

Glossary of terms

Advertorial
At a glance it looks like editorial journalism but it is in fact a version of advertising. Where pure journalism contains a balance of views and opinions, advertorial only draws on those views which are positive. Badly done, it has little value – everyone knows that it is just advertising dressed up as editorial. But skilfully done, it can play a useful part in the marketing mix. You will probably have to pay for the space, just like advertising, and the editor may insist that there is a slug along the top of the page which says 'advertorial' so that the reader does not confuse it with true editorial.

Audio
Sound material.

Banner
A big, wide headline, or the title of a publication, as in 'banner headline'.

Bleed
Technique of making the editorial run right to the edge of the page, rather than leaving a narrow, white border.

Blurb
Marketing or PR copy, or information about a product sent by a PR company.

Body copy
Main text of a feature or story.

Box-out
A box within a feature containing a short story or case study.

Broadsheet
Large-sized newspaper (23" by 16"). General term to mean the quality press, as opposed to the tabloids.

Bulletin
A short radio or television news item or programme.

By-line
The attribution of an article to a specific journalist: 'By John Smith' or 'by Sarah Jones'.

Camera-ready copy (CRC)
An image or page ready to be transferred direct to the printing process.

Caption
The short sentence under a photograph which explains who or what it depicts.

Case
In old print rooms, the capital letters were kept in the higher tray and the small letters kept in a lower tray, hence 'upper case' and 'lower case'.

Case study
A 'story' about a customer using your product or service. Ideally, from the journalist's point of view, case studies should include all the bad news as well as the good, but they invariably tell solely the positive side of the story. Include some background information, such as what the customer was using before they used your product, and mention other products they looked at before deciding on yours. Give quotes from the customer, and a contact number at the end. The person quoted must be prepared for the journalist to call for more details, and should know in advance what to say. The worst thing is if you give a contact point for a person quoted in a case study, and then they refuse to talk to the journalist or say, 'No comment'.

Casting off
A nearly obsolete term for a task made less necessary by new technology. In the old days, a journalist and sub-editor had to make sure their copy would fit the space allocated by working out how many words are required to fit a given space. A piece is then 'cast off' by being pruned to the right length. The term comes from a old printing expression meaning to cast a line of metal type to fit an exact space. Most stories have to be cut to fit, but these days this is done on screen.

Catchline
Keyword usually at the top outside corner of a page which indicates what is on that page, such as 'News', 'Feature', 'Letters', and so forth. Helps the reader find their way around the book.

Classified
Small advertisement.

Copy
The words produced by journalists. Mainly refers to the written word.

Copy flow
The route or process that the copy follows from journalist to page or broadcast.

Copy taster
The link on the editorial team between the journalists and the sub-editors. Reads every story submitted and selects those to be used. Usually a task performed by the editor on small titles.

Correspondent
A journalist covering a specific geographical or vertical market area.

Cover flash
A strip across the corner of a cover, or a bold star imposed on the top of the cover image, containing words which tell the reader that there is something special inside this issue. Can be used to indicate a sponsored competition or special offer.

Crop
To trim or cut photographs in such a way that the best parts are emphasised and unwanted parts are cut off and not printed.

Cross-head
Short sentence or one word set in bold and larger type in the text of a feature or news story, which indicates to the reader something interesting coming up. Intended to retain the reader's attention, or to catch the eye of someone casually scanning the pages. Sometimes taken straight from the body copy, or sometimes written cryptically like a headline.

Deadline
The absolute date or hour when a journalist has to deliver copy. After this time only a major crisis would warrant changing anything – and even then it is sometimes not possible. Some journalists are given false deadlines because they are notorious about delivering on time, and sometimes a journalist will tell you that their deadline is sooner than it actually is, in order to get you to talk. Even if you suspect that you are being told false deadlines, you can't take the risk and you have to behave as though that is the absolute cut-off point.

Defamation
Unfair or injurious comment.

Display
Large advertisement.

DPS
Double-page spread. A feature which is spread across two facing pages.

Drop quote
Like a pull quote, a quotation copied from the text and run enlarged to enhance the page design.

Dub
Copy a recording from one tape to another.

Editing
Amending and checking copy and tapes.

Editor
The most senior person on the editorial team, responsible to a publisher or producer. Legally responsible for all the contents.

Em
The basic measurement of width in newspaper layouts. Normally one-sixth of an inch (the 12 point em).

Embargo
Request to wait to publish or broadcast a story until a specific date or time. Not legally enforceable, except by the Government.

En
Half an em.

Exclusive
A story which no other publication or programme has.

Feature
A story which is not a news story. Usually includes analysis and multiple views.

Filler
A short story, usually at the bottom of a column.

Flannel panel
List of staff on the publication, sometimes with their contact details. Usually includes sales and production staff, and the publishers, as well as the editorial team.

Flatplan
Visual schematic of the contents of a magazine or newspaper, showing which pages are for advertising and which are editorial.

Folio
Has several meanings, usually taken to mean the page number or a page of copy.

Freelance
A journalist who is self-employed, usually working for several publications or programmes.

Gatefold
A page which folds out, usually to carry advertising.

Gutter
The join in the middle of two facing pages.

Headline
The short, snappy title to a story or feature. Usually written by the sub-editor, not by the person who writes the copy.

House style
A standardised set of rules for spelling, punctuation and handling of copy adopted by each magazine or newspaper to achieve consistency. Serves to standardise the text, with the same titles or captions always being handled in the same way, and gives the unique character to the publication. Essential when copy is written by many contributors or there are several or changing sub-editors.

Inside back
The page on the inside of the back cover.

Intro
Another name for the standfirst, or the two or three lines at the beginning of a story which come after the headline.

Kern
The space between letters and words. In word-processing software, kerning is automatic.

Layout
The design of an editorial page.

Leader
Another name for the editor's foreword. Sometimes the only piece written by the editor. Positions the magazine or newspaper in the eyes of its readership and advertisers. A statement of views or position.

Lineage
Small unboxed advertisement.

Literal
A typing mistake, or 'typo'.

Masthead
The paper's name and the standfirst running under it, which explicitly declares its target audience or the aim of the magazine or newspaper.

Morgue
Press cutting library or holding of back issues.

NIB
A nib is a News In Brief item in a newspaper or magazine, usually under 100 words.

Orphan
A single line at the bottom of a page which is the first line of the next paragraph, continued on the next page. Good subbing will remove all widows and orphans.

Overmatter
Wording in excess of the space allocated. The sub-editor will cut out the overmatter to make the piece fit.

Pagination
The number of pages in the publication. Split between editorial and advertising.

Perfect bound
When a magazine is bound together with glue at the spine and each page is separate.

Pix
Pictures or photographs.

Point size
The size of type. One point is approximately 1/72 inch.

Press day
The day that a publication closes and goes to the printers. The last day for news. Everyone in the editorial department will be very busy. Not a good day to telephone.

Press pack
Collection of press releases, photographs, product specifications and information.

Producer
Person responsible for putting a programme on air.

Publisher
The person who appoints the editor of a magazine or newspaper, and sets the pagination, yield and budgets on each issue. In law, the editor is more powerful. In practice, the publisher has ultimate power, but a strong editor will resist the publisher's attempts to influence and control.

Pull quote
A quote which is selected by the sub-editor and reprinted in a larger typeface, as part of the layout and design of a page.

Reporter
A journalist, usually working on news stories. The person responsible for compiling and writing (and, on TV and radio, presenting) the piece.

Running head
A running headline on each page of a feature, usually on the outside corner of the page, so a reader can flick through and see at a glance where the feature is located and what it's about.

Script
Broadcast journalist's copy.

Sic
A Latin word used by editors to indicate an apparent mis-spelling or doubtful word in a quote, to indicate that the editor is not responsible for the fault and to lay the blame on the source being quoted.

Sidebar
Short story run within a feature, often based on a case study.

Side-head
Another name for a cross-head, or a short caption which appears in the middle of a news story or feature. Often put in by the page designer as a visual to make the page more interesting, written by the sub.

Slug
A short caption which usually goes across the top of a page, either to highlight its content or to point out that it is advertorial.

Sound-bite
Short comment extracted from an interview to illustrate a report. Usually 7–40 seconds.

Spike
To 'spike' a story is literally to impale it on a spike of rejections. To reject.

Standfirst
The caption which goes under a headline or title, to give a little more information about it. So, for example, you may have a headline which reads, 'BBC in uproar' and the standfirst will tell you a little more about it: 'Journalists threaten strike because of cut in expenses'. Or the title of a publication may be 'Autocomputer' and the standfirst will be 'For users of automatic computers in industry'.

Stet
An editing term, taken from the Latin and meaning 'let it stand', cancelling a deletion or other change previously made in a page proof.

Story
A potential news item or article which has to be made to 'stand up'.

Strapline
The line underneath the title of a publication which explains who the reader is supposed to be, and at whom the contents are aimed. So, *PC Dealer* is 'The weekly newspaper for computer resellers'. Also used to refer to the catchline on the outside corner of a page to indicate the contents.

Style sheet

Several pages, or a small booklet, which define how the publication handles specific types of copy, such as spellings of job titles and names, the way pictures are captioned, handling of abbreviations. A detailed definition and description of a publication's style, which means that if a sub-editor gets run over by a bus, someone else can take over without any impact on the look and feel of the title. Prescribes accepted abbreviations, contractions and spellings. Should be regularly updated to reflect the changing use of language.

Sub-editor

The person on a publication who:

- Checks facts, names and places.
- Checks and puts right errors in grammar and spelling.
- Ensures that the style of the copy matches the style sheet.
- Cuts the text to fit the space allocated.
- Combines material from several sources to make a composite story.
- Rewrites part or all of the copy, if necessary, to achieve the right balance and style.
- Checks that the story is accurate and legally safe.
- Gives the right instructions to the production editor and printers to ensure the page looks right.
- Revises a story, if necessary, for later editions.
- Writes captions, headlines, standfirsts, cross-heads.
- Selects pull quotes and drop quotes from text.
- Makes sure the editorial copy is ready for deadline.

Tabloid

A small newspaper with pages half the size of a broadsheet. A general term meaning the down-market press.

Text

The main printed material.

Trade names

Registered trade names should be used with care, and always with a capital letter. It is better if possible to use the generic equivalent, for example:

Hoover (vacuum cleaner)
Sellotape (sticky tape)
Elastoplast (sticky plaster)

Coke/Coca-Cola (cola)
Fibreglass (glass fibre)

If in doubt, contact the Institute of Trade Mark Agents (0181 686 2052).

Typo
A spelling mistake, particularly one made at the keying-in stage, or blamed on the typist.

Web offset
A printing process.

Widow
A single word on a line, at the end of a paragraph. Sometimes a single word at the top left corner of a page, when the previous page's copy runs over. Good subbing will remove all widows and orphans.

WOB
White on Black – a block of text reversed so that white type appears on a black background.

INDEX

257